Murder Under the Microscope

Murder Under the Microscope

A Personal History of Homicide

Jim Fraser

Atlantic Books
London

First published in Great Britain in 2020 by Atlantic Books, an imprint of Atlantic Books Ltd.

Copyright © James Fraser, 2020

The moral right of James Fraser to be identified as the author of this work has been asserted by him in accordance with the Copyright, Designs and Patents Act of 1988.

1 2 3 4 5 6 7 8 9

A CIP catalogue record for this book is available from the British Library.

Hardback ISBN: 978-1-78649-594-5
E-book ISBN: 978-1-78649-596-9
Paperback ISBN: 978-1-78649-595-2

Printed and bound by CPI Group (UK) Ltd, Croydon, CR0 4YY

Atlantic Books
An Imprint of Atlantic Books Ltd
Ormond House
26–27 Boswell Street
London
WC1N 3JZ

www.atlantic-books.co.uk

For Ralph Skinner
12 October 1965–24 August 2017

History (hi.stori), sb. [Ad. L. *historia* narrative of past events, an account, tale, story, a. Gr.ἱστορία] a learning or knowing by inquiry, an account of one's inquiries … 1. A relation of incidents … narrative, tale, story.

CONTENTS

Author's Note

This book melds recollection with reflection and, with the passing of time, the accumulation of richer experience and of course the benefit of hindsight. My memory has been supplemented with research, including publicly available material, an unsystematic collection of notes, diaries and documents accumulated over the years and conversations with individuals. I have made every effort to check facts, but any errors that remain are mine. In most instances I have altered the names of individuals to preserve anonymity. I have used real names when the person is readily identifiable or has given permission. Most of the dialogue is re-created from memory, but some comes directly from notes or transcripts. My aim is to reproduce the character and content of dialogue rather than the literal words.

According to Janet Malcolm, the writer and journalist, 'Every journalist [when writing about murder] who is not too stupid or full of himself to notice what is going on knows that what he does is morally indefensible.'[1] I am not a journalist but it seems to me that there must be an element of truth in Malcolm's view; many accounts of murders appear to be inherently gratuitous and problematic. This raises for me a gnawing question, arguably a duty to justify my work. This is all the more acute because my experience is so indirect that I cannot do justice to the many victims in these cases. Nor is this something that I feel able to clarify with any richness; I simply felt that these were stories that needed to be told. I have written about these cases because I believe they are experiences that ought to be shared, and in a manner that explicates, clarifies and counters the superficial, technophilic simplicity of the many institutionally curated accounts of murder investigation. I firmly believe that only by weeding the forested thickets of myths and ignorance around the topic can we learn from these experiences.

Preface

'Working on an interesting case?' I asked my colleague sitting opposite me.

She looked up from her microscope. 'Not really,' she replied. 'There's blood on the knife matching the victim and cuts in the victim's shirt that the knife could have made. The suspect denies it but his fingerprints are on the knife. It's the usual murder stuff.' She smiled and went back to what she was doing.

I have worked as a forensic scientist for over forty years, during which I have dealt with some of the most terrible murders. The murder detection rate in the UK is about 85 per cent and most murders are not difficult to solve. There are three reasons for this. First, most people are killed by someone they know; the killer will be found within a small group of family, friends and acquaintances. Second, the crime is the end point of an escalating series of events that usually leaves behind abundant evidence. Finally, the police methods used to investigate this type of murder are highly effective.

Most of the murders I have worked on were pushed from memory to be replaced by others in my busy operational role. I gave evidence in only a small proportion of cases and it was rare for me to get to know the outcome of any trial. Apart from my memories, my only record of these cases, if I have one, is a line in a notebook or diary recording the date I attended the crime scene or court. My involvement was, in the end, relatively superficial, as was my knowledge of the case. The public profile of these cases also diminished, leaving the individuals directly involved to deal with their impact and loss. The cases in this book are different, for many reasons; they involve serial killers (very rare), child victims, miscarriages of justice, poor investigations or police misconduct, or they remain unresolved or contentious. All have attracted a great deal of attention from the media. My level of involvement was also very different. I was much more closely engaged, sometimes over a very long period, and I had extensive and detailed information about the investigation. I knew these cases intimately and had some sense of their often tangled trajectories.

A common theme in all of these inquiries is that they are multi-layered; small stories are enclosed in bigger stories that in turn are enclosed in yet bigger stories, like a set of Matryoshka dolls. In this book, I deal with three layers. The outermost layer could be called 'societal'. These are the biggest stories; public stories of expectations and beliefs, right and wrong, good and evil, justice and injustice. I do not spend much time on this layer, but all of the cases have some element of it.

The middle layer is what we might call 'institutional'; the systems that deal with murder investigation – for our purposes primarily the criminal justice system (CJS).* The CJS

---

* There are many important elements to the criminal justice system – social work, prisons, parole boards – but I confine myself to those I have had some involvement with; primarily the police and the courts.

generally presents us with an image of procedural rectitude, but these cases reveal a different reality under this polished veneer. Although the CJS produces a binary output of guilt or innocence,* this does not come from a mechanical or algorithmic calculus, but from something more organic and gelatinous. Component parts collide and merge in a loosely linked, constantly moving network, like distributed ganglia in some vast primitive organism. The CJS is all periphery and no centre, a system that is not a system,[1] a system that no single individual fully understands. Organisations cooperate or clash, muddle along or fail. My viewpoint of the CJS is narrow, framed by science and technology, a peripheral domain that is sometimes valorised, sometimes condemned. Science and technology in this context does not stand alone; it relies on human action, knowledge, imagination and fairness. It can also be attenuated by human inaction, ignorance, failure or prejudice.

The innermost layer of this book is the individual perspective; my individual perspective from my direct involvement in these cases. I have spent much of my working life looking down microscopes: low-power microscopes, high-power microscopes, polarising microscopes, comparison microscopes and microscopes connected to other scientific instruments that analyse colour or chemical structure. Looking at everyday things under a low-power microscope reveals an extraordinary micro-world. The surface of clothing yields an exotic array of particles: fibres from the clothing itself and the items it

---

* Strictly speaking, not guilty. And of course in Scotland there is the unique verdict of not proven.

has been in contact with, such as other clothing, furniture, bedding; hairs from you, your family and acquaintances; fibres and hairs from seats in your car; hairs from animals; minute quantities of skin or dust; sparkling fragments of minerals and crystals from domestic products, such as sugar or salt; glass fragments, particles of foodstuffs, plants and insects.

But low magnification only takes you so far. Like scanning the horizon with binoculars, it shows the trees and other features but does not identify them individually. Increase magnification a level and some of the debris can be more clearly seen. It becomes possible to distinguish different types of fibres and hairs, although it is hard to keep things in focus; they tremble and disappear when you try to pick them up with forceps. They are also more difficult to find. It's rather like trying to locate a star in the night sky with binoculars. At higher magnifications, the Petri dish containing the debris takes on the proportions of an airport long-stay car park, with vast areas to search. Sometimes you look straight at the thing you are hunting for but don't realise it because it completely fills the field in front of your eyes, like a giant cinema screen. You can't see the trees for the wood. In this world of higher magnification, it is easy to get lost. And if you don't know what you are looking for, you can't operate. You can't search for fibres when you don't know what colour they are.

The cases in this book are under the microscope. For most murders, those that are quickly resolved, low magnification suffices. But when the police investigate the more difficult homicides, or unexplained deaths, they enter the equivalent of the forensic scientist's micro-world. The more closely they look, the more they find, and the more detail they see. It becomes harder to stay focused and what they discover becomes more complicated and contradictory. Sometimes they don't know what they are looking for; but not looking is not an option. These cases can become so saturated with information, so fogged with detail that sometimes no sense can be made of them. There is so much inchoate data that logic and reason are overwhelmed.

These are cases that have puzzled me for many years, and I have written about them in an effort to understand them and see what they tell us about the business of homicide investigation. The book moves constantly between the institutional and individual perspectives. We shift from one lens to a second and occasionally a third. Having worked on these cases, I thought I knew their stories. I was wrong.

Introduction

I crouched over the body of the man lying in the doorway and slowly scanned around his head with the soft bright light from my lamp. Bloodstain spatters radiated outwards onto the wall and the pavement. The congruence between the bloodstain patterns and the position of the body was unmistakable; he had been repeatedly attacked where he lay. I turned to look at the trail of blood along the pavement and saw the crime scene manager walking towards me. I had just arrived; we hadn't spoken yet.

'What do you think?' he asked.

'I think I'm going to be here for a while examining the blood patterns,' I replied.

'The DI thinks he fell.' He pointed to a first-floor window above where the body lay.

'Maybe.' I nodded. 'But then somebody gave him a good kicking.'

The analogy of an unassembled jigsaw puzzle as a crime investigation is as inaccurate as it is clichéd. Even a straightforward investigation is an unfolding drama in time and space. You never have all the pieces, nor do you need them. Instead you must decide what is likely to be important and find those pieces – witnesses, or items of evidence such as drugs or weapons. From this evidence you need to construct a picture; more accurately, a story. Even then, the pieces may not give you the image you expect. An emerging picture that resembles one thing can change to something else as other pieces are added. And the picture that does explain the case will look different to different people: like the Necker cube or the 'old wife/young mistress' illusion.

A cryptic crossword puzzle is a better analogy; you have to solve individual clues, not just assemble them, and there is more scope for error and misinterpretation. Sometimes incorrect answers can falsely corroborate each other. But even this analogy breaks down, because the aim with a crossword puzzle is to answer *every* clue, to achieve a perfect solution. There is no need for a perfect solution to a murder investigation, no need to find every clue; just enough to present a credible prosecution and eliminate reasonable alternative explanations. Nor does the crossword analogy capture the sense of binary choices that an investigation can present; things not done that once forgone can never be recovered, the choice of bifurcations in a road that are lost once the alternative is chosen.

Crouching over the body that morning, I was presented with the clearest of evidence that the death was a murder. The man may have had some hidden pathology in his body that I couldn't know of that was connected with his death, but when he was being kicked, he was still alive, his heart was beating, his blood was flowing; otherwise I would not have seen the bloodstain patterns that were around him. If I had packed up my stuff and left, this evidence would have been lost.[1] Some hours after I had completed my scene examination, news filtered back from the autopsy that the man had multiple head injuries that could not have been caused by a fall.

At the start of a death investigation it is essential to balance all the possible explanations until one emerges as dominant: accident, suicide, homicide, murder. A forensic strategy identifies the central questions in an investigation and links them to forensic examinations that might resolve them. In most cases, like the example above, many of the questions are obvious. How did the person die? How did they come to be where they were found? Is there anything that makes the circumstances immediately suspicious? The questions are obvious but the answers may not be. At the outset, in the so-called 'golden hour',* much depends on the experience, knowledge and attitude of those addressing them. The person dealing with the investigation at that stage could be an inexperienced on-call detective. We are fed the solo investigator myth so widely that even those who do the job sometimes forget that they are part of a system where support and advice are available. One wrong decision can take an investigation down a road from which it may never recover and murder is written off as an accident or suicide. A Home Office study in 2015[2] identified a worrying number of cases that had been identified as murders after they had initially been categorised as non-suspicious. The main reason for the wrong decision was a lack of knowledge and bias of those first attending the scene.

---

* This is a much-used cliché but one that holds some truth. It means the early stages of a homicide investigation, before key evidence might be lost. No one seems to agree how long this period is, but I have seen suggestions that it is as long as 72 hours.

Even a *delay* in the early stages of the investigation can be a problem; witnesses vanish and forensic evidence is lost, leaving important questions impossible to answer. There is still scope for error once an investigation is stabilised, but there are more opportunities for fatal error at the outset.

Much of what we believe about murder investigation has been shaped by history and mythology. Around 1850, at the height of the public frenzy about the new individuals called 'detectives', Charles Dickens wrote about the 'science of detection' and the special skills that the detective was assumed to possess.[3] Are detectives exceptional individuals with skills and procedures that no one else has? Few believe this now, but a great deal of mythology shrouds these issues, much of which is created by those involved. Only a tiny proportion of people, mainly those with direct experience, get to know what actually goes on in an investigation. How many people have been to a courtroom or a crime scene? How many to a forensic science lab? Our information comes second-hand, filtered, presented and represented, partial; continually reinforcing the mythology. From the time of Dickens until now, little has changed. How murder is investigated comes to us more from imagination than from experience or fact.

The modern extension of the detective myth is best exemplified by the TV series *CSI: Crime Scene Investigation.* *CSI* makes such good TV because of its stories, characters and puzzles, and perhaps above all the style and visuals that accompany them.[4] It blends the detective myth with the mythology of science: objectivity, logical reasoning and truth; truth that cannot be seen by the eye, that can only be revealed by technology, that requires an expert for it to be found and understood. This, of course, is artistic licence, entertaining but oversimplified gloss, sometimes nonsense. *CSI* gives us a science that benevolently serves criminal justice – a belief-based science.

It's not only fiction that deals in stereotypes. *I'll Be Gone in the Dark* by Michelle McNamara[5] is a detailed account of the investigations into the Golden State Killer,* who was active in California between 1974 and 1986. It is well written and researched and reads more like a thriller. But even here, light and shade is lost and Day-Glo colours are used when the author compares detectives and forensic scientists: 'Cops thrive on action. They are knee jigglers ... The crime lab is arid ... there's no hard-edged banter ... Cops wrestle up close with life's messiness; criminalists† quantify it.' These are matchstick figures, a convenient shorthand but lacking in nuance. Such stereotypes also feed the mythology; it thrives still.

I spent the first 18 years of my career as a laboratory-based forensic scientist, scene investigator and expert witness in London and Edinburgh. I spent eight years as head of forensic investigation for Kent Police, running a large department, advising senior investigating officers (SIOs), reviewing cases and working on national projects. I spent 12 years as an academic, researching, teaching, reviewing cases and advising police organisations and governments. I have been involved in hundreds of murder investigations. Am I a 'quantifier' or a 'knee jiggler'? Neither is accurate, it seems to me.

---

* Also known as the Eastern Area Rapist, the perpetrator is believed to have committed at least 13 murders, 50 rapes and over 100 burglaries.
† A common term in the USA that in this instance means a forensic scientist.

'You don't talk like a scientist, you talk like an investigator,' said an Australian police officer I met when I was reviewing a case in Melbourne. I thought it was a compliment. Some forensic scientists would think not. Some detectives would be appalled at the idea of anyone other than a police officer being considered an investigator. Others would agree, because they are not confused by the artificial boundaries, the stereotypes. I want to cut through these stereotypes and mythologies, because only by doing so can the world I want to describe be understood.

This is neither a systematic nor a scholarly work, although it does have a logical rationale. Most murders are solved quickly and go through the courts speedily. When there is a guilty plea, or plenty of evidence, as there usually is, the full details rarely leave the courtroom. These are tragic events for a small group of individuals, but publicly we hear little more about them. The drama, pain, twists and turns of the story remain buried. When such details are left untold, at least to those not directly involved, it is difficult to know what aspects of the trial were salient. I want to explore these investigations in order to better understand them. I also want to enable the reader to draw their own conclusions about what these cases tell us; to achieve this, I need to point out some recurrent features of significance that will aid understanding. There is a difference between what an institution – for example, the police* – says it does and what it *actually* does. We need to apply this sense of *actualité* to the three domains involved in

---

* For clarity, this notion applies to *all* institutions, from the military to the Church.

murder investigation: forensic science, the police, and the criminal law and courtroom. How much weight is given to each of these domains varies from case to case, determined by the individual story.

Forensic science, our first domain, is a term that cloaks a ragged patchwork of assertions and beliefs. It covers activities that are unquestionably scientific as well as those that are unquestionably subjective or entirely intuitive. There is no single thing that can be straightforwardly categorised as forensic science. It is an ill defined collective. If we consider 'real' science to be the stuff that qualified, professional scientists do in laboratories using specialist equipment and procedures,* this leaves a large number of individuals in other roles commonly tagged under 'forensic science' who are neither scientists nor do any scientific work: fingerprints experts, crime-scene investigators, crime-scene managers and others. Nor is all of the work done by the people in white coats entirely scientific.

A good example of the kind of quasi-scientific work carried out by some forensic scientists (including me) is bloodstain pattern analysis (BPA), which crops up in several cases in this book. BPA has a scientific foundation and some elements of it can be considered to be objective. But a great deal of the BPA work done at crime scenes is completely reliant on subjective information, without which there can be no interpretation and therefore no evidence. Why does this matter? It matters because the courts and others accord

---

* This is, of course, a huge oversimplification of what science is but is fine for our purposes.

science a higher, perhaps the highest, status as a source of knowledge (and therefore evidence). Deciding what is and what is not science is important.

There is a myth that scientific evidence speaks for itself; that it is somehow free from the frailties of human agency, and that it occupies a special and incontestable place in the evidential canon. The modern origins of this idea can be traced back to nineteenth-century France, although it could have arisen earlier. Dr Alexandre Lacassagne, professor of legal medicine at the University of Lyon,* was amongst the first to see the potential of scientific and medical evidence to overcome some of the weaknesses of witness testimony: poor memory, prejudice and mendacity. He introduced a rational approach to homicide investigations that took into account observations and findings from crime scenes and post-mortem examinations. He coined the term 'silent testimony' to describe this new type of evidence.

One of his students, Dr Edmond Locard, nowadays more famous than his master, supplemented Lacassagne's idea with what is now widely referred to as Locard's exchange principle: 'Every contact leaves a trace.'† In 1953, Paul Kirk, an American forensic scientist, took Lacassagne's idea of silent testimony and Locard's principle of exchange and stretched them into one of the most pervasive myths of modern forensic science: that forensic science has all the answers, always.

---

* Lacassagne's school in Lyon operated from 1855 to 1914.
† What Locard actually wrote was 'Any action of an individual, and obviously the violent action constituting a crime, cannot occur without leaving a trace.'

Wherever [the criminal] steps, whatever he
touches, whatever he leaves, even unconsciously,
will serve as a silent witness against him. Not only
his fingerprints or his footprints, but his hair, the
fibres from his clothes, the glass he breaks, the
tool mark he leaves, the paint he scratches, the
blood or semen he deposits or collects. All of these,
and more, bear mute witness against him. This is
evidence that does not forget. It is not confused
by the excitement of the moment. It is not absent
because human witnesses are. It is factual evidence.
Physical evidence cannot be wrong, it cannot
perjure itself, it cannot be wholly absent. Only
human failure to find it, study and understand it
can diminish its value.[6]

This is not science, or rationality for that matter, but mythical
dogma portraying forensic science as a utopian project that can
only be corrupted by humans. Yet whatever forensic science is,
it can only be fulfilled by humans. It is true that humans can
mess things up. But it is also true that it is humans that make
forensic science and investigations work. It makes no sense
to describe what might be achieved if it were not for humans.

Our second domain is the institution of the police. There
are many myths about how the police operate, which can
be grouped under the heading of 'police culture'. One of
these is procedural integrity or thoroughness; following the
rules. However, the police, although very good at producing
documented procedures, are actually quite poor at following

them, even their own.[7] There are many practice manuals and policies in existence throughout the police service in the UK, but their role is often symbolic, or at best a rough guide to what might get done. The police delight in improvisation. For example, what was going through the minds of the detectives in the Jill Dando case (see p.215) when they opened the sealed packaging of a critical exhibit and compromised the forensic evidence in a case of great public interest and significance? I find it impossible to believe that they did not know what they were doing, and equally impossible to understand why they did it. If you find this surprising, you will come across even more extraordinary lapses in procedure in more than one case in this book.

Another aspect of police culture that is not widely appreciated is the preference for action over reflection. Action and being seen to act can be an end in itself; it relieves anxieties, avoids deliberation and is a visible signal that something is being done.

Finally, how the police use science and technology is an ongoing theme. Counterintuitive though it may seem, the police have quite a limited understanding of science and technology generally, and forensic science in particular. Furthermore, how they choose what technologies to employ and how they then use them is heavily influenced, even distorted, by police culture. If you can accept this, the mist will disperse. The current debate about real-time facial identification – how effective it is and whether it is ethical or legal to use it – is a good illustration of these issues.

Our third domain is the criminal trial, those 'great reckonings in little rooms'[8] that are such a dominant feature in the work of a forensic scientist. In my experience, the courts are theatres where the rational and the absurd compete for attention. If health and safety rules allowed it, I feel sure forensic scientists would be expected to wear white lab coats in the witness box; the symbolism and rhetorical power of such an image would be too much for the advocates to resist. Although it is rare for forensic scientists to appear in court, even as operational experts, the courtroom is a constant presence. All prior activities and considerations are framed with reference to this imagined future event. In the mind of an expert witness, it provides a continuous stream of narrative and counter-narrative, argument and counter-argument, guess and second-guess, determining choices, actions and judgements. This is also a significant feature of detective work; a recurrent theme of investigations is deciding what is to be attended to, what is to be chosen, prioritised, acted on or rejected on the route to resolving a case, with the trial in mind.

These three domains influence how police investigations, forensic work and trials are imagined, structured and operate. They interact, sometimes productively, sometimes destructively, in terms of the procedures, beliefs and epistemologies of the institutions involved.

—

The small selection of cases in this book are a snapshot from the thousands I have worked on, and are arguably exceptional. All have a public face and profile and have engaged and continue to engage a broader audience. They have been the subject of books, TV dramas and documentaries. There are websites and web forums about some of them. They have been pored over, picked apart and argued about. Their stories and their main characters have become public knowledge; they have an additional dimension. This information and the detail they reveal is rarely available; these cases can tell us in a direct way about how murder investigations happen, a way that can be reflected upon and from which we can learn.

The reasons for the public face of these cases vary but include the particular nature of the crime, the characteristics of the victim or the offender, the effectiveness or otherwise of the investigation and the fairness of the conviction. But none of these bland words captures the public emotion or drama involved when a crime is so horrific that its details can only be hinted at by media, when women and children are murdered, when a serial killer, whose mind is so different from our own that we can scarcely conceive of it, is on the loose, when errors are made that allow the guilty to escape justice, when the evidence for conviction appears so thin that views are divided as to its significance.

My direct experience of these cases was deep but narrow, exposing a particular view that sometimes made sense but more often did not. In this book, I explore them from the near distance, from shifting viewpoints and from the lived experience; what I recall and have established actually took place. Having undertaken this work, I am much better informed; still fascinated, yet still a bit puzzled.

CHAPTER ONE

Robert Black, the Killer of Childhood

[Each attack was] accomplished in the same circumstances, executed in the same way, and showed an identical operating procedure.

Alexandre Lacassagne[1]

As a child back in the sixties, I used to walk to primary school on my own. It was safe, and no one worried. Fewer than half of today's kids walk to school, and almost all of them are accompanied by an adult. The main reason parents give for accompanying children is dangerous traffic. The second most common reason, cited by almost one third of parents, is fear of assault or molestation; 'stranger danger'. Robert Black, a man now largely forgotten, is possibly more responsible for this change in parental behaviour than any other single person.

In July 1990, Black had attempted to abduct a six-year-old girl in broad daylight in the Borders village of Stow. A local man saw a blue Ford Transit van slowing to a stop on the roadside opposite him, its wheels partly on the pavement. He saw the girl's legs disappear as she walked past the van; she didn't reappear. The van then pulled away violently onto the correct side of the road and drove off north, towards Edinburgh. This witness called the police.

Constable John Wilson was one of the officers who responded to the alert and was by the roadside when he saw a blue van travelling south back into the village. He stepped out into the road and flagged it down. The driver of the van was aged about 40, bearded and balding. Wilson opened the side door and found the missing child in two overlapped sleeping bags. Her head had been pushed towards the bottom of the outer bag and the drawstring of the inner bag was tightened around her neck. Her hands were bound and she had sticking plaster over her mouth. As the child gasped for air, he recognised his own daughter.

In August 1990, Black was convicted of the abduction of Mandy Wilson and sentenced to life imprisonment at the High Court in Edinburgh. His arrest and conviction led to a child murder investigation on an unprecedented scale. He was suspected of abducting and murdering 11 children; seven in the UK and four in continental Europe. There were also a number of other abductions and assaults that fitted his *modus operandi*. A meeting was convened in Edinburgh for those UK police forces that believed he might be a suspect in any of their cases. By the end of the meeting, four cases were identified as being the main priorities of the investigation: the murders of Susan Maxwell, Caroline Hogg and Sarah Harper, and the attempted kidnap of Teresa Thornhill.

In July 1982, eight years before Black's arrest, 11-year-old Susan Maxwell went missing on her way home from playing tennis. She lived in Cornhill-on-Tweed, near the border between Scotland and England. Her body was found 12 days later, 250 miles away in Staffordshire. She had been raped and strangled. Her tennis racket and ball, blue plastic thermos flask and one of her shoes were missing.

Five-year-old Caroline Hogg went missing one evening in July 1983 from Portobello, near Edinburgh. Her naked body was found 10 days later in a ditch in Leicestershire, almost 300 miles away. She was so badly decomposed that the cause of death could not be established. Her lilac and white gingham dress, underskirt, pants, socks and trainers were never found.

In March 1986, 10-year-old Sarah Harper disappeared after going to buy a loaf of bread from her corner shop in Leeds. Her body was found a month later in the River Trent near Nottingham. Her pale blue anorak, pink skirt, shoes and socks were missing.

In April 1988, a man tried to kidnap 15-year-old Teresa Thornhill and force her into a blue van. Teresa was older than the murdered girls but was slightly built and looked younger. She managed to fight off her attacker with the help of her boyfriend.

All these cases had striking similarities to the abduction of Mandy Wilson. Black's snatch of the young girl in broad daylight had been meticulously planned. He carried equipment – sleeping bags, duct tape and other items – for this purpose. The three murdered children had vanished without trace, and two of their bodies had been found in similar locations. Six police forces were now involved in the investigation: Lothian and Borders, West Yorkshire, Staffordshire, Leicestershire, Nottinghamshire and Northumbria.

I had joined Lothian and Borders Police* in Edinburgh in 1989, after 11 years with the Metropolitan Police Forensic Science laboratory in London. At the time, the Met lab was one of the largest in the world, with more than 300 staff. My notebook records my first murder case in 1981, and a total of 62 by the time I left London eight years later. A crude analysis of these cases shows the most common method of killing as stabbing (22), with shooting and strangulation in joint second place (six each). Some of the cases are still unsolved, but there were no child murders recorded, and no serial murder cases.

Lothian and Borders was the second largest force in Scotland but was small by UK standards. I wasn't anticipating new opportunities in Edinburgh, but I needed a change. Although London was an exciting environment to operate in professionally, the management in the lab I worked in was stifling. The people in Edinburgh would be different and the problems would be different. I was head of biology in one of the smallest forensic science laboratories in the UK, with only 15 staff. The biology section had four full-time scientists, including me.

When I learned of Black's *modus operandi*, I thought about my own young children. How could I protect them from a man like that? My impulse was to jump in the car, drive to their school, take them home and lock them in. Only then would they be safe.

---

* In 2013, all Scottish police forces were subsumed into a single national force: Police Scotland.

—

'Every contact leaves a trace' is the snappy slogan of forensic science, the equivalent to 'Just do it' or 'I'm lovin' it' – and about as accurate. It is widely misunderstood by police officers, lawyers and jurors to mean that scientific evidence will always be found and that it will be definitive. We now know that if material is transferred, it can also be lost afterwards. Textile fibres transferred from a killer's clothing to his victim will stay in place if the body is undisturbed. But once the killer has left the crime scene, the fibres transferred to him (or her) will be lost within hours. Many factors determine if particles will be transferred and how quickly they are lost: the degree of contact between surfaces, the microscopic size of the particles, and the type of the surface to which they are transferred. Since all of this is a bit complicated, 'Every contact leaves a trace' has become the catchphrase to keep things simple.

I thought about the possibilities for forensic examination in the Black case. The most recent murder, that of Sarah Harper, was in 1986, four years before Black's arrest. The chance of finding scientific evidence was so small it could be discounted. There was other evidence that had much more potential, such as the missing items of children's clothing that Black might have kept.

The only comparable case to the Black inquiry was the Yorkshire Ripper investigation, which I spent a short time working on in 1979. Between July 1975 and November 1980, Peter Sutcliffe attacked 20 women and murdered 13 of them. At the time, the Metropolitan Police lab was the only one in the UK using a microspectrophotometer, an instrument that measures the colour of tiny particles as small as 10×10 micrometres.* It was a big breakthrough in fibre examination, overcoming two previously unsolved problems: the subjectivity of colour comparison – we all perceive and describe colour differently – and the microscopic size of fibres.†

By 1979, the Yorkshire Ripper, as he became known, had killed 10 women. The investigation was in a desperate state. Someone, somewhere, probably a forensic scientist, told the investigators about this new instrument and they came up with the idea that it might be a way of linking the cases and identifying the killer. That fibres from the killer's clothing might be found on the victims was possible, even likely. But the belief that the microspectrophotometer could be used to find this evidence was madness.

The idea was that by randomly analysing fibres that had been recovered from the victims' clothing, it might be possible to find fibres that were common to more than one victim and that could therefore be from the clothing of their killer. Given the number of victims involved, there would be tens of thousands of fibres to be searched through under a microscope and then analysed: among them might be a few hundred from the killer's clothing. But since the killer was unknown at the time, no one knew what he was wearing or what colour or type of fibre was involved, or indeed whether he wore the same clothes for each of the crimes. This was

---

* A micrometre is one millionth of a metre, $1×10^{-6}$m, usually abbreviated to μm.
† The microspectrophotometer can also be used to analyse inks, plastics, paint, glass and other minute coloured particles.

like trying to play a colossal game of 'find the pairs' on the deck of an aircraft carrier, with hundreds of different packs of cards. Yet it was something the Metropolitan Police immediately agreed to.

My boss was apologetic. He knew it wouldn't work, but he also knew the importance of maintaining good relations with the police. We agreed I would spend one day a week analysing as many fibres as I could; at the end of each day I would look for matches. In theory we were on board and supporting the investigation, but with minimal effort. This only went on for a few weeks; nobody truly believed that it would produce anything and it was gradually forgotten.

This desperate searching for a technological solution is a recurrent feature of police culture when investigations stagnate or stall. It seems to be born of two things: an overwhelming desire to do something – action always trumps reflection for the police – and the desire to be associated with new technology. Together these things stave off the anxiety of failure, and more importantly can be used to demonstrate that everything possible is being done, and everyone is busy doing *something*.

I heard an account at a national conference of forensic specialists by the senior investigating officer in the lengthy and successful investigation of the murder of a French student, Céline Figard, who was travelling in England when she went missing around Christmas 1995. She had accepted a lift from a lorry driver. Her naked body was found days later. As the tall Scot took us through the twists and turns of the case, he told us how they had investigated a mysterious yellow stain on

Figard's body. He emphasised the extraordinary lengths to which they had gone to establish the nature and significance of the stain. He also explained that it had been analysed by the only instrument of its kind in the UK. He waved in his hand the lengthy report that the scientists had produced. The stain was identified, but it played no part in the case. This report was not evidence; rather it was symbolic of how much effort had been put into the investigation and demonstrated how investigators were embracing innovation and the latest science.

The Yorkshire Ripper case was one of the most notorious and influential in UK policing history: notorious because it was ineptly investigated; influential because it led to the introduction of new working practices and the computerisation of major investigations. We know it went badly wrong, because it was followed by some very big changes. This only happens in response to two things: either a public disaster* that the police are intimately connected with, or changes in the law.† Even in the latter case, they often fail to respond in a timely way.‡

—

We find out about murders through the media, but what is presented to us is filtered, and there is an unstated hierarchy of presentation. Sexual murders are given more

---

* The Stephen Lawrence investigation and public inquiry is probably the most notable example.
† Such as the introduction of the Police and Criminal Evidence Act (PACE) in England and Wales.
‡ In 1996, the Criminal Procedures and Investigations Act was enacted in England and Wales. Part of this requires disclosure of evidence, yet it was many years before practices changed to reflect the law, and even longer before police attitudes changed.

prominence than non-sexual ones; murders of women receive more attention than murders of men, especially if the woman is white, middle-class or portrayed as undeserving of what has happened. Some women are deemed less equal than others; prostitutes make the news less frequently, unless there is someone notable involved or the crime is especially violent. The Black investigation was at the top of this unspoken hierarchy, even when compared to the Yorkshire Ripper investigation. The children were victims of a serial offender and the cases involved abduction, sexual violence and torture. The press pursued the case relentlessly.

The deaths of these three children were no ordinary murders. Black was a loner with no living relatives, who spent most of his life on the road. No one knew his routines or habits. He was highly secretive. All of these factors would hamper the usual approach to an investigation. There were other complications. The crimes were spread over six years and dispersed across the UK, involving six police forces and two jurisdictions, Scotland and England, whose legal procedures were quite different. Like the Ripper case, the Black investigation would generate vast amounts of information, and there was considerable potential for important evidence to be overlooked or lost. The forces involved would all have different practices and perspectives. Each came to the investigation with the assumption that they could do a better job than anyone else. Inter-force rivalries would need to be controlled to prevent them impacting on performance and cooperation. The labs were not much better than the police at cooperating, and this worried me. The lab in Edinburgh could not possibly cope with this case without support from other labs, but I couldn't see how this would come about.

The Black investigation was led by Deputy Chief Constable Hector Clark of Lothian and Borders Police, and was the first serial murder investigation since that of the Yorkshire Ripper. A formal inquiry into the Ripper case had been conducted by Sir Lawrence Byford.[2] Clark had the benefit of a personal briefing from Byford and had also been involved in the Ripper case. He wrote about his experience of the Black investigation when he retired. In his book,[3] he described the disastrous Ripper investigation as 'a very good investigation, in the main, led by excellent detectives from an efficient police force'. He felt free to make these comments knowing that the Byford report was at that time unpublished.

His explanation for the numerous failings was that the police were overwhelmed by information and, in the absence of a computer system, were unable to track and cross-reference data. This is only partly true. West Yorkshire police were indeed overwhelmed with information, but some of the officers were incompetent or lazy and failed to do their job properly. Interviews of Sutcliffe by police officers were conducted half-heartedly and were poor. Before his eventual arrest, Sutcliffe was interviewed on nine occasions, and although he was never eliminated from the inquiry, he was never identified as a suspect who merited further investigation. Many of the women who were killed were prostitutes; as early as 1969, Sutcliffe had a police record for incidents involving prostitutes. His car had been seen in the red-light district in Leeds, but when he was asked about this, he simply denied even having a vehicle, a lie that no one bothered to check.

Byford made many recommendations to prevent the recurrence of these failings. Among these were the call for standard operating procedures for major incidents, and a computer system for all UK police forces. The newly introduced system was called HOLMES – the Home Office Large Major Enquiry System. Its functionality[4] included document management, record management, task allocation, exhibit tracking* and preparation of case files for court. What Clark entirely missed was that any investigation system was completely dependent on humans being willing and able to follow agreed procedures, retrieving and inputting data and then acting on that data. My experience is that police officers commonly fail to follow agreed procedures and on occasions entirely disregard them, as we will see in later chapters.

Murder investigations put the victim and suspect at the centre of a process known as TIE – trace, interview, eliminate. This involves tracing potential witnesses and interviewing them by posing some basic questions to see if they can be eliminated as witnesses or suspects. Investigators will establish where they were at the time of the incident and if they can prove their whereabouts, or whether further inquiries are needed to corroborate this.

The main questions of a criminal inquiry are well known to any reader of crime fiction: Who is the victim? Who is the suspect? Where did it happen? When did it happen? What happened? Why did it happen? The answers to some of these

---

* The equivalent term for exhibits in Scots law is 'production'.

are often obvious. In most cases the identity of the victim and the suspect will be known, although they need to be checked. The body is usually found where the murder took place. If you know who the victim is, you can investigate their family and social circle to find the killer. Knowing where or when someone was killed narrows the scope. If the victim was killed in their home, the killer must have had access, although they don't necessarily live there. If the murder was on a weekday, it was probably committed by someone who had free time during the day. Of course, inquiries may later show that someone was supposed to be at work but called in sick that day, and this would put them back in the frame for TIE. Most people are killed for depressingly predictable reasons: money, jealousy, revenge, sex, hate, excitement – or a combination of these.

TIE is superbly effective in most cases because we are all constantly weaving an invisible fabric that leaves traces of our every move. Who we live with, associate with or meet, what we buy and how we travel: our secrets are quite easy to unravel. But it doesn't always work. Prior to the arrest of Black, the Maxwell and Hogg murders in 1982 and 1983 had been linked but remained unsolved. The investigations had been going on for many years but not in the narrow circumstances of a typical murder inquiry. The police had no idea who had killed the girls, or how their killer might be connected to where they were abducted from or where their bodies were found. They didn't know where to look, but obviously they couldn't stop looking. In these cases, TIE can go badly wrong. A witness mentioned a Ford Cortina near the bridge where Susan Maxwell was abducted, and the police, believing it might be involved, traced the owners of 15,000 similar vehicles. The effort was enormous but it was misplaced. A similar TIE led to the tracing of 19,000 other vehicles that turned out not to be involved. Yet sightings of a white van, 'probably a Ford Transit', seen on both sides of the bridge were not followed up because it 'would have been utterly futile'.[5]

Another common method of identifying an offender is by what the police call *modus operandi* (MO) suspects: individuals with convictions for offences related to the one being investigated. The skill with this approach is in making the pool of TIE individuals – or 'nominals', as the police call them – big enough to contain the offender yet small enough to be practical for investigation. Too small a pool and the offender may not be there; too big and you'll never get around to interviewing them. The size of this pool is governed by two parameters: the conviction you choose as being similar to the offence under investigation; and geography. For a minor crime such as housebreaking, police might just look for convicted housebreakers in their local division, which could amount to 20 or 30 people. Prior to Black's arrest, in the linked Maxwell and Hogg cases, MO suspects were identified as 'people who had murdered, indecently assaulted or abducted young children, living in a certain area and within certain age parameters'.[6] Across the UK, hundreds, possibly thousands, of convicted offenders would fall into this category.

—

I stood in the main hall at Lothian's police headquarters, a space usually reserved for formal celebrations or social events. In the hundreds of plastic crates being carried in were some 4,000 carefully labelled packages. As I walked around, I could read some of the labels that identified their contents: shirts, T-shirts, trousers, underwear, socks, belts, shoes, postcards, pens, pencils, notepads, toiletries, photographs, magazines, films, darts ... The crates held the entire material world of one person – Robert Black. The Metropolitan Police had seized the items from his lodgings in West Bank, Stamford Hill, London, and transported them to Scotland. The largest investigation of child murder that had ever taken place in the UK had been shifted from the largest police force in the country to one of its smallest. I had never known such a thing to happen before.

Recognising one of the London detectives who had accompanied the items to Edinburgh, I said, 'Hi, John.'

'Hi,' he replied. 'This is a joke, isn't it? How are these numpties going to investigate this case?'

He was scathing. Only one police force could investigate this case properly and that, of course, was the Met. I knew the Met culture well. They were the biggest force in the country, but they confused being the biggest with being the best, a problem that still lingers to this day.

My boss had been at a meeting to decide how to deal with the thousands of items from Black's lodgings. Keen to know how we were going to approach the case, I went to see him in his cramped sixth-floor office.

'What's the plan?' I asked.

He gave a broad smile and leaned back in his chair with his hands behind his head. 'I'm the Byford scientist,' he responded.

In his report, Byford had recommended that a new scientific role should be created to oversee all forensic work in serial murder investigations. This role was popularly referred to as a 'Byford scientist'.

'It's a very important remit,' he continued, looking out the window towards Edinburgh's Royal Botanic Gardens in the distance. 'We've just to get on with it, start the examinations.'

'Get on with what exactly?'

'Everything,' he replied.

'How can we examine everything?'

'That's what has been decided.'

'Did you explain how long that would take?'

'We've just to get on with it,' he repeated. 'We'll be working in teams of two, a scientist and a police officer. Everything. We start tomorrow.'

He went back to reading the papers on his desk, giddy with his new titular role.

—

In forensic science, one of the important decisions in a murder investigation is whether trace evidence (usually fibres and hairs) is needed. This decision is important for two reasons. First, recovering trace evidence, let alone examining it, takes a lot of time and effort. Second, if the traces are not captured from the start, the evidence will have been lost or the item contaminated. If you are not concerned with trace evidence, you can move on quickly. If the suspect and victim in a case are known to have been in contact before the incident, trace evidence can't be used because you would expect to find it anyway; it could be explained away. There was no known connection between Black and the victims, but to recover all the trace evidence from the items in Black's possession was going to take a monumental effort.

Most cases involve some discussion, negotiation and sometimes argument about what forensic work is worth doing; the examinations that might answer a question, prove or eliminate a theory or identify someone. Unproductive work is usually deeply resented by scientists, as time and resources are scarce. But some investigations are different, and this was one of them. Pointless or not, there was an unstated acceptance by all that something of exceptional importance was at stake. Many years later, when I was working for Kent Police, a senior detective said to me that it must have been a privilege to work on this investigation. We both knew that 'privilege' was not the right word, but we both understood.

We worked in pairs – four forensic scientists and four police officers (CSIs) – and examined each item in turn. The lab wasn't big enough, so we were based in the hall where the items were stored. Trestle tables covered with a protective layer of the glossy paper that we used in the lab were used as examination benches. They were wiped down between items to cut down contamination. We placed a pop-up lab in a corner of the hall. This had high- and low-power microscopes and chemical tests to identify blood and body fluids such as semen and saliva. A lot of stains can look like blood or body fluids and this basic kit would exclude false alarms and enable us to carry out initial identifications. We could also have a quick look at hairs, fibres and other traces using the microscopes, to get an idea if they were of interest. The items had been packed by the Metropolitan Police in an assortment of ways: envelopes, brown paper bags, plastic bags, boxes. Each had a unique exhibit label that described what the item was, where it came from, when it was recovered and who had taken possession of it. These labels were for use in English courts, so anything that was going to court in Scotland needed to be re-labelled. All this would need to be sorted out when we knew where the trial would be.

As well as the detailed forensic examination, there were other items we were keen to find. Serial killers sometimes keep trophies from their crimes. One of the USA's most infamous serial killers, Ted Bundy, kept the heads of some of his victims. Other killers keep underwear and jewellery. We didn't know if this was one of Black's practices, but we knew there were items missing from some of the children that he might have held onto. Finding one or more of these would crack the case wide open. Pictures of the missing items were circulated so we all knew what we were looking for. We also knew that Black had carefully planned the abduction of Mandy in Stow, so there might be evidence of his planning of the other murders: maps, notebooks, photographs, etc.

In addition, we needed to be alert to evidence we might stumble across unexpectedly. This was one of the reasons we were working in pairs – it meant we could quickly confer about the significance of anything we found. The detective sergeant I was working with showed me a postcard Black had received that referred to 'noncey pictures'. Nonce is prison slang for a child sex offender. However, many of the items were of no relevance; just things he used in his everyday life – toothpaste, soap and so on.

Each time I came across an item that needed a full examination, I followed a standard procedure. Taking the item out of the crate – let's say it was a T-shirt – I wiped the table and noted the label details, how it was packed and sealed. None of this was of much interest at this stage but would be important when it came to writing reports and giving evidence. I gently laid the T-shirt out on the table, to minimise loss of microscopic particles that could be evidence, and taped its surface. Taping involves using strips of Sellotape to remove the loose surface debris, in the same way you would remove fluff from an item of clothing. I covered the whole surface front and back, systematically, then stuck the tapes to clear plastic sheets and wrote on the sheets where they came from: upper front, lower front, upper back, lower back, right sleeve, left sleeve. Among the loose fibres on the tapes could be fibres from the children's clothing, although I didn't believe there was any prospect of this.

The T-shirt was old, worn and faded. Black had a reputation for being untidy and poorly dressed. As a child he was nicknamed 'Smelly Bob', and that reputation continued into his adult life. This T-shirt wasn't especially smelly, but it hadn't been washed for a long time and was in very poor condition. Most people would have thrown it out long ago. I made notes describing it so that, together with the label details, I could identify it in court. I looked for blood and semen stains using a bright soft light, slowly scrutinising every part of it in turn. It's like painting a wall with transparent paint; you can't see where you have been, so you follow a set pattern to make sure you don't leave any gaps. As I did this, the voices and movement around me dropped off into the background.

After a while, I found a hair. Robert Black was greying and almost bald, so any hairs from the children should be easy to spot and easily distinguished. With fine forceps I lifted the short, light-coloured hair from the surface of the T-shirt, put it in a clear plastic bag and labelled it. Then I walked over to the pop-up lab and looked at it under a low-power microscope. It wasn't a head hair; it could be a pubic hair, perhaps from Black. I made a note. I hadn't seen the hair samples from the girls, but it couldn't be from any of them because of their age. I couldn't see blood or anything that looked like semen on the T-shirt, so I folded it, put it back in the paper bag it came from, and closed it with some Sellotape. In the bottom right-hand corner of my notes I wrote the date and my initials.

'Have you seen this?' asked a colleague, handing me a colour Polaroid photo.

Black was obsessed with inserting things into his anus and had been doing this since he was eight. As an adult, he also photographed some of his 'experiments'. As I looked at the picture, I was handed a second. I winced. The first photo featured an old-style telephone handset, the second a table leg. More of Black's sexual obsessions were found in the contents of a blue suitcase he kept on top of his wardrobe. It contained 110 magazines, 4 cine films, 10 movies, a scrapbook and loose photographs; all of them portrayed the sexual exploitation of children.

Later, I went into the lab and saw Deputy Chief Constable Hector Clark standing between two benches of analytical instruments. He had his back to me and was looking at the view of Edinburgh's exclusive public school, Fettes College. Stocky and square-jawed, in full, tight-fitting uniform, he turned as I walked in. I had never known him to be in our makeshift lab before. The summer sun fell on the towers of Fettes. He stretched his hands out to rest on the benches either side of him, saw the years of unidentifiable chemical stains and brought them back to his sides.

'You've got more equipment here than you know what to do with,' he said, distastefully taking in all the lab's paraphernalia.

The instruments hummed and the aroma of decomposed body parts and bodily fluids from the toxicology lab drifted around us. I updated him on progress, such as it was. I also told him we were trying to get help from the other labs in Scotland. This man was leading the triple murder investigation; it was my first and only encounter with him.

—

By the end of the second day, we had examined about 30 items between us. The senior detectives were not happy and pounced on my boss, who pounced on me.

'What did you expect?' I asked. 'You said everything needed to be looked at. If we have to recover trace evidence, it's going to take us forever.'

'We need to work faster,' he replied.

'No, we need to change the plan,' I said.

I had been discussing this with other colleagues. The usual

procedure would be to look for fibres transferred between the clothing of the victim and the suspect. You wouldn't normally do this if the delay between the incident and seizing the items was more than a week. Even then it would be a long shot. The fibres on tapings from the victims had been deposited years ago, when they had been in contact with their killer. But there were only a few items of clothing from the victims. In the case of Caroline Hogg, there was just one tape, with around 50 fibres on it.

We knew that Black kept his clothes for years. Was it possible that some of the items from his lodgings were as old as some of the offences? If we reversed the usual practice and, instead of targeting individual fibre types, removed all the fibres from the tapings of the victims and looked to see if these matched any of Black's clothing, we might have a better chance of finding some evidence. Equally, it could be a huge waste of time and effort. We could only do this if we stopped examining things in detail and targeted items that might be worthwhile.

In the corporate language of today, we were proposing a risk-based approach, but we didn't call it that at the time. If we coupled this approach with a search for items that were missing from the children, we would have the best chance of finding evidence – if indeed there was any.

The police reluctantly agreed.

CHAPTER TWO

The Many Roads to Justice

> Even the clearest and most perfect circumstantial
> evidence is likely to be at fault, after all, and
> therefore ought to be received with great caution.
>
> Mark Twain[1]

Robert Black was born in Falkirk in central Scotland on
21 April 1947. The name of his father is not recorded and his
unmarried mother gave him up for adoption when he was a few
months old. He spent much of his youth in Kinlochleven, in
the western Highlands, with a foster parent. His foster mother
died when he was 11, whereupon he was moved to a children's
home near Falkirk. During his stay there he attacked a young
girl with what appeared to be a sexual motive, and was moved
to another institution, in Musselburgh, near Edinburgh, where
he was sexually abused himself. When he was 17 and working
in Greenock, on the west coast of Scotland, he choked a 7-year-
old girl until she was unconscious and digitally penetrated her.
He was convicted of this offence and admonished – effectively

warned to be of good behaviour – a sentence that is difficult to understand even by the standards of the time.

He was then moved back to the Falkirk area, to Grangemouth, where his birth mother had lived. Around this time, he formed his only adult heterosexual relationship, but remained fixated with children and was caught abusing his landlord's granddaughter. He moved back to Kinlochleven and there was convicted of abusing a child in the house where he lodged. He was sentenced to a year in Borstal, after which he was moved to a probation hostel in Glasgow. When he left the hostel, aged 21, his regular contact with criminal justice and social services in Scotland ceased.

—

DS Gary Hooper was from West Yorkshire Police. He was wearing a trench coat in the lab. Some cops think they can't contaminate evidence. He held a small plastic bag up for me to see. Inside was a short piece of green braided yarn, about 30 mm long.

'It was found in Sarah's stomach,' he said in a strong Yorkshire accent. 'I've been told not to let it out of my sight. The pathologist said it must have got into her stomach around the time of her death.'

I wasn't sure how the pathologist could know this, but let it pass.

'We think it's a decorative part of some kind of fabric or clothing, piping from a cushion, something like that,' he said.

They had obviously made inquiries in the textile industry. Only someone with specialist knowledge would know that

kind of stuff. He seemed indifferent to my opinion, but I
agreed with what he had been told. It wasn't a common item
to encounter in a forensic lab. Because it could have come
from a number of different things, it was hard to add anything
to what they already knew.

'I've got a microscope slide as well,' he said, putting it on
the bench beside me.

I slipped the slide under the microscope and adjusted the
light. As I focused on the fibres, I wondered about how well
the different forces were cooperating. This item wasn't being
formally submitted for me to examine and hadn't been recorded
with the items from the rest of the case. West Yorkshire were
holding onto it.

'Do the Met know about this thread?' I asked.

'What do you mean?'

'The Met have seized Black's stuff from his bedroom, but
what about things in the other parts of the house? This braid
could have come from an item of furniture that wasn't in
Black's room.'

'Not much chance, though,' Hooper replied.

I continued to stare down the microscope.

—

The children Black abducted were from different locations
and their bodies were found around the country. The earlier
investigations were carried out by different police forces and
forensic science labs. Two of the bodies were found by the
roadside; the range of artefacts that can be encountered if
you search a roadside is extraordinary. What the police are

willing to collect and send to the lab for examination is even more extraordinary, such as items rotted or covered in moss that could not possibly be connected with the offence. We already had more work than we could cope with and I wanted to make sure that we screened out any needless examinations.

I travelled to Staffordshire with a detective sergeant from Edinburgh to triage the items from the scene where Susan Maxwell's body was found. The exhibits were stored in a disused police station. My notes list 56 items, found in a white-ceramic-tiled cell. There were body samples from Susan and a few items of clothing. There was also outer clothing, underwear, tights, pieces of cloth and fabric, a cassette tape, plastic, tarpaulin, rope, string, thread, buttons, tissue paper, carrier bags, yellow insulating tape, pieces of shoe, spectacles and a dildo. I examined some of the items there and picked out 20, including the dildo, to take back to the lab for detailed examination.

We continued to screen the items from Black's lodgings and selected 312 – mainly clothing, bedding and other items made of cloth – for detailed examination. The idea was to see if any of the fibres from the bodies of the victims matched anything from Black's room. We were also looking for other evidence: anything that might be the source of the green braid found in Harper's stomach, missing clothing from the victims, any items with missing buttons that might match buttons from where Maxwell's body was found. All 312 items would also be examined for blood and semen.

We then removed every single fibre from the tapings of the victims' clothing and categorised them by type – cotton, nylon, wool and so on – colour and other features, such as cross-sectional shape and diameter. We did the same thing with the 162 items from Black's room that we thought might be possible sources of fibres on the victims. The 162 items were then categorised into four groups. The main group consisted of 70 pieces of outer clothing that shed their highly coloured fibres. This group also included any items that matched descriptions from witnesses. These were the most likely fibres to have transferred in any contact. The other groups were less likely to yield evidence so were set aside for the moment.

All this information was put into a database, which then churned out what fibres from the victims needed to be individually compared with items from Black's lodgings. Four scientists worked on the comparisons. It was slow, detailed and tiring work, like moving a building from one spot to another one brick at a time. All the comparisons were recorded, since anything found could form the basis for evidence in court and be subject to challenge.

—

Robert Black was an unusual killer. As part of his planned appeal against conviction in the Mandy Wilson case, he was interviewed by Ray Wyre, an expert in sex crime and paedophilia. Black also allowed Wyre to interview him after he withdrew his appeal because it was likely to fail. These interviews were later published. Sexually motivated murderers are usually men, and their sexual development is laid down in puberty. They tend to be more solitary throughout their lives, and often have schizoid personality disorder. Many like to cross-dress. Black targeted girls, and his main motivations were paedophilia and sadism. Sadists want to humiliate, hurt and torture their subjects. Victims are wholly objectified; their only purpose is to serve the fantasies of their attacker, who exhibits no empathy for their suffering. Fantasy plays an important role, and because fantasies are strongly visual, the appearance of victims is important. Fantasies are honed and practised: Black told Wyre that he masturbated to visions of young girls. He found the torture and murder of a child sexually arousing. During the interviews, he repeatedly normalised his behaviour, as do many paedophiles. He never admitted guilt for any of the murders.

His van contained everything he needed for indulging and achieving fantasies of cross-dressing, paedophilia, torture and murder. He slept overnight in it. He dressed in women's and girls' clothing, masturbated and inserted objects into his anus. He travelled the country identifying locations for abducting victims. And he tortured and killed his victims in his van. This prosaic delivery vehicle was a physical manifestation of his perverted murderous fantasies. It travelled the public highways undetected for years.

Thirty-seven items were taken from the van. My case notes describe them in detail: a child's printed cotton dress, adult women's clothing (skirt, underskirt, tights), sleeping bags, rags, bags, towels and a few items of Black's clothing. One of the items was labelled 'Sock containing pencil, three wooden handles and two plastic objects'. This was not a random assemblage. These objects were carefully chosen by Black for purposes most of us could never contemplate nor understand.

The banality of their legal description shrouds and diminishes their purpose: the torture of children. Ray Wyre asked Black if he knew whether the children were alive or dead when he was assaulting them. Black's response was chilling. He said that if they were dead, they couldn't be hurt. He knew that what he was doing was inhuman, but he couldn't or wouldn't confront his actions.

The most common means of murdering someone in the UK is with a knife. I have examined thousands of knives. It doesn't require much thought: you usually know what you are looking for (blood) and where to look (the blade). That the weapon has killed someone – a mother, a father, a brother – is a remote prospect that doesn't need consideration. I examined Black's torture kit for blood, but I also needed to look for other body fluids and tissues: semen, vaginal deposits, saliva and faeces. The primitive tests to find these deposits, still in use today, required me to imagine what he might have done to his victims with these items and how I might establish this from any traces left behind. The bodies of Maxwell and Hogg were too decomposed to reveal how they had met their death, but I knew that Sarah Harper had horrific injuries. I also knew Black was obsessed with inserting items into bodily orifices.

Forensic scientists for the most part operate at a distance from the real trauma and drama of investigations. Our work is indirect: the clothing from a rape victim or samples from a suspected murderer or paedophile. We don't have to deal with the people themselves. The work is done in a lab, with occasional days out to crime scenes or mortuaries. It can be distressing, but not as bad as the trauma experienced by some other professionals in criminal justice. The worst that can happen is that we pass out at a post-mortem. The only time I ever came close to passing out was when watching a video of a crime scene in the lab. A 17-year-old schoolboy had gone berserk and killed his younger sister and brother. I made the mistake of thinking about what had happened in human rather than forensic terms. The detachment needed to do forensic work is easier to develop when you are focused on the task in front of you. Counting the bloodstains on a body in a pool of blood is then not so difficult.

—

Six months into the investigation, we had worked our way through most of the fibre comparisons and many of the other examinations. The main ones left to do were hair comparisons. Since I was the most experienced in this field, my colleagues returned to their home labs while I continued to work exclusively on the case for another few months. I became worried about keeping track of all the examinations and how these would be used to produce a report for court. We still didn't know when or where the trial was going to take place. I was concerned that something would be missed or forgotten, so decided to consolidate all the examinations and results into a report. A report compels you to check everything before you can start writing; the act of writing clarifies your mind about what any evidence might mean. This wasn't a legal document, just a summary of all the work that had been done and what we had found.

Now working alone, I examined the hairs found on the clothing of the victims. I compared them with the victims' own hair to see if there were differences. All the hairs from Hogg and Harper matched their own samples. One hair found on Maxwell's panties was different from her own. It wasn't a head hair; it could be a body hair or pubic hair.

Hair comparison is considered by many forensic scientists to be more like alchemy than science. Certainly there isn't much science involved: you simply compare the characteristics of the hairs – colour, thickness, texture and so on. Each recovered hair is compared individually with a sample from the person they are thought (or alleged) to have come from. There is no analysis, just microscopic comparison.

The difficulties are inherent in the physical characteristics of hair. Although a person may have blond or brown hair, when a sample of their hair is examined under a microscope, many differences in colour can be seen. A person who has mid-brown hair will have individual hairs that range in colour from white, which is colourless or transparent under a microscope, to dark brown, occasionally even black. A second problem is that the range of hair features from one person will overlap with those from someone else, even when the colour of their hair looks very different to the naked eye. To make matters worse, one never has a sample with enough hair in it to be confident that the full range has been obtained.

Deciding if a hair microscopically matches or not is always a tentative business. Given this, why is it worth bothering? Hair comparisons are like eyewitness accounts, which are held by courts to be so unreliable that if a case rests solely on eyewitnesses, judges are required to warn juries. The same warning should be applied to hair evidence*, but everyone is caught in a mindless machine. Police officers and lawyers want hairs examined because they think they are good evidence, and there are enough scientists either with a professional investment in their examination to keep the party going or, like me, without the influence to change things.

—

The months dragged into years.

I had completed all the necessary examinations, and after extensive discussions between the police and prosecution authorities in Scotland and England, it was decided the case would be tried in Newcastle. By this time my sole contact in the investigation was DCI Robin O'Neil. Robin was an experienced and capable detective who had been involved in the case from the outset. He knew it inside out and had personally interviewed Black, so had some insight into the man he was dealing with.

In early 1994, almost four years into the investigation, Robin brought two pieces of news to one of our meetings in the lab. Both items were bad news. The first was that Black had sacked his defence counsel and replaced him with a QC from London, Ronald Thwaites. There were thousands of items of evidence in the case and the prosecution team had spent years working with the defence to agree as much material as possible in advance of the trial. Thwaites had revoked these agreements. Six weeks before the trial, the police were almost back at square one.

---

* Nowadays DNA profiling can be used on hairs.

I had encountered Thwaites before, when he defended alleged armed robbers at the Old Bailey, in the days when people used to steal real money rather than digits from a database. Such cases attracted a small group of highly skilled and challenging barristers, who had no time for the police, were well prepared and made their points determinedly, occasionally aggressively. Between them they terrorised many witnesses, including a number of my colleagues in London. It was so bad that some of the senior staff in the London lab refused to take on armed robbery cases and they then fell to more junior staff, such as me. Fortunately, I was working with a group of very experienced scientists, some of whom relished these encounters. I never learned to relish them, but I did learn how to deal with them.

I recalled an occasion when Thwaites had been irascible and aggressive with me when I gave evidence. My impression was that he was also cantankerous and threatening in real life, but you can never be sure what is real and what is tactical in courtroom encounters. After a particularly combative session at the Old Bailey with one of his colleagues, during which I was accused of all sorts of misdeeds and incompetence, the same man was quite happy to make idle chit-chat with me as if nothing had happened just a few minutes previously.

Robin's second piece of news was that the hairs from Susan Maxwell had previously been examined by another scientist, who had come to a different conclusion from me. I had heard this on the grapevine but had ignored it in the hope that it was wrong. I knew I ought to act but was paralysed by the prospect of it, because I could think of no outcome that didn't leave me in peril. The first scientist, Robin told me, had concluded that there were several hairs on Susan's clothing that did not match her hair. The implication was that they were from her killer. It was perfectly believable to me, despite all the care we had taken, that in working our way through the mountain of items some mistakes had been made. But I was the only one who had examined the hairs. Mistakes aren't always the end of the world: they just usually are. I knew a few scientists who never recovered from the mauling they got in court for an error. Your best hope is that you won't be called to give evidence. In most cases you are not. But in this case I was certain to be called.

I travelled with Robin by car to North Yorkshire the following week. The first scientist to examine the hairs from Susan's clothing was based in a lab in Birmingham, and he had agreed to meet us halfway, at the forensic science lab in Wetherby. Norman was a very experienced scientist and I had met him on a few occasions previously. I carried in my briefcase a set of control hairs from Susan and the hairs found on her clothing. We arrived at the lab, but Norman was delayed. A temporary reprieve, I thought. Robin suggested we go for some lunch, and we drove the short distance into the town.

As we ate, Robin drew my attention to some framed pictures on the wall of the pub. 'Do you recognise that picture?' he asked.

'No,' I replied.

'It looks like one of Black's photographs.'

Black possessed a large collection of photographs, but I had paid them scant attention because they were largely irrelevant to my examinations.

As we paid for the meal, Robin asked the barmaid about the picture. She said it was a place at the edge of the town and told us how to get there. We drove through the town, across a bridge over the River Wharfe, and turned right onto a narrow, unpaved track along the river edge. As the car pulled to a stop, we fell silent. We both knew that Black had been here: at the end of a lane was a children's playground and a tennis court, two of his favourite haunts.

We got out of the car and looked back along the river towards the town. 'It was taken here,' Robin said, making a frame with his thumbs and index fingers. The scene was identical to the picture in the pub. We stood on the same spot where Black had taken the photograph. Was he identifying this as a location to snatch another child? Or had he already decided it was a good spot, and was planning an escape route? Or was it just to refresh his memory some time later? A horrific thought came to me: this was a man whose single aim in life was to abduct, torture and murder children. All his actions were predicated on these outcomes. Actions that would bring indescribable pain to his victims and their families, actions that were cruelly and coldly calculated and were beyond their comprehension and mine.

When we got back to the lab, Norman had arrived and we were shown to a room with a comparison microscope, which is two microscopes side by side, linked together by an optical bridge. The control sample is placed on one microscope and the recovered sample on the other. When you look through the two eyepieces on the optical bridge, you see a split image, with one half from each microscope, allowing a detailed comparison of the two hairs at the same time under the same lighting. I placed the hairs on the bench and got my notes out of my bag.

'Will I go first?' said Norman, taking a seat at the microscope.

I handed him the slides in cardboard trays. 'These are the control samples and these are the hairs from the body.'

He slid a sample under each microscope and pulled the light cord to darken the room – ambient light can be distracting. If Robin was tense, he gave nothing away. Norman continually adjusted the slides as he worked, comparing the individual features – colour, thickness, pattern of pigmentation – as these changed along the hairs.

'OK,' he said eventually, drawing the slide out slowly as if to indicate how much care he was taking in the comparison.

I could foresee no reconciliation of this that didn't involve serious complications. If he matched any of the hairs to Black, the defence would pitch the two of us against each other to diminish the significance of the evidence. At best the result would be confusion. If Norman decided they couldn't be from Black, the defence could suggest that someone else was the killer. I had concluded that all but one hair matched Susan and the remaining one didn't match Black. Overall the hairs were of no value, one way or the other.

Norman began the process again with a new slide, working his way through each sample in turn. The last sample had only been on the microscope for a few seconds when he turned and, leaning forward to see us in the dark, said, 'I agree.'

At first I wasn't sure what he meant. He went on to explain that when he was comparing the hairs originally, he was on the lookout for anything that might not be from Susan and might be a lead for investigators. So he erred towards identifying any hairs where there was the slightest possibility that they might be from someone else. Now that he was comparing them with hairs from Susan and with Black as a suspect, he agreed with me. I wasn't sure about his logic. I had never come across this approach before, but I felt myself relax.

—

I stepped into the witness box in the Moot Hall, Newcastle, on the morning of 15 April 1994. To my immediate left and above me was the judge, Sir William Macpherson, who later chaired the Stephen Lawrence public inquiry and introduced the UK police service to the concept of institutional racism. On the far left, level with me, was the jury. Below me in the well of the court were prosecution and defence counsel.

'I swear by Almighty God that the evidence I shall give …' I read the oath from the card in front of me.

Breaking the silence is like a surgeon's first cut. Everything has to integrate into a single faultless gesture, in which posture, eye contact and voice pace, pitch and volume must be wholly convincing. It has to convey a whole complex of things: 'I work here, I know what I'm talking about, I won't be messed with, but I'm not cocky.' Bombast doesn't work in court. There are already too many people there who make a career out of it and will be better at it than you. Much of the skill involved in being an expert witness is about structuring time, managing the onrushing present, learning not to jump in too quickly with responses. Like learning a musical instrument, with experience you realise that you can find time, even in the fastest of pieces.

'Can you tell the court your full name, please?' asked the prosecution counsel, continuing with introductory questions to establish who I was, where I worked and my level of experience. I took a file from the case that contained my papers and placed it on the edge of the witness box.

'Do you wish to refer to your notes?' he asked.

'I do.'

'When did you make your notes?'

'At the time of my examination.'

He glanced at the judge, who nodded. Another legal technicality was out of the way – my notes had been accepted as contemporaneous, so could be used to refresh my memory. I settled in and adjusted my posture, legs slightly apart, knees slightly bent, occasionally shifting weight from one foot to the other, like a soldier on guard duty. If you don't do this, you end up with a nasty pain in your lower back, which is imperceptible while giving evidence but all too noticeable when you are finished.

Gradually prosecution counsel worked his way through the case: how many items had been examined, what evidence had been looked for, how many people were involved, how long it took, the hair found on Susan's clothing, and one particular item from Black's lodgings: a copy of the *Nottingham Evening Post* newspaper, on which I had found a small stain that tested positive for seminal fluid.

I had used the standard screening test for semen, which detects an enzyme that is present in high concentrations but needs to be confirmed by the presence of sperm. I couldn't find any sperm. In fact the stain was so small that I couldn't even confirm the screening result when I repeated the test. The newspaper was found together with items of Black's that had faint smears of faeces and pubic hairs on them. On these other items I also found a few small stains that tested positive for seminal fluid. The stain on the newspaper could be due to contamination from these other items. Some scientists would have ignored this result because it seemed so inconsequential, but my experience was that it is best to default to the truth, even when that might be awkward to explain. What made the newspaper interesting was that it contained a report of Teresa Thornhill's attempted kidnap, and that it had been purchased by Black on 27 April 1988, when he had stopped to refuel on a subsequent trip to Nottingham. Knowing Black's obsessions and habits, it was easy to reach the intuitive conclusion that the newspaper was a trophy kept by him and used to relive the attack and feed his fantasies. The hints of semen seemed to confirm this.

There is a strange and tangible silence between the end of the prosecution evidence and the start of cross-examination by the defence. Time stretches out, rather like a slow-motion car crash that actually takes no more than a few seconds. Having relaxed to a degree over your testimony so far, a sense of vertigo comes upon you, like walking along a cliff edge. In this balancing act, it can feel safe to pull away from the edge by conceding to an assertion or question. This is often, though not always, the wrong thing to do. The trick is to balance, concede when it is correct to do so, but otherwise hold the line and walk the cliff edge.

Thwaites rose to cross-examine me. There would be no need for aggression on this occasion. The hair on Susan's clothing was the first issue he wanted to deal with. Since it wasn't a match for Black, he suggested that I ought to have excluded him as a source. I explained I could not, because the hair samples from Black were taken several years after the murder and may not have been representative of his hair at the time of the murder. He didn't press me too hard on this. It wasn't evidence against his client, just a loose end that he would have preferred to tie up by eliminating Black as the source. He went on to reiterate the amount of time and effort that had been put into the forensic examination, the hundreds of items, years of examination, the number of people involved. The implication was that if any evidence was present, it would have been found. He then asked:

'Have you been able to make a scientific link between this man' – he pointed towards Black – 'and any of the murders?'

'No,' I replied.

The prosecution counsel returned to this point on re-examination, asking me if I would have expected to find any evidence, given the time between Black's arrest and the offences.

'No,' I repeated.

—

'I got you a sandwich,' said Norman, who was waiting to give evidence next.

'Thanks,' I said. I wasn't ready to eat yet, but hunger would come quickly once the adrenalin wore off. One of the court ushers approached us.

'The press want to come and talk to you,' he said, looking at me.

'What about?' I asked.

'They're desperate to get some pictures and they think you're going to sneak out the back way like all the other witnesses.' The other witnesses had been whipped away by the police, but I was being left to my own devices. 'They want to know if you would be willing to talk to them before you leave the building.'

'Who is out there?' I asked.

'Everyone – all the national newspapers, TV, radio,' he replied. 'They want to send a representative to speak to you.'

I had to get from the court to Newcastle Central Station – about a 10-minute walk. I imagined they had already worked this out. It seemed to me that I would probably be harassed on my way out, but if I spoke to them, I might minimise this. I agreed to talk and the usher went off to speak to the press.

A reporter from the *Yorkshire Post* came in as I was munching my sandwich.

'We'd like you to come out the front entrance so we can get some pictures,' he said.

'You want me to walk into the lion's den?' I responded. 'The usher says there's hundreds of you out there.'

'No, there's only forty or fifty of us. We're just trying to do our job, but the police have managed to get every witness out of here without us getting near them.' He was almost pleading.

'OK. If I come out the front door, I need a guarantee I won't be harassed or manhandled, and I need that from all your colleagues as well as you.'

'And you'll let us know when you're coming out; you won't run or hide your face?'

I agreed.

Twenty minutes later, I walked out into the corridor of cameras. There seemed to be a lot more than fifty of them. I walked steadily, not rushing, looking ahead. As I passed them, many of the photographers ran backwards to stay in front of me and get more shots. One of them, carrying a hefty video camera, tumbled backwards over a parked car, ending up on the pavement in front of me. I continued, stony-faced; the last thing I needed was to have my smirking mug in the national newspapers, having just given evidence in the biggest case in the UK in decades.

—

John Milford QC skilfully presented the case for the prosecution.

On Thursday 29 July 1982, Robert Black drove his white Ford Transit van from London to Glasgow via the M1 and M6. He then travelled to Edinburgh. These were his typical routes. Around 4.15 p.m. on Friday 30th, a witness saw a white Transit van on the main road by the bridge in Coldstream. Susan Maxwell crossed that bridge at 4.30 p.m. that day and was never seen alive again. The next morning, a similar white van was seen in a lay-by at Loxley near Uttoxeter. A witness also described a man resembling Black near the van. Susan's body was found 13 days later, in trees near the same lay-by. On 6 August 1982, Black submitted a claim for a bonus that was paid to drivers for the Scottish run, corroborating his movements.

In 1983, Black was driving a grey Ford Transit van, and company petrol receipts charted his movements around the country. On 7 July 1983, fuel for this van was purchased at a service station in Northampton and paid for with BP Agency card No. 009. The same card was used to buy fuel later that day at a service station near Hull. Company records showed that card No. 009 had been issued to Robert Black and no other driver could have used it. Black then travelled towards Scotland, stopping for fuel near Gateshead, in Northumberland, and later at a service station near Berwick-upon-Tweed, by the Scottish border. He went on to make deliveries in Edinburgh and Glasgow. Caroline Hogg was last seen on Portobello promenade in Edinburgh, around 7 p.m. on Friday 8 July, about a mile from where Black had made his Edinburgh delivery. Witnesses saw her with a man fitting Black's description. Black then left Glasgow and made deliveries in Carlisle and Stafford before arriving at his London lodgings on Saturday 9 July. All of these journeys were corroborated by petrol receipts. His next journey, on 12 July, took him to Bedworth, to the east of Birmingham, about 11 miles from the lay-by where Caroline Hogg's body was found. A witness testified to seeing a similar grey van that day near the lay-by.

Black changed his van the following year and now drove a white Ford Transit. On the day that Sarah Harper went missing, 26 March 1986, company records and petrol receipts showed that Black delivered to premises in the Leeds area, arriving around 6 p.m. The premises were 150 yards from where Sarah was last seen. Later that evening, around 7.30, a witness described a man matching Black's description getting into a van outside Sarah's house. Another witness saw him in the shop where Sarah had been at around 8 p.m.

In 1988, Black's van changed again, to a blue Ford Transit. On 23 April that year, he set out on another northern run, to Warrington, making a final delivery on his way back in Radford, near Nottingham, on the evening of Sunday 24th. A CCTV camera showed a dark blue Ford Transit van at the spot where Teresa Thornhill and her boyfriend described the attempt to kidnap her. Teresa gave a good description of Black that matched a photofit.

All of this evidence placed Black at the scene of the abductions but not at the sites where the bodies were found. Since 1971, he had lodged with the Rayson family in London, and some of the Rayson children had grown up and moved on. For several years, one of them lived in the area of Donisthorpe, in the Midlands. Some of the family testified that Black would drop in on them while on his deliveries, occasionally staying overnight. This evidence showed that he regularly used the roads where the bodies of Caroline and Susan had been found. His visits to the Rayson children only partly explained his odd routes: the true reasons were more sinister.

Each case on its own was circumstantial; taken together, they formed a pattern. When Black's Scottish conviction for child abduction was added, the case against him was stronger. The conviction for abduction was allowed under the English common law of similar fact evidence, where a number of offences that appear to be connected can be considered together. The prosecution had taken this approach because it would make a more persuasive case. At the opening of the trial, Thwaites had tried to get the cases split up and treated separately, but the judge had rejected this.

Some years later, in the foreword of a book about Black's case, an experienced Scottish High Court judge expressed the view that this strategy would not have been allowed in Scotland and that the circumstantial case against Black was unlikely to have resulted in a conviction.

Black's defence was that his presence in the areas where the three girls were murdered and the fourth kidnapped was coincidence. John Milford QC for the prosecution described this as 'an affront to common sense'.

The jury returned verdicts three days later, on 19 July 1994, finding Black guilty on all counts. They were convinced that the evidence connecting him to the locations of the abductions and where the bodies were found was sufficient to establish his guilt beyond reasonable doubt.

—

It had taken 12 years to bring Black to trial. Almost 200,000 people had been interviewed, 60,000 statements had been taken, and hundreds of items forensically examined. In Clark's book, recounting an investigation that must have involved several hundred professionals, he selected 15 people for his *dramatis personae*, listing their formal qualifications and appellations in full. All were senior police officers, some of whom could only have had a passing connection with the investigation, four of whom were knights of the realm. None of the 'backup services', as Clark called them – pathologists, psychologists, scientists – are listed, nor is any police officer below the rank of detective chief inspector. He did not address the obvious and important question of how a man like Black could operate for over a decade below the radar of the UK police service, only being caught due to an observant member of the public. It would take more than a new computer system to address the issues identified in the Yorkshire Ripper report, and these issues continued to plague murder investigation in the UK for many years to come.

The forensic work had always been a long shot, but like everyone else, we knew that if there was any evidence, an effort should be made to find it. We didn't succeed, but the evidence fails to appear in many cases, and the chances in this one were very slim. Not finding evidence, not getting an 'answer', is not something that has ever bothered me. I long ago relinquished the idea that there is always something to find and I ought to be the one to find it. But I admit that I would have liked to have found something in this case. I would have liked to have contributed more directly to the conviction of Robert Black.

CHAPTER THREE

The Chillenden Murders

If there is one belief (however the facts resist
it) that unites us all … it is the conviction that
somehow … if we could only detect it, everything
will be found to hang together.

Frank Kermode[1]

Around 9.00 p.m. on 9 July 1996, Shaun Russell picked up his
home phone and called the police. His wife Lin and his two
daughters, six-year-old Megan and nine-year-old Josie, had
now been missing for several hours. The girls had been at a
swimming gala in Canterbury that day and Lin had gone to
meet them at school on their return. He then contacted local
hospitals and his neighbours; no one knew where his family
were. Over the course of the coming hours, Shaun Russell
would confront unimaginable loss.

—

The morning of 10 July 1996 was bright and warm as I drove
to Surrey Police Headquarters in Guildford. Traffic on the
M25 motorway was moving freely for a change. I answered the

phone and heard the voice of my deputy, 'Geordie' Wright, head of crime scene investigation.

'We've got a bad one here, Jim. I need you to do some scene examination.' Geordie was a man with a complicated reputation: big, loud, direct, but highly respected for his experience and for defending his troops. He was the most loyal person I had ever worked with.

'What's the story?' I asked.

'It's a double murder, a mother and her six-year-old daughter. Another daughter has serious head injuries; she's unlikely to survive.'

'Are the bodies still at the scene?' I asked.

'They are,' Geordie confirmed. 'We need you here right away. It looks as if one of the victims was tied to a tree. Oh, and there's a dog,' he added.

'They killed a dog?' I asked.

'Yeah, the dog's at the scene as well, we're trying to find a vet to examine it.'

'Any suspects?' I asked.

'None so far. We're not sure how many were involved; could be more than one.'

'OK, where are you?' I asked.

Geordie described the location and how to get there. It would be obvious when I arrived, he said; there was a large police presence. As I made my way back around the M25 towards Kent, I wondered what I would face at the scene in Chillenden.

—

The doctrine of scene examination is that attentive, dispas-
sionate observation, gathering minute details – 'leaving
no stone unturned' – will reveal what has taken place. The
assumption is that the answer to every question lies in detail
– 'trifles', as Sherlock Holmes called them. Gradually the
detail accrued shifts the balance from opacity to clarity, from
incomprehension to understanding, like building up a digital
image, pixel by pixel. The amount of information at most
scenes is overwhelming and confusing, and the opportunities
for error and misunderstanding are great. So the process has
to start slowly and steadily. At the beginning no one knows
the answers, but they emerge as the collective knowledge of
everyone present distils information from a combination of
experience, skill, imagination and guesswork. Holmes sees
it all instantaneously because his act is a trick; his cleverness
comes from his omniscient creator.

But sometimes reality mimics art, and on these rare occasions
the interpretation of a crime scene can be instantaneous, like
a 3-D image snapping into focus when you put on those special
specs. This has only happened to me occasionally, but when
it does, it leaves an indelible memory.

In the early nineties, I was asked to examine the bloodstain
patterns at the scene of a murder in a bedsit tenement flat
in a smart area of Edinburgh. The doorway in which I stood
was in the corner of the room. Diagonally opposite me was
another door to a small kitchen. There was a double bed in
the middle of the wall facing me. The body of a man in his late

forties was sitting upright on the floor with his back against the wall to my right. I walked over to the body; the man had been battered and his face was covered in blood, but there was no blood staining on the wall behind him. Two CSIs, suited and gloved, busied themselves with their own work.

'Who moved the body?' I said to no one in particular. Both CSIs turned towards me and then to each other. There was no response. This possibility hadn't occurred to them.

I moved closer to the body and looked at the floor in the gap between the bed and the wall that led to the kitchen. There was a small bedside table by the bed, next to the kitchen doorway. On the floor between me and the bedside table were some flattened and bloodstained cardboard boxes. Iain, a perennially miserable photographer, was standing in the doorway photographing the kitchen.

'Have a look under the bedside table,' I said to him. 'There should be some blood there.'

He gave me his usual 'I'm really busy, can't you do it yourself?' look before he realised I would need to walk over the bloodstained cardboard boxes. He got down on his knees and shone a light under the table.

'How did you know it was there?' he asked.

'Splashes?' I asked.

'Yes,' he replied.

Splashes on the underside of the table could only have come from below, so I knew the victim must have been attacked on the floor near the bedside table. I had made a working assumption that all the blood was from the victim. I hadn't yet searched the place, but I hadn't picked up anything that suggested otherwise. As I left the scene, I passed my provisional conclusions about the blood pattern to the crime-scene manager: the victim was battered on the floor near the bed and then the body was moved and propped up against the wall.

Some days later, the DCI in charge of the scene examination unit came to see me. Alec was a capable and affable character; we had worked well together on a few cases. We chatted for a bit, then he went quiet. 'How did you know there was blood under the bedside table?' he asked.

I explained that if the victim had been attacked on the floor by the bed, there was likely to have been blood under the table.

'But how did you *know* it was there?' he persisted.

'I didn't. I just thought that was the most probable place for it.'

My powers of deduction, as Holmes might call them, had been the subject of debate and speculation for several days in the crime-scene unit, and the DCI had taken it upon himself to clear the matter up for everyone.

I had been at the scene for a few minutes and in that time had integrated conscious observations (the lack of blood behind the body) with unconscious observations (there was no obvious blood anywhere else in the room) and combined these with intuitive judgements (he was attacked on the floor beside the bed). This kind of reasoning happens all the time, but not usually so quickly. And there is no problem with it. Imagination and intuition only become a problem when you fail to step back and test them with evidence. If Iain had said there was no blood under the bedside table, I would have abandoned my hypothesis and come up with another.

Imagining hypotheses is fine; failing to abandon them when you have no evidence to support them is not. Even worse is ignoring evidence that contradicts your theory.

—

Chillenden is a hamlet in the parish of Goodnestone that is recorded in Domesday Book. It is midway between Canterbury and Dover, on the edge of the North Downs, with a population of around a hundred people. This is archetypal rural England; there is a twelfth-century church, a village hall, a pond and a nineteenth-century windmill. The Russells' home, Granary Cottage, and the location of the crime scene, Cherry Garden Lane, emphasised the extraordinary conjunction of tourist-brochure England and multiple murder.

I arrived at 12.15 p.m. and Geordie walked me from the rendezvous point to the scene. We ducked under the outer cordon and walked up the track. There was lush woodland on our left and a field of ripe corn on our right swaying in the warm breeze. It was bright and sunny. The track was just wide enough for a single vehicle and obviously didn't get much use. Geordie talked me through what had been done so far and what he hoped I could help with. As we spoke, I tried to find a frame of reference for a double murder and attempted murder like this. I could find none. A sense of how unusual the case was, and how newsworthy it would become, was dawning on me as we spoke. I had also heard that two SIOs had turned the case down before DCI Dave Stevens had accepted the job. It seemed I wasn't the only one who sensed the difficulties ahead.

DCI Stevens was intelligent and thoughtful but not vastly experienced at this stage of his career. But few SIOs anywhere in the country would have previously encountered such a case. Stevens was under intense pressure. He had to deal with a team of investigators who all seemed to have different theories about the case, as well as internal police politics and external demands from the media.

High levels of media attention generally lead to problems. The police try to control information in investigations, particularly before any arrests. But murders like this are hot news and the less scrupulous journalists are quite happy to interfere with witnesses, evidence and police procedures to get a story. Ironically, one of the main sources of information for journalists is the police themselves. Many police organisations are extraordinarily porous, and the media often get information from insiders that investigators would rather they didn't. Years later, around the time of the Leveson inquiry, I joked with a senior police officer I knew well that I might leak information to the media. He laughed. He didn't need me to leak stories, he said; there were plenty of individuals in his own organisation who were already doing it.

Stevens had to apply for an air exclusion zone over the scene to prevent a national newspaper from capturing images from a light aircraft. The media were the SIO's problem, not mine, but in cases like this, the pressure diffuses out to everyone involved in the case. It's not usually explicit, but it is always on your mind, like a vague sense that you have something important to do but can't remember what it is.

We stopped at the inner cordon to log in. I watched as Geordie carefully checked his scene suit – 'The bastards sometimes deliberately give me a suit that's too small to wind me up,' he said – but it went on without difficulty. This wasn't the time for japes. We then left the track and walked into the woods along the common approach path – the route that everyone would take in and out of the scene. Deciding on this path can be tricky. The idea is that you find a way in and out that does the least damage to the scene and avoids the route used by the perpetrator. Sometimes this is obvious – in houses, most people come in and out of doors or occasionally windows. Sometimes there is evidence that provides a clue to the perpetrator's access and exit, such as shoe marks or a blood trail. The common approach path is the first part of the scene to be examined, before everyone starts tramping over it.

The inner scene was smaller than a child's bedroom in a modern house – about 1.5 metres by 2.5 metres. Inside a circle of trees were the bodies of Lin and Megan Russell, and Lucy, their small white dog. As I listened to Geordie, I was already thinking about some of the possibilities and how I might go about testing any hypotheses. Two people had been killed in this tiny space, and a third, left for dead, was fighting for her life in hospital. The bodies had been found by a police search team at around 1.30 in the morning. The horrific injuries, visible only by torchlight, led the officers to believe that all three of the Russell family were dead. But someone thought they saw one of the children blink, and a doctor confirmed that there were signs of life. Josie, gravely injured and suffering from hypothermia, was cradled in the arms of a young police constable and driven at high speed by the doctor to the nearest hospital in Canterbury.

The sun threw shifting shafts of light onto the bodies; wrens chirruped in the background. I was already getting warm inside my scene suit. Geordie was asking questions. Did I think there could be any blood from the killer? Could I tell him in what order the attacks had taken place? Had the bodies been moved, or were they attacked where they were found? No obvious answers were jumping out; it would all need careful examination and reflection. Theoretically, bloodstain pattern analysis can help answer these questions, but multiple attacks so close to one another would make the examination difficult. Blood pattern would overlay blood pattern, one casting a shadow on another, adding an extra layer of complication and uncertainty, blurring any interpretation. My instinct was that there were too many imponderables for me to make sense immediately of what had taken place. I would only find out after a detailed examination.

Scene examination is about the present tense: start somewhere and work out what to do next while doing that. I would start by looking for blood that might have come from the killer and that could lead to an identification. This would transform the investigation. But to shed blood, the killer would need to be injured, and we had no indication that was the case. The sequence of events – who was attacked first, and where – might emerge, but I wasn't convinced. That information is more useful after someone has been arrested, because it can be used to test their story.

By the time I arrived, everyone else had been at the scene for a few hours. They had already absorbed all the important information and were busy at work. I was still trying to work out what might be significant. From where I stood at the edge of the circle of trees, I could see six dried pools of blood. There were pools beside the bodies of Lin and Megan. Examining them might tell me if they had been attacked where they lay. Geordie pointed out another pool of blood just outside the trees. This was where Josie had been found. Questions kept popping into in my mind and distracting my thinking. Who was attacked first? Where were they attacked? There were more pools of blood than there were victims; were any of them attacked in more than one place? Did any of the victims move themselves, or did someone else (the murderer) move them? Trying to work this out is like working backwards in a completed game of chess that you weren't involved in at the beginning. I was never very good at chess; I could never hold enough moves in my head at one time.

The trick for me is to combine the brain work with practical work. Doing is thinking. Start with the basics, sketch the scene, walk around it slowly, view it from different angles and positions. Buy time to think. Gradually information builds and creates the foundation needed for logical analysis. Listen to everything that is going on around you, talk to people to get a sense of how capable they are. Work out if you can trust them. Engage them but say nothing about what is in your mind until you can back it up solidly.

How much you tell people depends on who they are, how confident you are, how straightforward or complicated your findings are. You will tell forensic colleagues a lot more than a detective, although it depends very much on who the detective is and how well you know them. I had worked for Kent Police for less than six months at this time. I hardly knew my own team, let alone anyone else. If you don't know anyone at the scene, a common experience for a forensic scientist, you have to make a judgement based on a few hours working together. If you have a tricky point to explain and you get the impression that the crime-scene manager or SIO will not grasp the nuances of it, you tell them nothing and spin some yarn about needing lab results first before reaching a conclusion. The alternative, giving them all the details, is taking a risk that your evidence will be misinterpreted or misunderstood and overplayed. It is *never* underplayed; possibilities become probabilities, probabilities become certainties, everyone seems to want a definite answer when there isn't one to be had.

—

A body is the defining element of a crime scene, physically, psychologically and legally. No image or description can substitute for its presence in engaging you with your examination, in enabling understanding of the space you are exploring or the significance of the enterprise you are undertaking. An individual has ceased to exist and has been transformed into an object of acute professional, legal and scientific questioning. Who has died? How did they die? What events led to their death? Was someone responsible for their death? Who was responsible? The exact disposition of the body in space and time will be recorded, pored over, discussed, theorised, interpreted. Later, all of this will be anatomised in court. More mundanely, when writing reports, you are able to refer to the person by name because you saw them *in situ,* which is much easier than the cumbersome 'the body of the person I now know to be …'

I crouched down to look closely at the nearest body. The first wave of blowflies had already arrived. Human gestation takes nine months, but in fewer than nine hours, an entire ecosystem of decay begins to dismantle the body and recycle it. The parade of marauding insects, arachnids, fungi and mammals is as predictable as waves washing against a shore, but it has the destructive power of a slow-motion tsunami. Only the most intractable of debris will remain if this process is not disturbed. The flies buzzed, the maggots writhed and tumbled; sparrows cheeped.

The clothing on the first body was extensively bloodstained and there was a pool of blood around the head. I could see signs of a ligature on the right wrist. It looked as if the victim had been attacked where she lay. I searched for the small bloodstains that would confirm this. They would form a pattern radiating outwards from the pool, dispersed by the force of the blows. I could see lots of tiny blood splashes on the ivy on the ground, but could make no sense of the pattern. There *was* no pattern. In response to the changing light, the ivy leaves had moved since the blood was deposited.

Some of the bloodstains on the upper clothing had run down her T-shirt; they must have been made when she was standing up. Amongst all this blood, one spot caught my attention: a small round speck on the inner face of her right arm. This didn't fit in with the other patterns of bloodstains. It was circular so had dropped onto her arm once she was lying on the ground. It could have dripped from a weapon, in which case it would probably be from one of the victims. But it could be from the killer if he (or she) had injured themselves. I asked the nearest CSI to sample it.

I moved on. On the ground between the two bodies was a pair of children's red jelly shoes. The face and body of the second victim were covered in smeared blood, but there were no signs of the tiny bloodstains typical of violent blows. There was a pair of blue tights tied to a tree about 60 cm from the ground. I couldn't see any blood on the tights, but they would need to removed and examined in detail in the lab.

I scrutinised the dog, its brown collar and lead still attached to it. I could see blood around the muzzle and a lot of tiny bloodstains on its back. The tiny bloodstains were caused by a blow but not to the dog. The dog was present during the attack. But exactly where it was would be impossible to establish. I imagined it running around frantically.

I looked at all the blood pools in turn and then at the pool outside the circle of trees where Josie had been found. Then I went back to the first body to start again: check my observations, rethink possibilities, let the ideas incubate.

Excluding the dog, there were three victims and six pools of blood. What were the options? Even if I could work out all the possibilities of where the bodies might have been, how would I decide which was most likely? If there was no one explanation with clear water between it and all the others – which was what seemed to be the case – I wasn't going to try. To some extent the scene spoke for itself: half a family had been wiped out of existence. What more did I need to say? The bodies had been moved, but I didn't know in what order. I wasn't sure there was much I could add to what any untrained observer would see.

—

The motive[2] for the attack on the Russells was a recurrent and pressing question, subject to much speculation by the investigation team. Categorising a crime by way of a motive can help identify possible offenders, particularly offenders who have previous convictions for similar crimes. Motive also provides the foundation for a narrative: 'he attacked him to rob him' is a convenient way of explaining a crime so that it can be understood. But in terms of *the* causal factor for an attack on an individual and their subsequent death, it is an oversimplification almost to the point of childishness. The law understands this and avoids the problem by not requiring proof of motivation.

But how does one categorise an extremely unusual crime, one that occurs a few times in a century? None of the investigation team had any previous experience of an attempted triple homicide. Nor was there at this stage much evidence to support any individual motive. None of the typical motives for murder – robbery, hate, violence, revenge, sex – fitted this crime easily or precisely. The question of sexual violence was the most pressing and significant. Clothing from the victims and swabs from their bodies would be sent to the lab to be tested for semen, but that would take a few days.

The post-mortem examinations were scheduled for nine o'clock that evening. I tend to avoid post-mortems unless they are essential – for example, to understand the victims' injuries and how they might have bled at the crime scene. It wasn't necessary in this case because I saw the bodies at the scene. I'm not sure why I went. Maybe it was because it was such an exceptional case and I thought it might be important for me to do so. I have no recollection of the examinations. When I think about them, my mind conjures up an image of me standing in the foreground in the mortuary, some distance from the table, looking at the silhouette of a child's body, its limbs flexed, held in place by rigor mortis.

—

I went back the following day to complete my scene examination. By this time two of my colleagues, CSI Simon Gallagher and SCSI Ian Carroll, had found more bloodstains on the track leading to the copse. There were four groups of stains, all of which were downward droplets in what I would call drip patterns. It seemed likely these were from one or more of the victims, but until they were analysed, we wouldn't know.

We wondered if there could be any semen at the scene. One of the problems with locating seminal stains is that, unlike blood, they are often invisible to the naked eye. In the lab there is a simple chemical test that can indicate the presence of semen. I have carried out this test at scenes on a few occasions, but it is complicated to use and some of the chemicals involved are carcinogenic. It wouldn't be practical to try it in this case. Some seminal stains fluoresce when illuminated with ultraviolet (UV) light, but the fluorescence is faint and can't be seen very well in daylight. We decided to examine the scene that night. This would give us the best chance to see any faintly glowing stains.

Three of us in white suits scoured the scene in darkness with UV lamps. I had never done an examination like this before and I have never done one since. It's amazing how many things in a wood fluoresce when you shine UV light on them. We checked each time with white light, but none of the stains looked as if they could be semen. We sent a few to the lab to be double-checked, but the tests were all negative. Finding semen would have established a sexual element to the murders. But its absence did not exclude a sexual motive. We were no further forward.

—

Megan and Josie were on their way home from school with their mother, Lin, when the attacks happened. Amongst the most poignant items at the scene were a pair of matching lunch bags. Inside each was a small plastic lunch box and a flask. Both bags were zipped closed and there were bloodstains on the inside and outside of each of them. A fingerprint in blood was found on the lid of one of the lunch boxes. Any parent with a school-aged child could connect with these lunch bags; they could have belonged to *their* child. On the face of it, no one at the scene gave these items any more thought than any of the other evidence. But there was something forlorn about them that was impossible to ignore, set alongside the coldness and brutality of a person who could murder children and search through their personal belongings in this way.

On the afternoon of the second day, a black bootlace was found in Cherry Garden Lane, about 45 metres up the track from where the bodies lay. It was 97.5 cm long and knotted in three places near the middle. It did not belong to any of the victims and was bloodstained. It was unquestionably connected with the offence.

A number of witnesses came forward in the days following the murders. Each recalled incidents that had happened shortly after they were believed to have occurred. One of the witnesses described how she was forced to slow down suddenly when a beige car pulled out in front of her unexpectedly. As she followed the car, she could see an angry man looking at her in his wing mirror. She helped detectives make an e-fit of the driver.

Another witness saw a man standing by a hedgerow near the murder scene beside a beige Ford Escort. Later that evening, when the witness was walking his dog, he looked into the hedge and found a string bag containing strips of bloodstained blue towel.

A third witness, a woman driving nearby, saw an agitated man by the roadside carrying a claw hammer.

Few expected Josie Russell to survive the horrific attack, but after weeks of intensive medical support, she was out of danger. However, her prognosis was unclear and because of her injuries it would be months before she was able to give detectives any information about what had happened. Two Kent police officers, Pauline Smith and Ed Tingley, remained with Josie and Shaun throughout her hospitalisation and recovery. They acted as family liaison officers and provided protection and security in the face of constant media intrusions. On one occasion a journalist posed as a parent in an attempt to get to Josie.

—

There is a common misconception that what needs to be forensically examined in a case is immediately obvious. Sometimes it is – a knife that is believed to have been used to stab someone would always be a candidate, as would a gun that is thought to have shot someone. In a murder there will usually be many more items than these obvious ones; sometimes hundreds, occasionally thousands.

Sometimes the problem is made worse by the way items are recovered by the police, who on occasion resort to mindless dredging rather than thoughtful harvesting. The dominant anxiety for those involved in this process (usually crime scene investigators) is that they might miss something of importance, a cardinal sin that can wreck a reputation, occasionally a career. How to avoid this transgression is drummed into CSIs and cops early on: bag and tag *everything*.

Once the police have all this stuff, the problem then becomes what to do with it next. This is a much bigger problem than anyone outside of the forensic world appears to credit. It all seems to work so logically and seamlessly on *CSI* or … (insert your favourite cop/forensic programme). One of the reasons why this is such a problem is because the police don't understand forensic science; something else that is counterintuitive to anyone outside the business. Take this for granted at the moment, but my supporting arguments from forty years' experience will gradually unfold over the course of this book.

The situation is further compounded by police culture, because the police are always anxious to *do* something and less keen to reflect on *what* to do. Most investigators just want to get everything examined; after all, they have collected everything, haven't they? This was how it was with most cases when I worked in Edinburgh. As much as a third of the work I carried out in the lab at the time was utterly pointless. All it did was make a busy lab even busier, more frustrated and demotivated. At the same time it relieved investigators of the responsibility to make decisions and passed the problem to someone else; it ticked all their boxes. One murder I recall from Edinburgh involved around a hundred items for examination: clothing from the victim, clothing from the accused, blood samples from the victim and accused, bloodstains from the crime scene, weapons, hair samples, skin swabs and much more. This was weeks and weeks of work. The accompanying paperwork with the case had a simple but witless instruction: 'Usual murder examination.'

Another complicating factor in the Russell case was that the forensic work for Kent Police was done by an external supplier: the Forensic Science Service (FSS), a government agency. When I worked in Scotland and London, I was based in a forensic lab that was part of a police force. If I was at a crime scene, I *was* the lab. In England and Wales, outside the capital, the arrangements were different: there were regional forensic labs who did the work. The relationship between the police, who are obsessed with control, and forensic scientists, who are obsessed with process, is a tricky one. Every SIO has a story of how he or she has been let down by false promises and failed deliveries from a scientist. Every scientist has a story about how they were compelled to carry out pointless work or how their evidence was misunderstood by the police.

My role in Kent was different from working in the lab. Yes, I was still doing some forensic work, but I was also running a big department that included crime-scene investigation, photography and imaging, and fingerprint examination. I was no longer *the* forensic scientist in a case; more a forensic consultant to the SIO and other investigators in every case where advice was needed.

What added friction to the already tricky relationship between the police and the external labs was that, in 1990, the FSS started charging for their services. Every examination had to be paid for and so needed to be thought through and justified in a budget. This isn't a bad idea in itself, and with the right relationships it acts as a reality check on the more extravagant examinations that often arise in a murder inquiry. Individually, not all scientists or investigators have the skills or temperament for these negotiations, which is why it is so important that teams are involved. Crucially, a great deal of trust is needed, and in the tense process of a difficult and high-profile investigation, this is easily damaged. When I worked in England, I encountered many investigators who believed that the FSS would advise them to do more work than was needed, just to make money. I never found any evidence for this, but it was an idea entrenched in the minds of some and it eroded trust. I probably encountered an equal number of investigators who blindly followed what the FSS proposed when this was not always the best way forward for either the force or the investigation.

A good proportion of scientists didn't like the charging arrangements either and were happy to provide 'back-door'

services by doing things for free or undercharging to make
their lives easier. Gradually this black market was squeezed out
and there were no more favours to be had from old pals. This
meant I was often caught in the middle of negotiations where
the police made demands for disruptive and time-consuming
tests that weren't necessary, or a scientist failed to grasp the
significance of an examination to the inquiry.

—

In the days and weeks following the murders, the forensic results
began to trickle through. Many of the analyses were initially
unsuccessful or uncertain. Testing of the blood droplet I had
singled out from the scene failed; further analysis would be
needed. The bloodstains from the clothing and from the scene
could all be attributed to the victims. Nothing from a possible
offender had been found. The six strips of bloodstained towel
found in the string bag were all part of the same towel.

The blood matched* the victims'. No semen was found† on
the swabs from the victims or on their clothing. Nor was any
semen found on the girls' swimsuits, the towels or the string
bag. The blood on the dog's teeth was dog blood. There had
been hopes that it might be from an attacker who had been
bitten. Initial tests on the bootlace showed the presence of
blood from Josie and Megan, but further work was needed.

---

* Strictly speaking it is the DNA profiles from the bloodstains and the DNA
profiles from the victims that match. This phraseology can be cumbersome
in a book of this type so I have simplified the language in many instances.
† In fact a tiny trace was found on one item, but this was put down to a false
positive reaction in the test or to contamination, similar to the findings in
the Robert Black case.

Many hairs were found on the clothing and shoes of the victims. Most of these matched one or more of the Russells, but some appeared to be different and were subjected to further tests.

The focus of the investigation and forensic work had been on the main crime scene where the bodies were found, but an extended search of the surrounding area had also been carried out. This uncovered bottles, crisp packets, pencils, sweet wrappers, plastic bags, beer cans, newspapers, sales receipts and porno mags; all the usual human detritus that turns up in a search of this kind. A black balaclava was also found, in Nooketts Wood, half a mile from the crime scene. There was no blood on the balaclava, but tests suggested there were traces of saliva, although this couldn't be confirmed. Twenty-two hairs were found on it; some inside, some outside. All of the hairs were different from the victims' and some were suitable for DNA testing.

A red cotton fibre and a blue synthetic fibre were also found on the outside of the balaclava. The red fibre matched fibres in Megan's jumper and the blue fibre matched fibres in Josie's cardigan. The SIO, Dave Stevens, came to see me. 'The forensic scientist says the fibres are not significant, but I don't agree,' he said. So what? I thought. It's not your call, that's why we use experts. 'I think we should contact the expert and challenge this.' What he meant was that *I* should contact the expert and challenge it.

I have interpreted fibres evidence many times. The general approach takes into account the number and type of fibres found and how common they are. When small numbers are involved, what you are trying to do is distinguish between fibres that are present by chance, part of the background, and evidence of something that is connected to the events being investigated. Imagine trying to listen to very faint music from an analogue radio with lots of hiss. You are trying to distinguish the music from the interference. It's similar with forensic evidence: there needs to be enough information to separate the evidence (the music) from the background (the hiss). In this case, the two fibres were in the background; they were not enough from which to draw any reliable conclusions.

I explained that there was no point in me phoning the expert since I agreed with him. And there was no point in Stevens phoning him since he didn't really understand the evidence and the expert would stand his ground. It could make him look biased. All the discussion would do was damage relationships, and maybe even the case when it came to court. Stevens was desperate to find evidence in this demanding and frustrating case, but this wouldn't help. I had no problem with him challenging the evidence; it's part of the process of making sense of things and I have encountered it many times. What was important was that he listened to my argument, which he did.

—

PolSA (police search adviser) is an acronym I had to look up before writing this. I had heard it used hundreds of times before, and I knew what a PolSA search was, but it had never occurred to me to find out what the letters stood for. PolSA teams are the guys who search the drains before the Queen or the Prime Minister arrives in town, to ensure there are no hidden IEDs. They are also deployed in major investigations to find evidence of various kinds, such as drugs or weapons, and in searches for missing persons or bodies. PolSA teams carry out carefully planned, detailed and systematic searches, so when they search for something, they find it. Or do they? Two months to the day after the murders, some local residents found a hammer in a hedge near the crime scene. The hedge had previously been searched by a PolSA team. The locals had held a seance and the Ouija board had told them where the hammer was. The PolSA team searched the hedge again. They found a purse that they had missed first time around. The purse had been stolen from a local house three years before; it wasn't connected with the murder.

On 6 November, long after the hammer had been found and the inevitable review of the incident was completed, I went to a meeting about what had gone wrong with the searches. The author of the review, a superintendent, concluded that the purse should have been found, but if the hammer had been there at the time it would have been found. I thought about this. We missed a purse that had been in the hedge for three years, but we didn't miss the hammer? It didn't quite stack up for me. I was glad I was a peripheral player in this farrago.

Procedural thoroughness, the idea that the police consistently use a systematic and detailed approach, is a myth. Try typing 'detectives left no stone unturned' into Google and you will find page after page of examples. What has struck me more frequently during my career is how ad hoc police practices are. They vary enormously from county to county and country to country. Each individual force is confident that it has the best way of doing things. There are many manuals, policies and guidelines, some of which purport to set national standards, but their role is largely symbolic and they are rarely consistently followed.

A forensic examination established that there was no blood on the hammer. It was ruled out of the investigation.

—

Three months into the case and there was little sign of an arrest. Most people are killed by someone they know, and it was inevitable that some suspicion would surround Shaun Russell until he could be confidently eliminated. He was aware of this. One of the police officers, Ed Tingley, who had become a constant part of Shaun's life, providing support and security, had told him that 'the vast majority of women-and-child murders are carried out by spouses or lovers'.

During the mid 1980s, the use of psychological profilers in major crime investigations had become fashionable. This practice was picked up from the FBI, who had developed some of the techniques used. Like many trends in policing, it relied more on advocacy and anecdote than evidence that demonstrated its worth. Some of the individuals involved were professional psychologists or psychiatrists, some were not, and SIOs were divided about whether the process added anything to an investigation. My experience was similar: sometimes this advice added clarity or confirmed decisions already made, sometimes it was a distraction; occasionally it was a source of problems.

The most notorious example of psychological profiling going wrong was in the investigation of the murder of Rachel Nickell in 1992 (see Chapter Nine), a case that some of the media were now suggesting could be linked to the Russell murders. About three months into the investigation, DCI Stevens told Shaun Russell that they were using a forensic psychologist to 'build a picture of the killer'.[3] Shaun, hoping to get some understanding of who had attacked his family, asked if he could meet the profiler. Stevens was initially reluctant but eventually agreed, and the three men met in the Russells' back garden one afternoon. Shaun asked the psychologist about the techniques he used in his work. The profiler instead turned the questioning round and tried to elicit information about Shaun's background and emotional state. Shaun felt cheated by this and wondered if the meeting had been a set-up to test him further as a potential suspect.

Few believed that Shaun Russell was the killer, but formally eliminating him as a suspect was problematic. One of the very simple tools detectives use in a murder inquiry is a timeline on which they plot key events based on witnesses' accounts, phone calls, CCTV and so on. This can corroborate events, but it can also throw up discordances for further investigation. Resolving these discordances lies at the heart of many police investigations.

A receptionist at a local hospital had said that Shaun called the hospital enquiring about his family at around 6.00 p.m. on the day they went missing. This was only shortly after the murders had happened and two hours before Shaun had said he had returned home. Many months into the investigation, Stevens confronted him about the call.[4] He denied making it. But if he didn't make the call, who did, and how did the caller know the family name? If you believe that all things are knowable, that all circumstances will yield to rational inquiry, as many people do, this leaves you with a large and unresolved problem. The alternative is to accept the frailty of human memory and the ability of others to judge the veracity of such claims. The claim about the call was never explained.

—

Almost a year into the investigation, much of the forensic testing had been carried out and we had a long list of results. The bootlace was stained with Megan's blood, but as yet, nothing from a possible offender had been found. Two hairs had been found on one of Josie's jelly shoes that didn't appear to match any of the Russell family. These hairs and some other hairs found at the scene had been DNA-tested, but without success. Standard DNA profiling needs a hair root; it doesn't work on hair shafts. Mitochondrial DNA (mtDNA) testing, however, a new technique that had become available, worked on hair shafts. It was expensive and took a long time, but some of the tests were successful. Yet there was no mtDNA database, and until there was a suspect to compare the results with, this information would take the investigation no further.

The blue tights belonging to Josie were stained with her own blood. The towelling pieces from the hedgerow were stained with blood of one or more of the victims. Hairs were also found on the towel, but all of them looked microscopically similar to hairs from the victims. The towel pieces were examined for varnish fragments that might have come from the shaft of a hammer: no such fragments were found. Hairs and blood on the string bag matched those from the victims. Some red fibres found at the scene were of interest but, like the mtDNA, until a suspect was arrested and their clothing obtained, they were of little use in taking things forward. The blood from the trail found in Cherry Garden Lane matched Lin Russell. The fingerprint in blood found on one of the lunch boxes did not have enough detail for identification. The pattern of the mark was similar to Lin's so it could possibly have come from her. Another finger mark found on a drinks bottle inside one of the bags matched Josie. There were some other fragmentary fingerprints on the lunch bags and on the jelly shoes, but there was not enough detail in them to be of any use.

The prospects of an arrest looked as slim as ever.

CHAPTER FOUR

The Trials of Michael Stone

… even where decisions are rationally based, they
are not the product of any objective state of affairs
but of our *perception* of those states of affairs.

Michael Frayn[1]

On the first anniversary of the Russell murders, a BBC *Crimewatch*
programme appealed for witnesses and information. The
murders were described as unprecedented in British criminal
history. It's hard to know what this means. What exactly was
it that was unprecedented? The number of victims? The age
of the victims? That it was a single family? That they were
murdered at the same time? None of these characteristics was
unique; all have occurred before in the UK in the past hundred
years. Shaun Russell was suspicious of the media attention the
case attracted. He had lived in Africa and encountered death
almost daily. He believed the public representation of his case
was more to do with the relationship between the media and
the police, and Josie's photogenic appearance.

Amongst the 600 or so phone calls received from the public
was one from Dr Philip Sugarman,[2] a psychiatrist. Sugarman

had treated a man called Michael Stone and said the e-fit shown on *Crimewatch* resembled him. On 14 July, detectives tracked Stone down at his mother's house in Gillingham, Kent. Stone denied the offence. A magistrate granted the police time to interview him further. Stone was interviewed for 22 hours in total; he answered every question put to him and maintained his innocence throughout. Detectives had to decide whether to charge him or release him.

On 20 October 1997, Michael Stone was charged with the murders of Lin and Megan and the attempted murder of Josie. Over the course of the next few days, around 40 officers from Kent Police would log into the Police National Computer to obtain details about Stone and the case. Few of these officers were involved in the investigation; they had no right to the information.

At the time of his arrest, Michael Stone was 37 years old and living in the Medway towns in Kent, 40 miles from where the attacks had taken place. He had been brought up in an environment of domestic abuse and had been physically and sexually abused in care. He had been involved in petty crime from the age of 12 and his criminal activities became more serious as he grew older. He was a heroin addict with a lengthy criminal record for misuse of drugs, robbery and violence, and had been in prison a number of times, for assault, armed robbery and – crucially for the prosecution in the Russell case – attacking a man with a hammer in 1981. In 1994, he had been sectioned under the Mental Health Act, although it was later decided that he could be released. His lifestyle was chaotic and revolved around his drug use and criminal activities.

Weeks and months passed in the investigation with no
progress despite enormous effort. The crime-scene borders,
which had previously determined the priorities of what was
to be forensically examined, became more and more porous.
Items from further and further away from where the bodies
were found were being sent for forensic examination. Amongst
these items was a sweatshirt found in a lay-by a few miles from
the scene. What was its relevance? I didn't know. Maybe there
was intelligence that hadn't been shared with me, but I wasn't
convinced this would yield anything. It looked to me like the
usual mission creep that happens in a struggling inquiry, with
detectives becoming increasingly desperate for evidence.

On 1 July 1998, scientists at the FSS found a DNA profile on
the black bootlace that didn't match Stone. Ten days later, a
DNA profile matching the one on the bootlace was obtained
from a hair on the sweatshirt found a few miles from the crime
scene. This opened multiple new lines of inquiry. Who did the
sweatshirt belong to? How and when did it get in the lay-by?
Could the owner be traced? The sweatshirt and the lace were
linked by DNA and the lace was believed to have been left by
the killer. The new findings now provided a means to directly
identify the killer by a mass DNA screening.

—

The first DNA mass screening in the UK had taken place in
1987. Two 15-year-old schoolgirls, Linda Mann and Dawn
Ashworth, had been raped and murdered in rural Leicestershire.
These murders resembled the Chillenden case in some ways:
uncommon and violent crimes in a rural setting. Although

the murders were three years apart, the bodies of the girls had been found within a few hundred yards of each other, and the cases were linked by the blood group of the semen found in both cases.

Richard Buckland, a local boy with learning difficulties, was interviewed and appeared to have let slip details about the crimes that had not been made public. He confessed to one of the murders but not the other. Detectives, convinced that the same person had killed both girls, concluded he was lying and charged him with both. After the initial court hearing, investigators became concerned about Buckland's continued denial of one of the crimes and how this might affect the trial. They contacted Dr Alec Jeffreys, whose lab at Leicester University was only five miles from where the murders had taken place. Jeffreys had discovered a new technique that he had called DNA fingerprinting,* and investigators wondered if this could be of use to them. Until then, DNA fingerprinting had only been used for immigration cases but never in a criminal case.

Jeffreys analysed samples from both cases. His results were astounding. He confirmed that the two murders were linked – the semen on both bodies matched – but the DNA was not from Buckland. The police, convinced that the killer was local, embarked on the world's first DNA mass screening, in which over 5,000 men gave blood samples. Colin Pitchfork persuaded another man to provide a blood sample in lieu of his, but their discussion was overheard and reported to the

---

* This was his original term, which has now been abandoned in favour of 'DNA profiling'.

police. Pitchfork was arrested and subsequently convicted of raping and murdering both girls.

DNA fingerprinting had provided evidence where hitherto there had been none. It had unequivocally linked the cases, identified the killer and exonerated a vulnerable suspect. It probably prevented a miscarriage of justice and resulted in a confession from Pitchfork, avoiding the time and cost of a trial. The two villages at the heart of the murders could now return to some form of normality after years of suspicion and fear. The modern miracle of forensic science had arrived – the biggest breakthrough in crime investigation since the discovery of fingerprints; the cure-all, the catch-all, the cold-case caduceus.

DNA fingerprinting would bring unquestionable benefits to the investigation of crime, but it was to be a long and hard road. Understanding the technology was beyond all but a small group of experts, and there were many challenges ahead that would befuddle the police and confront the courts with major difficulties in weighing up evidence. In time, however, it would revolutionise how crime was investigated and prosecuted.

—

DCI Dave Stevens was keen to rule out contamination. The only person from Kent Police who had been directly involved with both the sweatshirt and the bootlace was CSI Simon Gallagher. The DNA was not from him. Nor was it from anyone else who had been at the crime scene. Having excluded the possibility of contamination, Stevens convened a meeting to plan the DNA mass screening. Was there any chance that there had been contamination in the lab? asked one of the

investigation team. 'We have to take this result at face value,'
I replied. 'There is no reason to believe there has been any
contamination.' In my experience, most contamination was
caused by police sloppiness before the samples got anywhere
near a lab; I thought it could be safely ruled out here.

There were over 6,000 names in the investigation database
and we needed to decide how to prioritise sampling and
analysis to identify the individual as quickly and efficiently as
possible. The planning would take several days. I was driving
to a meeting near Canterbury when Geordie rang me. 'Where
are you?' he asked. 'Pull over.'

'I can't,' I replied. I could hear the urgency in his voice.
'What's the problem?'

'It was contamination,' he said. 'The DNA match was contamination. I need you back here, they're baying for blood.'

One detective in the investigation team tried to throw
the blame my way. I had reassured them, they said. But the
argument was a sideshow. What we needed to know was how
this had happened.

It transpired that an assistant scientist had managed to
contaminate both the lace and the sweatshirt with his own
DNA, probably from a couple of loose hairs from his arms or
hands, making it look as if there was a connection between
the two items.

It took six weeks to get this story from the FSS, who were
defensive and reluctant to respond. In the process we found
out that the FSS didn't routinely check staff against DNA
matches, so there could be misleading DNA results circulating
in investigations around the country. It wasn't just a Kent

problem. Nor did they have a full DNA database of their staff to eliminate them.

The police were not much better at this either. Providing an elimination sample to check whether a police officer had accidentally contaminated an item was voluntary, and many police officers who went to crime scenes were reluctant to do so. From that day on, gloves, overshoes, face masks and over-suits with the hood up were mandatory at major crime scenes in Kent. When the story spread around the country, most other police forces adopted the same measures. The poor response from the FSS and the excessive demands of the police* sent the relationship between the two organisations into a downward trajectory.

—

The trial of Michael Stone started on 5 October 1998 at Maidstone Crown Court. The modern court in the centre of the town was built in 1983 to replace the original, which became Kent County Council headquarters. As I waited to give evidence, my memory drifted back to a time when I had given evidence in the old court many years before. It was in a robbery case, and it wasn't one of my best performances.

Under pressure from the police to meet a deadline, I released my statement before the scientific tests were completed. There was only one test outstanding, but it turned out to be critical; I had misidentified a fibre. You only make such a mistake once,

---

* It was suggested by Kent Police that they should be compensated by a complete analysis of the DNA on the lace, which would have cost around £70,000.

and I quickly corrected the error in a second statement. I had found fibres that incriminated the two suspects, and at the trial I was taken through my evidence in detail by prosecution counsel. This gave me the chance to correct my error in person and apologise to the court; however, I hadn't found many fibres so the evidence was not strong, and I had handed a Christmas present to the defence.

At the end of my evidence in chief,* defence counsel rose from his seat, adjusting his gown. He took me through my statement in detail, page by page from beginning to end, except for my conclusions – the part that tells the court what the evidence means. There was no mention of the error. Then he stopped and bent over to confer with his junior counsel. Was this a genuine conversation, or for dramatic effect? I wondered. You can never be sure. I waited. I looked at the jury. Some of the jury members were looking at me, some were lost in their own thoughts. I glanced at the judge, who had completed his note-taking and was now watching defence counsel. The court was almost silent; occasional whispers from the defence team were audible from where I was standing in the witness box.

At last defence counsel turned away from his colleague and, standing upright, looked directly at me. 'Could I ask you to turn to page four of your statement.' Here we go, I thought; the whispers were tactical, a deliberate pause to raise tension. 'Could you please read out the second sentence in paragraph three, in order that the ladies and gentlemen of the jury may hear it.'

---

* This is the first stage of giving evidence, which may be followed by cross-examination from the other side.

This was the only sentence in my report that I didn't want to read out. I wanted to forget it. It was the misidentification of the fibre. I read it out, then started to explain, but I was interrupted.

'Is that sentence correct, Mr Fraser?' I started to respond. 'Is that sentence correct?' he asked again, now looking towards the jury.

There are many tactics that counsel can use in a situation like this; I call this one 'ritual humiliation'. Unlike football, cross-examination is a game where it is perfectly legitimate to go for the man if you can't get the ball—

'James …' A woman's voice cut through the daydream. I was on my feet before the court usher got to my surname.

The courtroom was packed, the press gallery full. Every national newspaper must have had at least one reporter present. The prosecution team was Anne Rafferty QC and junior counsel Mark Ellison. Rafferty subsequently became a judge and now sits in the Court of Appeal. Ellison is now a senior QC and was the advocate who led the successful prosecution in the Stephen Lawrence case.

Ellison skilfully took me through my evidence in chief. He began with my qualifications and experience, inviting me, with the judge's permission, to refer to my notes. He then set the scene with a few introductory questions. He was doing all the work. He knew exactly what he wanted from me. Did I go to Cherry Garden Lane on 12 July? Did I make a detailed examination of bloodstains in the copse and lane? His substantive questions focused on my conclusions and avoided the details of my examination. Did I form a view as to whether one or more of the bodies had been moved from the places where they were attacked?

'Yes,' I replied.

What did I mean by 'moved'? Had the victims just fallen down?

'No, the bodies had been moved from where they had been attacked.'

Was there any evidence that someone had been attacked while tied to the tree with the blue tights?

'No, there was no evidence of that.'

He then asked me to look at the scene photographs and told the jury to refer to photo 19. Did I place the various markers on the track where the bloodstains were found?

'No, that was done by CSIs.'

What had I concluded about the bloodstains on the track?

'They were in a linear pattern, typical of someone bleeding or holding a weapon dripping with blood.'

There was no cross-examination from William Clegg QC, who was representing Stone. I had found nothing to incriminate his client.

I am not an anxious expert witness, but neither am I a regular star performer (I have had occasional moments). My approach is simple: get in and get out with minimal drama, tell the truth and do your best to hold your line when necessary. Don't get emotional, don't get angry when abused, don't make jokes no matter how friendly the judge seems to be; try not to make mistakes. Sometimes it's OK and you come out with an extraordinary feeling of lightness and release. Sometimes it's horrible and you come out indignant

and angry. You can never tell until it's over. This time it
was OK.

—

Neither Shaun nor Josie had to give evidence in person. Shaun
made written statements and was interviewed by video. In the
months following the attack, Josie slowly regained her memory
and speech. Her account of what happened on the day of the
murders was recorded and the video shown to the jury. She
described how the family were walking back from school after
the swimming gala. They crossed a rape field, went through
Woodpecker Wood and into Cherry Garden Lane. As they were
walking down the lane, they had to step aside to let a car pass.
Josie waved to the driver but he didn't wave back.

When they came around the corner, the car was parked
across the lane blocking their way. A man got out and took a
hammer from the back of the car. He threatened them, he
wanted money, but her mum didn't have any with her. Her
mum said there would be money in the house if the man
would come with them, but he said no and became angrier.
Her mum told Josie to run but the man grabbed her and hit
her with a hammer. They were forced into the copse and tied
up with strips of towel, a shoelace and a pair of tights. Josie was
tied up with a shoelace. The man went through their lunch
boxes looking for things. He then attacked all of them in turn
and killed the dog.

The jury was also shown a video of an ID parade. Stone was
lined up with another nine men. Shaun was with Josie and he
could see that she was frightened[3] in the dark, claustrophobic

viewing gallery. Behind the two-way mirror could be the man who had tried to kill her. She rushed through the gallery with her head down, hardly looking at the men. She didn't pick any of them out.

The prosecution case was largely circumstantial. Stone resembled an e-fit of a man seen driving a car near the scene shortly after the murders. He was a man with a history of violence and had made a hammer attack in the past. He was an intravenous drug user and the bootlace stained with the blood of the victims and used to tie Josie up was said to be a drug user's tourniquet. He had connections with the area in his past; he had been in foster accommodation with his sister locally. He was a known shed burglar who had stolen lawnmowers; a lawnmower had been stolen on the day of the murders. A witness had seen blood on his clothing around the time of the crime, but the clothing had never been found and the date was uncertain.

The circumstantial evidence was supported by a key witness who said that Stone had confessed to the crime. Damian Daley, a 23-year-old with a reputation for being a hard man, had been remanded to Canterbury prison. He was in a cell on the bottom floor of the segregation unit and Stone was in the adjoining cell. According to Daley, Stone had told him through pipework between the cells that he had attacked the Russells. He mentioned using wet towels and a shoelace to tie them up and that a dog was continually barking.

Another prisoner, Barry Thomson, who was almost at the end of his two-year sentence, said Stone had spoken to him on a few occasions in the exercise yard. On one of these occasions, he had threatened him: 'He looked menacingly at me with his eyes rolling into the back of his head and said "I made a mistake with her, I won't make the same fucking mistake with you."'[4] Before his arrest, Stone had visited a friend, Mark Jennings, who was in prison serving a life sentence for murder. According to Jennings, Stone told him that he (Jennings) should have killed the witnesses to his crime. Stone said he would kill anyone including women and children if it kept him out of jail.

—

In a criminal trial, the prosecution need to prove their case, and an accused person is innocent until proven guilty. The defence is not required to present a case, nor is the accused required to give evidence.* At the end of the prosecution case, the defence faced the crucial decision of whether to put Stone in the witness box or not. Stone wanted his day in court; he wanted to prove his innocence. The accused person has to decide in line with advice from their legal team if giving evidence is the best move. For Clegg, the advice was easy; Stone would have been a disastrous witness. His mental health problems would have made him a soft target for the prosecution. Clegg's account to the jury was that Stone had already explained his position and there was nothing else to add. He had been interviewed by the police for 22 hours, he had answered all their questions and given a full account. He had not said 'no comment'. Clegg emphasised the position of

* There are some notable exceptions to this; for example, when the defence case is self-defence.

the defence: there was no direct evidence against Stone and the circumstantial evidence was weak or doubtful. He believed the likelihood of conviction was slim.

At the end of the 14-day trial, Mr Justice Kennedy summed up for the jury. In essence, he told them that if they did not believe the prison confessions, there was not enough other evidence to convict Stone. The jury deliberated for two days before finding Michael Stone guilty, by a 10–2 majority, of the murders of Lin and Megan Russell and the attempted murder of Josie. He was given three life sentences. When being sentenced by the judge, he shouted from the dock, 'I didn't do it, Your Honour.'[5]

Within 48 hours, the case took a dramatic turn. Barry Thomson, who had convictions for dishonesty and intimidating a witness, contacted a *Daily Mirror* journalist and admitted that he had 'told the jury a pack of lies'.[6] The family of Mark Jennings had been paid £5,000 by *The Sun* newspaper and were expecting to receive a further £10,000 for his story if Stone was convicted. Jennings could not benefit from the cash personally because he was serving life imprisonment for murder.

In November, Stone's defence team lodged a formal appeal. In the meantime, I continued to work with DCI Dave Stevens to review the forensic evidence, particularly in light of some developing DNA techniques that might be useful. We also had a case conference with the new prosecuting counsel, Nigel Sweeney QC.

The appeal was delayed until February 2001 due to the investigation of Thomson for perjury. Prosecution and defence agreed that if Damian Daley's account of the confession was true, it was an admission by Stone that he was the murderer. At the trial, parts of Daley's evidence had been corroborated by Thomson. Now this had been thrown into doubt because Thomson had been lying. According to Clegg, the prosecution 'more or less admitted'[7] that the conviction was unsafe but insisted there should be a retrial.

Clegg argued that the amount of publicity the case had received would make it difficult for Stone to get a fair hearing. Sweeney presented evidence about the number of articles that had been published around the time of the trial, trying to minimise their impact by saying that not all of them were hostile to Stone: some had raised the issue of mental health; others the problems with cell confessions. Clegg derided this view; it would be impossible for Stone to get a fair trial in what had become one of the most publicly notorious cases in recent memory.

In making their decision, the judges referred to several equally notorious cases: Ronnie Kray, Rosemary West, and the Guildford Four. The court decided that there should be a retrial but that it should not take place in Maidstone. The change in location and the lapse of time between the first and second trial would be safeguards against adverse publicity.

—

The retrial began on 5 September 2001 at Nottingham Crown Court, 170 miles from where the first trial had been held. The judge ordered the media not to refer to it as Stone's *second* trial, or to the outcome of his first trial. It was as if this could roll back time and undo what everyone already knew.

And so it began again, with each side preparing its story, this time better informed about how to set out the plots and sub-plots, what evidence would be important and what less so.

The prosecution needed to present credible characters and a causal chain of events to convince the jury that Stone was guilty beyond reasonable doubt. They needed to convince the jury that he had been in Cherry Garden Lane that day, that he was there for a reason (the mainspring of their narrative – his motive), that this reason was murderous and that he attacked the Russell family, killing two of them. The central characters in this drama included Stone, the victims, and the key witness: Daley. Other secondary characters might appear in court personally or by proxy via statements or videos. But some of the key props of this drama were missing: for example, where was the hammer?

—

I waited in the witness room with DCI Dave Stevens, Dr Mike Heath, the forensic pathologist, and a few others. Waiting is the worst part, and on this occasion it wasn't helped by lost sleep caused by a fire alarm in the hotel during the night. Sometimes the waiting is eased by the presence of colleagues, sometimes not. Conversation can be a helpful distraction from the endless introspection about what might happen when you get into the witness box. But I prefer to be a solitary waiter. I have my own rituals: the constant reading and rereading of my notes, the frequent trips to the toilet. These behaviours can look odd to others. On one occasion a fellow scientist asked me why I kept studying the file when we had both read it a couple of times before we left the lab. I knew why, but was unable to articulate my answer. It's just what I do to manage my demons: stage fright, the prospect of failure, the terror of error.

There is also the possibility that you will get caught up in a conversation with someone who has just finished giving their evidence and has returned to the witness room. Although witnesses will have made statements before a trial, their evidence is what is heard *during* the trial.* If something unexpected comes up, the temptation to warn a subsequent witness can be huge. This is taboo; witnesses should be uncontaminated prior to their testimony, not forewarned so that they can avoid difficulties or shore up a particular point. This lesson was ingrained in me after witnessing its consequences many years ago. It is something I have never forgotten.

I was sitting on the marble bench facing the door of Court 4 in the Old Bailey with a CSI and a couple of detectives. A detective sergeant burst out of the courtroom. 'You saw the floor, didn't you? It was wiped, wasn't it?' He looked along the line at each of us in turn.

I had met this DS on and off over the course of the investigation; he was straight out of *Life on Mars* with his talk of lags, blags and slags. When you work closely with cops, you get to know many of them well. Generally it works fine, although there is always a need to keep some distance for those inevitable occasions when you have to tell them that the evidence you have found is not what they had hoped for. This DS was an

---

* In some instances the statements are accepted by both sides, in which case there is no need to call the witness.

exception. He wasn't just an amusing stereotype; he was dangerous, and I didn't trust him. I wasn't sure if he was stupid, manipulative or both.

I closed my case file, which was on my lap (yes, I was reading it), put it in my briefcase, got up and walked to the opposite side of the atrium and looked out into the street. I didn't hear the ensuing conversation.

After I gave my evidence, rather than leave, I sat in the court to watch the show and recover from cross-examination by Michael Mansfield, one of England's top defence QCs. The CSI who had been sitting beside me on the bench was called next. He stood in the witness box and took the oath. He looked quite young and inexperienced; I hadn't noticed this before. He was only asked a few questions by prosecution counsel, the final one being 'Did you notice anything about the floor?' To which he replied, 'Yes, it was wiped.' His evidence was short and, on the face of it, inconsequential.

Mansfield rose to cross-examine him. The CSI's brief and exact answers had made him suspicious. He asked the CSI if he had discussed his evidence with anyone else before coming into court. The CSI said no. The question was repeated and the denials continued. Not only was the CSI committing a procedural breach, he was lying, and somehow Mansfield had sensed this. Having now encouraged the CSI to dig himself in, Mansfield proceeded to extract the truth from him. It was like watching a cornered animal waiting to be dispatched by a terrifying predator. When the judge reminded the CSI that he was on oath, I could watch no longer and left the courtroom. I couldn't face the *coup de grâce*.

At the mid-morning break in Nottingham, one of the lawyers came into the witness room to tell us their plan. He spoke to Stevens and Heath in turn. Both were important witnesses; the story could not be told without them. 'And you're on straight after lunch,' he said, punching me chummily on the shoulder.

'I'm not being funny,' I said, 'but why am I here anyway? I don't really have any evidence of any use.'

'It's a retrial,' he replied. 'Most of the evidence is on paper, which is very dull for everyone involved. So every now and then the jury need an interesting live witness to keep them awake; today you're it.'

My evidence in chief was as straightforward as it had been in Maidstone. In cross-examination, Clegg challenged my interpretations of the blood patterns and how I had chosen between alternative explanations of how the bodies may have been moved. He was implying my judgements had been rash. I wasn't sure what his point was. In re-examination, prosecution counsel countered this, asking me to remind the court what I had said about the alternative explanations. I repeated the words I had used: deciding between them 'was a finely balanced judgement'.

Perhaps this exchange was what had been meant by keeping the jury awake. Clegg had injected some drama into the proceedings, but for what purpose? Were the circumstances not dramatic enough – the virtual slaughter of three members of a family? Was it possible that this fact would be lost in the dreary succession of papers that were being presented to the jury? My evidence had gone unchallenged in the first trial because I'd found nothing to incriminate Stone. Why challenge it now?

Did Clegg want to disrupt the evenly unfolding narrative from the prosecution, or was he just a little dyspeptic?

—

On 4 October 2001, after almost 11 hours of deliberation, the jury found Stone guilty of all three charges by a majority verdict. He was sentenced to life imprisonment on each of the charges. The word everyone reached for was 'evil'. The *Guardian* described him as an 'evil man';[8] Dave Stevens said, 'Josie's survival was a triumph over evil.'[9] Another detective said, 'It is difficult to know if Stone really has forgotten in a haze of drugs that he did it, and is mentally disturbed, or if he is just truly evil.'[10]

Few doubted that Michael Stone was the type of man who could have committed such a crime. He had a long history of violence and mental health problems, and his need for drugs could have driven him to desperate acts. To prove he was the killer, the prosecution had to weave a story from a network of indirect evidence. What was the evidence for and against him?

The e-fit of the man seen near the scene at the time of the murder resembles Stone. The lips and nose look about right, as do the eyes and ears. But Stone's face is more elongated. Is it him? The e-fit was created from the memory of a single witness. The encounter was brief and emotionally charged, both factors that affect accuracy and recall. The woman who created the e-fit did not pick Stone out in the ID parade. Does it resemble Stone because it *was* him or because it just happens to look like him? How many other men does it also look like? A forensic scientist in weighing their evidence would want to know this probability, because it has an important bearing on the judgement. These are not factors that courts tend to entertain. Some people have pointed to a resemblance to Levi Bellfield, a man convicted of multiple murder who also used a hammer. Is this chance also?

Another witness saw a man with a claw hammer near the scene at the time. The hammer used to commit the crime was never found. The man seen dumping the items stained with Lin and Megan's blood in the hedge was clearly involved in the attack. He had been seen beside what was described as a beige Ford Escort. Stone owned a white Toyota. There was no evidence in the Toyota to connect him to the crime. He had no access to another car, nor was there any evidence that he borrowed or stole a car to commit the crime.

Stone was seen by a police officer over 40 miles away in the Chatham area just before and just after the murders. It was possible that he could have travelled to Chillenden to carry out the attack and then returned to Chatham, but did he know the area? He had been fostered as a child about four miles from where the attack took place. According to his sister, though, they were never allowed to leave the home. Even if he knew the area and was there around that time, *why* was he there? To steal the lawnmower that went missing that day? The lawnmower was never found. Or was it to rob the victims? Of what? There was little to be had, and he left Lin with her watch and necklace. Motive does not need to be proved, but it can be used as armature to weave a story around, to make it more explicable, more comprehensible, more credible.

The key evidence before the juries in both trials was the

testimony of Damian Daley, a known liar and a man with a long criminal record. Daley recounted a conversation with Stone through pipework in Canterbury prison. The suggestion was that he knew things that were not in the public domain and could only have been told to him by the killer. In fact, everything he told the police and the court was already in the public domain. In the first trial, Daley's evidence was supported by two other convicts. In the second trial it stood alone, but he was in the witness box at least twice as long as on the first occasion.

The jury in the second trial went to Canterbury prison and listened through the pipework to see if they could hear someone reciting an extract from *Harry Potter and the Goblet of Fire*. Were these the same circumstances as the alleged confession? No. Was it the same person speaking? No. Were the cells in the same condition? No, the walls had been repaired. This was not experiment; it was theatre. The jury could determine if it was possible to hear when they were present, but not if this was possible at the time when Stone and Daley were there. The Nottingham jury also went to Cherry Garden Lane, to the crime scene. This was more theatre. *Mythos* and *logos* reside comfortably side by side in a criminal trial.

In both trials the judges made it clear that the most significant evidence was the prison confession. If the jury did not believe this, then they must acquit Stone. The criminal justice system still prizes witness testimony, the emotional recollection of an individual, above almost all other types of evidence. But Daley was not a typical witness. In a system where character as well as testimony comes into play, his was not an unmarked character. He was a self-confessed liar, so this was no easy decision.

Stone answered all questions put to him by detectives and has never changed his story. Does his record suggest he was so desperate and violent that he would try to kill a family of three for what seems to be no reason? Who knows? There was no direct evidence against him: no eyewitnesses, no identification, no forensic evidence. If the jury did not believe Daley, there was not enough other evidence to convict Stone. But they did, on two separate occasions, some years apart and in different parts of England. Not all of them agreed, however, and if one more person had dissented in either trial, Stone would have been acquitted.

—

I had more reflections, reconsiderations, discussions and meetings about this case than any other I have been involved in. The investigation spanned the entire time that I worked for Kent Police, from 1996 until 2004. It was constantly under review even after Stone was convicted. DNA profiling* was rapidly evolving during this time, working on smaller and smaller samples and giving better and better results. The possibility that some forensic evidence might be found that would link Stone to the murders was continually under consideration. I was frequently engaged in advising and helping make sense of each new set of results. There was also the possibility that

* The standard form of DNA profiling in 1996 was SGM (second-generation multiplex). That same year, mitochondrial DNA and Y-STR testing were introduced. In 1997, SGM Plus was introduced, and in 2000 low-template DNA analysis became available. All of these techniques were used in the case.

we would find something that would cast doubt on Stone's conviction or exclude him as the killer. If there was a concern about this, no one mentioned it to me. What everyone wanted was some clear and definitive sign, one way or the other.

Long after Stone had been convicted, in one of the many memos that formed a paper trail of all this ongoing activity, Dave Stevens, by now a detective superintendent, summarised the situation. He listed all the forensic work that had been done, the numerous experts involved, and detailed the information that had been established to piece together how the crime had been committed. A single sentence on the last page summed up the outcome: 'No items seized from Michael Stone … or another person can be positively linked to the murder scene.'

Perhaps the most surprising aspect of the case, and the one that baffles many people, including me, was that no forensic evidence was found to incriminate Stone. If 'every contact leaves a trace', where was the trace? Did someone miss evidence at the scene? Did *I* miss something at the scene? Was something lost in the lab? Or was there nothing to be lost? Stone was arrested a year after the crime. This might explain why no evidence (blood, fibres, hairs) was found on him. But what about the other way around? Why was there nothing from him left at the scene? What about the bootlace? It was stained with blood from the victims and Josie described how it was used as a ligature. Why was there no DNA from Stone on this if it was something he owned and handled regularly before as well as during the crime? Samples from the lace were tested as recently as 2017,[11] yet only minuscule traces of DNA were found, too little to connect it to Stone or to anyone else.

The surprising truth is that, although scientists can predict the trajectory of a bullet, or measure the path of subatomic particles and the expansion of the universe, it is impossible to accurately predict in many circumstances whether DNA will be found. A crime is a unique event that is not amenable to this type of scientific analysis or prediction. Sometimes no DNA is found when everyone expects it, and sometimes it is found when no one expects it. DNA from one person can be found on another when they have never been in contact because it was transferred indirectly. Prediction about DNA transfers relies on the subjective opinion and experience of the individual scientist in the individual case.

Did Stone attack the Russell family? Only two groups of people have heard the full story; those present at his two trials. Most of the jury thought he was the killer; some did not.

CHAPTER FIVE

The Murder of Wendy Sewell

It is in the nature of an hypothesis ... that
it assimilates everything to itself, as proper
nourishment; and from the first moment ... grows
stronger by everything you see, hear, read or
understand ...

Laurence Sterne[1]

On 7 February 2001, the journalist Don Hale stood outside
the Royal Courts of Justice in the Strand, London. His
smile was a little stiff, but his arm was raised in triumphal
salute, his fist clenched as he faced the flashing cameras.
He had led a long campaign to free Stephen Downing,
who had been convicted of murder in 1973 and had spent
27 years in prison. The Court of Appeal had just ordered
his release on bail pending appeal.

Such events are extraordinarily rare. Downing had
unsuccessfully appealed in 1974 and Hale had been campaigning
for him since 1995, the same year that the law had established

a new body, the Criminal Cases Review Commission (CCRC), to review possible miscarriages of justice. The CCRC had the power to refer a conviction back to the Court of Appeal if a case could be made. Even so, the odds were slim – about 50/1 against referral – and there was no guarantee that following referral the Court of Appeal would agree with the view of the CCRC. There was also the possibility that a successful appeal would result in a retrial and the whole process would begin again. A year later, Hale and Downing's legal team completed a grand slam; the case had been referred, his conviction overturned and no retrial was ordered. Downing was free to return to his family and community.

—

Wendy Sewell had worked in the offices of the Forestry Commission in Bakewell, a small market town in Derbyshire with a population of about 3,000. She was walking in a nearby cemetery during her lunch break when she was attacked on Wednesday 12 September 1973. She suffered multiple skull fractures and other injuries from a pickaxe handle that was found near her almost lifeless body. Her clothing had been disturbed; she was naked from the waist down and her top had been pulled up above her breasts.

Downing was 17 years old at the time. He worked in the cemetery as a gardener and lived nearby. He was described variously as backward, of limited intelligence and having a low IQ. Nowadays he would be classed as a vulnerable individual who needed support. He had told one of his fellow workers that he had found Sewell lying bleeding on a path through the cemetery. He took his colleague to see for himself. The two men were joined by other workers, who noticed that Downing's clothing was bloodstained. Shortly afterwards, the police and an ambulance arrived. Downing agreed to go to the local police station to be interviewed as a witness. Two days later, Sewell died of her injuries.

Downing was questioned throughout the day and late into the evening. He was not given access to legal advice, although his father was allowed to see him for a short time. At 10.45 p.m., he was cautioned by the police and confessed to attacking Sewell. The police wrote his statement out in pencil and he signed it in ink. He was still awake in the early hours of Thursday morning when the official records show he had his fingernail scrapings taken.

Downing later withdrew his confession and at his trial denied both the attack and making comments to witnesses that appeared to incriminate him. But he admitted that when he found Sewell he put his hands between her breasts to see if her heart was beating, and also put a finger into her vagina. He said that he confessed to the police because he was tired and hungry. The most compliant of scapegoats are those who cannot cope with their accusers or speak for themselves. The police said Downing had not been mistreated and his barrister stated in court that there was 'no suggestion … [of] any improper behaviour on the part of the police'.[2]

A forensic scientist, Norman Lee, examined the blood on Downing's clothing. He said the pattern of staining was a textbook example of what might be expected given Sewell's injuries.

For many years, the issue had been whether or not Downing had killed Wendy Sewell. Following the quashing of his conviction, the issue was now who *had* killed her? The release of Downing had left the police with a problem: a high-profile unsolved murder. On 25 March 2002, Derbyshire Constabulary asked me to review the case. I was asked to carry out a comprehensive forensic review and commission any further testing that was required. I was also to re-examine the bloodstain pattern evidence, which was one of two reasons why the conviction had been overturned.

—

There are three reasons why a case might need to be reviewed: it is unsolved, it is a possible miscarriage, or it is problematic and there is a need for reassurance. Sometimes more than one of these reasons applies, although this is not always explicit. Whatever the reason for review, historic cases carry significant baggage and practical problems. Items from the case go missing or are damaged by poor storage. Statements disappear or no longer comply with the law. Witnesses, detectives and others move on and sometimes die. What may have started as complicated becomes more so with the passage of time.

Another problem is that past judgements, actions or inactions will come under scrutiny; individual and organisational reputations may be at stake. Not everyone wants to cooperate with a review, although few will openly admit this. I have known of instances where what was expected was that the original investigation be rubber-stamped rather than scrutinised. The reviewer can also be a danger to themselves. It can be flattering to be asked to review an especially tricky case. So before you start, you need to pose yourself some demanding questions and answer them honestly. Do I truly have the skills to do this work? Do I want to wade into what might be an irresolvable historic mess? Will there be publicity, and if so, how will I handle it?

Weighing against all these negatives and complications is the possibility that you might crack a problem that has so far resisted solution. This is a rare event, but not unheard of. The trick is to imagine this possibility, because it is a source of motivation, but not to let your imagination run wild. There is no guarantee that a case many decades old can be solved in the traditional sense – with a trial and subsequent conviction. Sometimes more evidence is found but it is still not enough. Sometimes a suspect is too old or infirm to stand trial; sometimes they die before the trial can take place.

All of this means that the first step is to attend to some practical details; terms of reference between you and your client. If there is any unwillingness on their part to agree terms of reference, I don't take the work on, no matter how interesting the case appears to be.

I was approached to review the murder of Jodie Jones, who was killed near Edinburgh in 2003. It was a case that attracted a great deal of media attention because the accused, Luke Mitchell, and the victim were both only 14 years old. I had also picked up some rumours about problems at the crime scene that could add some tension to any review.

I had been contacted by the SIO, with whom I had worked in the past. We had a friendly chat and I agreed in principle to review the case. Later I was contacted by a detective sergeant to discuss the details – or so I thought. What exactly did they want me to review: the lab work – biology, chemistry, toxicology, etc.? The scene examination? The lab work *and* the scene examination? What kind of report did they want and when did they want it by? Might I be called as a witness, or would I stay in the background? Would I have free access to all the case information? I sensed her impatience with these questions, and when I stopped, she said, 'Are you saying you don't want to review the case?' I wondered what the problem was. 'No, I just want to know exactly what you want me to do,' I replied. I never heard from her again, nor from anyone else involved in the case.

Luke Mitchell was later convicted of killing Jones, in what was the longest trial of a single accused in Scottish legal history. He appealed twice and was refused in both instances. In the first appeal judgement there were echoes of the Downing case. One of the appeal judges said, 'The police … plainly embarked upon a campaign … to force a confession from the appellant.'[3] There seemed to have been an expectation that I would stroll into the middle of this controversial case without a plan.

—

Don Hale, then editor of the *Matlock Mercury*, had been voted journalist of the year in 2001 and awarded an OBE for his campaign on the Downing case. In 2002, he published *Town Without Pity*,[4] an account of the campaign to free Downing. The book reads like a thriller and Hale comes across as an intrepid, single-minded sleuth in pursuit of the truth. Starting in

1994, he reinterviewed witnesses, tracked down new witnesses, traced documentation and highlighted defects in the original investigation. He also received a number of anonymous letters about the case. He was in regular contact with Downing and his family throughout his investigations and in his book gives a detailed account from Downing of what happened on the day of the murder. He explains how he drew on his wide network of contacts in the media and the police, including some informants in Derbyshire Constabulary, to build a compelling case to secure Downing's release.

All of this work appeared to put him at some personal risk; he recounted numerous death threats from anonymous individuals as well as actual attempts to injure, if not kill him. As someone from outside the system, he encountered extensive bureaucratic resistance, denials and obfuscation from Derbyshire Constabulary, the Home Office and the prison service. I have seen this before; the system maintaining itself, countervailing with the simple expedients that everyone claims to be the victim of a miscarriage, that there is a procedure to be followed, or in some instances that there is no procedure and therefore nothing to be done. At best this is frustrating, at worst it is cruel.

The Sewell case had polarised the local community; many believed Downing was guilty, others believed him to be innocent. Whatever the case, the appeal court had decided to quash the conviction for two reasons: his confession was deemed inadmissible because it was oppressive, and the bloodstain pattern evidence of the original forensic scientist was considered to be unreliable. Yet the conviction had been defended for many years by Derbyshire Constabulary, so who would trust them to reinvestigate the case adequately now?

This problem was not a new one. In London, a string of high-profile failed investigations, such as the Stephen Lawrence inquiry, had resulted in arrangements to ensure review processes were transparent, engaged the local community and engendered trust. Following this model, the Derbyshire reinvestigation would be overseen by an independent advisory group that included a leading criminal barrister selected by the Downing family, Downing's legal adviser, a recently retired senior SIO from a different police force and an independent representative from the Crown Prosecution Service.

The terms of reference agreed by the independent advisory group were: 'to review all available evidence … relating to the death of Wendy Sewell … [and] conduct any necessary further inquiries to establish who may or may not be responsible'. What this meant for me was a complete reconsideration of all the forensic evidence, including examining important items that were still available, commissioning new analyses and re-evaluating all the findings in light of any new information.

—

DI Chris Sutton was my link to Derbyshire Constabulary. 'What do you need from me?' he asked when he came to see me at police HQ in Maidstone.

I gave him the potted version of what had become my standard terms of reference for any review: that Derbyshire Constabulary respond adequately to any reasonable request from me to progress my review. I added, 'And I need the primary materials, not a summary someone else has produced.'

Sutton took a bundle of files and papers from his briefcase and showed me what he had brought with him: forensic and witness statements, scene photographs, maps, plans and graphics of the scene, press reports and more.

'I need the original statements from the witnesses at the scene, and a timeline,' I said.

'All here,' he replied, leafing through the papers and pointing to the documents.

'Have you got the original case file from the lab?' I asked.

'Gone,' he shrugged, 'and the scientist is dead. We think he kept the file as a souvenir. It's probably sitting in someone's loft in Nottingham, where the lab was at the time.'

There was a lot of material, but it was manageable. Sutton's responses and businesslike manner were reassuring at a time when I needed to place my trust in him. So far, so good. I asked him to talk me through the case. He started at the beginning, and over the course of a couple of hours told me the whole story up to date.

Among the papers was also a stack of printed media articles about the case. I didn't read them at the time, as they were irrelevant to what I had to do. Looking at them now, there is a summary of Hale's book, as well as pieces from *The Times*, the *Independent*, the *Guardian*, the *Daily Mail*, the BBC and, of course, the *Matlock Mercury*, where Don Hale worked. *The Times* had been running with the story since 1998, before Hale published his book, and the others had picked it up later. The main themes of the pieces were Downing's innocence and his return to everyday life. There were other big issues the case had raised: how Downing had been treated in prison and refused bail before release, the parole process that required him to admit his crime, the role of the CCRC, and calls for Jack Straw, then Home Secretary, to resign and for a public inquiry into the case.

—

Science is founded in experimentation, and repetition is at its heart. Carefully crafted experiments, where variables are controlled and uncertainty is measured, give it its predictive power. We know how blood droplets behave and interact, we can calculate angles and distances and establish points of impact. But this rarely goes to the crux of things in a BPA case. Bloodstain patterns arise from people being kicked, punched, battered and physically assaulted in a variety of ways with a variety of weapons. We can't set up scientific experiments to analyse these events, let alone repeat them. That's not to say that *no* experiments can be done, but these are proxies, pale images of the true events, usually compromised in some way or another – by using (dead) animals, animal blood or human blood that contains anticoagulant rather than fresh blood. There is no guarantee that an experiment that works in a laboratory will also work when it is tested in the real world. That's why we have clinical trials for new drugs that use real patients and not animals or tissue cultures. If you cannot test the science in the field, its power is reduced, possibly in ways that you don't understand.

BPA usually involves looking at all the patterns together, considering how they relate to each other and what they might tell you about the case. Another way of approaching the interpretation is to consider the patterns, in light of what is known about the case from witnesses, the victim, the accused and maybe others. This information conditions judgements by grounding them in the question of whether the findings support one version of events or another. This is more craft than science; sometimes it's all craft and no science.

A common explanation from an accused person who is found to be bloodstained is that they encountered the injured person, who was already bleeding, and tried to help them. In these circumstances, the question that grounds the interpretation is: does this explain all the bloodstain patterns and do the blood patterns corroborate this version of events? Or are there bloodstain patterns that cannot be explained or point to another explanation, perhaps a more direct involvement by the accused? Sometimes these questions can be answered; often they cannot.

As bloodstains age, their redness fades; they become browner in colour and harder to recognise. The bloodstains on the items from the Downing case were almost 30 years old and most were dark red and brown-red in colour. A screening test can be used to give an indication that something is blood, but this doesn't always work on old bloodstains.

There was heavy blood staining on the pickaxe handle at its broader end, extending back for about 20 cm along its length. I could see lots of tiny spots and splashes radiating out from this heavy staining. I have seen bloodstain patterns like this on many occasions; they are characteristic of the item having been used to strike someone repeatedly. There was no doubt that this was the murder weapon, but had it been wielded by Downing in the attack? And if not Downing, who?

The handle hadn't been fingerprinted in the original investigation. I wondered why. Was it because Downing might have had handled the pickaxe in his work and fingerprints matching him would be ambiguous? Was it because he had confessed, so it wasn't necessary? Wood isn't an ideal surface for fingerprints, but the pickaxe was varnished, so it would retain prints. The examination would have been straightforward at the time and could have been done by the force fingerprint bureau. I tried to imagine a situation in a case I had been involved in where investigators would not want to corroborate such an important element of the crime; the connection between the weapon and the accused person. I couldn't think of one. The words that came to mind were: lazy, incompetent, indifferent.

I arranged for the pickaxe handle to be fingerprinted. I wasn't sure what it would tell us now. The item had been found in the police museum in Derbyshire so could have been handled by any number of people since the murder. Any original fingerprints could have faded or been rubbed off and supplanted by others that were not connected with the case. But who knows? The point of a review in a case of this type is not to make such assumptions. Do the tests and see what the outcome is. Fingerprints of significance have been found many years after an offence in some cases. In this instance, a partial palm print was found. This didn't match Downing or any of the other individuals of interest. There was no national palm-print database at the time, so it was not possible to take this any further.

Downing had been wearing a short-sleeved mustard and cream pin-striped T-shirt, which I examined using a low-power microscope. In the process I found some additional tiny bloodstains on the front and back that had not been noted before. There were also two small bloodstains on the lower left back of the T-shirt that Lee had marked in his original examination.

Downing's jeans were worn and grubby. They were extensively bloodstained, although this was sometimes difficult to see. Most of the blood was on the front and below thigh level. There were large areas of contact blood staining on each knee; the type that is caused when two items touch each other and one is wet with blood. There were also many tiny blood spots below knee level and around the bottom of the trouser legs.

I didn't fully examine his black boots, because it was too difficult to see bloodstains against the dark background. I could see some blood where it had been marked in the original examination. I re-tested some of these stains and they gave positive results. The case file, which would have contained detailed records of the original forensic work carried out by Lee – notes, diagrams, tests results – would have been very useful here.

—

Bakewell is a small market town in the heart of England. The cemetery where Wendy Sewell was attacked lies on its western side. It is long and narrow, with a single main drive that leads from a lodge house at the entrance to an unconsecrated chapel at the far end.

The scene photos were in black and white. I wondered why. This was the oldest case I had reviewed, but colour photography had been available at the time. When I started working for the Metropolitan Police in the late seventies, all the scene images were in colour. Were other police forces still using black and white in 1974? The images had a graphic simplicity and power that colour images sometimes lack, but it felt as if I was looking at something from another era. They also had a major drawback: it wasn't easy to distinguish the bloodstains.

The numbered sequence of monochrome images presented a sombre narrative that began at the entrance to the cemetery and ended at the locus of the attack. Two images showed the site of the attack on a gently curving path at the edge of the graveyard. In the first, there was a heavily bloodstained pickaxe handle in the foreground, lying across the path at 90 degrees. In the second, taken from the opposite direction, Sewell's clothing was strewn across the path in the foreground. In the middle of the path were her plimsolls, and to their right her trousers and panties. The bow and clasp from her bra were on the path about halfway between the pickaxe handle and the clothing. The plastic 'bones' from the bra were lying a few metres apart. This was a sexual attack.

Two fragments of the pickaxe lay on the path near the blood staining. The weapon had been wielded with such force that it had splintered. The distance between the clothing and the pickaxe handle was about eight metres. Amongst the papers I had been given was a single-page graphic that overlaid photos onto a plan of the scene. Whoever had made this was trying to distil all the information, but in doing so they had got the plan scale wrong; I set it aside. There was heavy blood staining in several places on the path, nearer to the clothing than the pickaxe handle. I could see staining characteristic of spatters from blows; large pools with blood radiating from them. Some of the staining showed that Sewell was moving while she was bleeding.

One image showed a single bloodstain near the top edge of a gravestone about two metres away from the nearest pool of blood. She had been attacked more than once and in different positions in this area. Later in the sequence there was a single image of where she was found, a few metres from where she was attacked. There was no body *in situ* by the time the photo was captured; she had been taken to hospital. She was seen by witnesses in this spot, standing upright before she fell and hit her head against a gravestone. The fact that she was standing after being attacked seemed extraordinary given the extent and seriousness of her injuries. Small cardboard labels had been placed in two locations indicating where blood was found.

No forensic scientist was called to the scene to examine the BPA. This isn't surprising. I know of many cases that would have benefited from a scene examination where a BPA expert was not called. Having a scientist at the scene slows things down and only happens if it is obviously essential at the time. But you don't always know at the beginning of a case what is going to be essential, and sometimes it is too late to backtrack. In England nowadays all the forensic science labs are private; cost is the primary consideration for the police for most forensic work. An experienced SIO I was working with a few years ago told me that making decisions about forensic science is not about investigation, it's about finance. My recent research also confirms this.[5]

How did Sewell get to where she was seen? Did she walk or crawl? Was she dragged? None of the images, plans or sketches showed blood between the attack site and where she was seen standing. It seemed very unlikely that she walked this distance given her head injuries. If she crawled or was dragged, I would have expected the grass to be bloodstained between the two locations. There were no signs of cordons, no extant notes of the scene examination, no scene log of who was present. Was the scene examined thoroughly? Not by today's standards, and probably not by the standards of the time.

Only the killer knew what had happened here; there were no other witnesses. I had Downing's account* as recorded in statements to the police and to others who were present at the time. Some of this evidence had to be problematic given that it came from his confession, which was later withdrawn and was deemed oppressive. But there were also witnesses to what he had said at the scene before he went to the police station to be interviewed. In these statements Downing said that he found Sewell lying injured and that there was a pickaxe near her that he had been using that morning. He also said that he moved the body and had been wearing gloves at the time. I compared the relevant sections from the papers to see where they corroborated or contradicted each other.

* Downing was no longer an accused person, but I had been asked to review the bloodstain patterns in light of what had been said by other forensic scientists, so had to review the original accounts.

There were also detailed accounts from Downing in Hale's book. According to Hale, Downing said:

> [There] was someone lying on the bottom path ...
> I threw my jacket down at the victim's feet and then
> I knelt at her side ... I rolled her over towards me.
> There was quite a lot of blood on the path and her
> hair was heavily soaked in it. I felt for a pulse at the
> neck but found none ... She raised herself up, and
> I too reacted by getting to my feet.
>
> It was at this point that I felt something
> sharp pressed into the small of my back ... I was
> ordered not to turn around and was told that if I
> was to say anything my sister would get the same.
> [T]he next thing I knew was that ... they made
> their escape down into the woodland area.* I ...
> picked up my jacket and ran over to the lodge ...
> [and told] Wilf Walker ... that a woman had been
> attacked.

Downing returned to the scene with Walker and others, and one of them went to call the police. Downing continued, 'I had my back to her and turned to look. She was already on her feet and managed to take a few steps.' When the police arrived, they asked him if he had touched anything. 'I said

---

* This story did not emerge until February 1974, when Downing told it to his father on a prison visit. It was thought to be grounds for an appeal, but Downing's counsel was unconvinced by the new information. Why had he not mentioned it in any of the meetings he had had with his solicitor or the prison psychiatrists, or to his father earlier? Crucially, why had he not mentioned it in the witness box?

I hadn't except for turning her over and showed him my bloodstained hands.'

—

I selected bloodstains from the pickaxe handle and Downing's clothing for DNA profiling. There was no sample from Sewell available, so the DNA was compared with two of her relatives. The DNA profiles in these situations are more complicated to interpret. There was no dispute that the blood on Downing was from Sewell, but I wanted to confirm the results of previous testing. Most of the tests failed, but the blood from the pickaxe handle, one stain from the jeans and one from the T-shirt worked. These tests found partial profiles of female DNA that could be linked to Sewell.

I considered all the blood staining as a whole rather than each stain or group of stains individually. There were various ways of explaining the individual blood patterns: tiny stains on his trousers, heavy contact on his knees, spots on the back of the T-shirt. For example, the bloodstain pattern that can result when someone kicks another person who is bleeding has two main elements: an area of contact staining (usually on the front of a shoe or boot), and splashes that are associated with this contact staining. If you interpret the two elements separately, which is what lawyers arguing with you in court will always try to do, the significance of the evidence is diminished. If you consider the two patterns to be coincident in time (and sometimes this is obvious), then they are more characteristic of kicking and the evidence is stronger. There is a sliding scale in the degree of correspondence between the patterns and a proposed action. Each case has to be considered on its own merits and each alternative explanation carefully weighed.

I had to consider the alternative accounts of what was said to have happened to Sewell at the crime scene. The consistent elements of the story were that Downing knelt beside her and handled her body, and that at some point when he was close to her, she shook her head. There were several accounts, and there were features that were in some versions of the story but not others: Downing was wearing gloves or not; Sewell gurgled at some point; the precise positions of each of their bodies in relation to one another.

I distilled the stories into two alternative versions. The first was that Downing handled the bleeding body of Sewell while she was alive but didn't assault her with the pickaxe handle. This accords with the account he gave to Hale in their correspondence. The alternative was that he battered her before he handled her body. My opinion was that the second of these more fully explained the blood staining on Downing's clothing and was the more likely. How much more likely? Not much. If there were to be a retrial, it could go either way in court, depending on how imaginative and skilful the lawyers were.

In his book, Hale misinterpreted the forensic evidence on almost every occasion. For example, he said that there was hardly any blood on Downing's clothing. I was the fifth forensic scientist to examine Downing's clothing; we all agreed that there was a lot of blood staining present. Hale also said that 'with such a ferocious attack, Stephen's clothing would be extremely bloodstained'. This is a common misconception. I have seen cases where individuals have literally been kicked to death and no blood was shed. I have also encountered cases of horrific and repeated battering where a lot of blood was shed but very little transferred to the assailant. How blood is sprayed around during an attack and whether it is transferred to an attacker's clothing depends on many things, including the amount of blood present as a blow strikes, the shape and texture of the surface that is bloodstained, the shape and surface texture of the weapon, the force and angle of the blow and the precise spatial relationships between the attacked and the attacker.

Another important issue is that the shedding and transfer of blood is a *process*, not an instantaneous event. The variables can and usually do change as an attack goes on: the amount of blood, the angle and force of the weapon, the positions of those involved. There is much more blood after an attack than there is during it, because the bleeding continues after it is over. The amount of blood left afterwards is rarely a good indication of how much blood was shed during the attack.

—

On 27 February 2003, Derbyshire Constabulary published the report of their reinvestigation into the case. It described an extensive investigation that included a public appeal for new information, house-to-house inquiries, reinterviewing surviving witnesses and the identification of 360 new witnesses. None of the surviving witnesses altered their view; all stuck to their original statements. Much of this, of course, was rather late in the day; some might say better late than never, others too little too late.

To the new information was added a page-by-page analysis of *Town Without Pity*, plus reviews of other documents from the courts and the Downing family, and anonymous letters the police had received. Downing and Hale cooperated with the police. In the course of the investigation, 22 men had come to the attention of the police via Hale or by other means. All of them were eliminated from the inquiry. The police report listed each of them individually and explained why they had been ruled out. Some of the individuals that Hale had told the police about denied having spoken to him. Others gave a different version of events to the police from what Hale had attributed to them.[6] Hale denies this was the case. The mystery of Sewell's missing handbag, which Hale had identified, was explained: it had been returned to her husband when the original court case was completed.

Stephen Downing was the only person who was not eliminated by the new investigation. Downing was in an odd legal position. Detectives couldn't interview him under caution* because he couldn't be reinterviewed about a crime he had already been convicted of (even though the conviction had been quashed). The police wanted to speak to him about various issues. There was evidence that he had admitted the offence to a number of people after his release, including his father, and during a phone conversation with another person that had been recorded. The police also wanted information about the person he had said stuck something into his back in the

---

* This has now changed in England and Wales following the introduction of the Criminal Justice Act 2003, popularly referred to as 'double jeopardy', which provides for second trials in exceptional circumstances.

graveyard and threatened him and his sister. Having initially
agreed to cooperate with the review, Downing declined to
speak to the police on legal advice. Hale said: 'He's a bloody
fool. He has let down me and all of his supporters. If he has
nothing to hide, why doesn't he talk to police?'[7]

The reinvestigation took 10 months and cost around half a
million pounds. The independent advisory group commended
what had been a difficult and detailed process and unanimously
accepted that Stephen Downing was the only person who could
not be eliminated from the new inquiry.

The following year, Hale's role changed from being the
inquirer to being the object of inquiry, from the storyteller
to the story. The *Daily Telegraph*[8] reported that he was having
second thoughts about both his investigation and Downing's
innocence: 'I made mistakes as any journalist would … With
hindsight … I would do things differently.' The police had
been critical of some of his methods. The *Daily Telegraph* also
reported that a number of women had been stalked or attacked
by Downing, incidents for which he provided an alibi.

In 2016, Hale hurriedly updated *Town Without Pity* before
appearing in *Judge Rinder's Crime Stories*,* a TV show about the
case. The new material is tagged on to the end of the book and
is headed 'Important Addendum'. It is a sloppy collation of
bullet points and scattered paragraphs. The tone is indignant
as Hale sets out a long list of grievances about the case, with no
signs of the regrets reported over a decade earlier. In contrast
to the rest of the book, the addendum reads like the stuff of

* This programme is no longer available, so I have had no opportunity to
view it.

an internet chat room. Hale comes across as a man-in-the-pub conspiracy theorist; he repeats old beefs, speculates wildly and exposes his limited understanding of many important issues.

The only significant new material in the addendum are extracts that purport to be from Sewell's autopsy report, which Hale suggests had been suppressed for 40 years. According to Hale, Sewell had been strangled before being attacked with the pickaxe handle, an idea that he originally got from a clairvoyant who visited the graveyard with him.[9] Hale cites retired police officer, Chris Clark, who claims to have a copy of the autopsy report. Clark states in his own book:[10] 'In plain English … Wendy had been strangled with a knotted garrotte before being struck on the back of the head.' The pathology report would not have been written in plain English but in highly technical medical terms, and Clark is no forensic pathologist. All Sewell's injuries are entirely explicable given how she was attacked and later treated in hospital. In his use of the word 'garrotte', Clark, who styles himself 'the armchair detective', has slipped into melodrama and the tropes of crime fiction. I have never heard a forensic pathologist in this country use the term 'garrotte'. The typical term to describe a cord or something similar would be 'ligature'. A ligature would leave bruising on the skin of the neck, and there was no such bruising visible on Sewell's neck because she was not strangled.

—

There is no doubt that Downing was vulnerable and was denied his legal rights. He was mistreated by the police and forced to make a confession; a confession that does not accord with the facts of the case, such as the number of injuries to the victim. He was also badly let down by his legal defence team, who failed to challenge the police evidence and procedures.

Hale was critical of the police investigation but his was also flawed, and the seeds of his failings were sown on the day of his triumph outside the Court of Appeal in London. If he had read the appeal judgement carefully, he would have seen that while the court believed that Downing's conviction was unsafe, they did not consider the question of his guilt 'in the somewhat bizarre circumstances of [the] case'.[11] Had they done so, they might well have found his story that he encountered the heavily bleeding, fatally injured Sewell and sexually assaulted her, but did not attack her beforehand, to be incredible.

Downing withdrew his confession that he attacked Sewell but he admitted in court that he had sexually assaulted her. He also admitted this to two consultant psychiatrists* after he had been convicted, although he later changed his story again and denied the offence. He never explained this discrepancy and Hale never asked him to do so. This issue is so discordant with Downing's innocence that it begs an explanation, but Hale did not explore this. He also fell into the same trap that he accused the police of: having a closed mind. He ignored important evidence that contradicted his view that Downing was innocent and focused on inconsistencies that made him *look* innocent. Some of the inconsistencies he identified were simply wrong; others were irrelevant. A list of inconsistencies

---

* Although he admitted the offence, neither of these psychiatrists was completely convinced that he committed the murder.

is not a coherent counter-argument to support someone's innocence.

If you believe a story at the outset, before you begin to investigate and establish the facts for and against it, you are vulnerable to all sorts of wishful and fallacious thinking. And you are particularly vulnerable to such errors if you are on your own, as Hale was. Criminal investigation is a collective enterprise if it is to be done adequately; even then, skilled investigators make these mistakes and drift into group-think. There are examples of this in this book. Every case has inconsistencies and inexplicable elements and the Downing case is a mass of contradictions. This is partly because Downing's accounts have continually changed. The version that included the man behind him in the graveyard did not appear until after his trial. It was never mentioned in the many meetings he had with his defence team or in court.

By the time Hale updated his book, he seemed less interested in testing the truth. He was content to take information at face value, even highly technical information that he did not understand, passed to him by another person who did not understand it either, if it supported his predetermined view. He was no longer an investigator but an evangelist.

In 1990, Downing was assessed by a visiting prison psychiatrist, who noted: 'He presents as a mentally immature solitary … and relatively unworried man who is trying to live with his offence by a childish fantasy, absolving him of all blame. His attack was an impulsive act, followed by sexual exploration, and his statement strongly indicates that this was the motive for the assault.'

The main challenge I faced in this review was to cut through the technical fog that had arisen from multiple earlier reviews of the BPA evidence without the original case notes. The apparent argument and counter-argument arose not because of major differences in interpretation but more from the different information given to the BPA experts at different times, and the different terminologies used to express the findings. I came down on one side, but there wasn't much in it.

CHAPTER SIX

The Murder of Damilola Taylor

> We cannot help expecting with part of our mind
> that the world will make sense, and [feel] cheated
> when it does not. Perhaps this is why injustice
> which is a kind of senselessness makes us so furious.
>
> Terry Eagleton[1]

'It wasn't my imagination … It's your fucking imagination,'[2] replied Bromley to Courtney Griffiths QC in Court 12 at the Old Bailey.

'Bromley' was a code name. Mark Dennis QC, for the prosecution, described the 14-year-old girl as 'a courageous child, the only person … brave enough to come forward'[3] after having witnessed the murder of Damilola Taylor, who had died from a single stab wound to his leg in November 2000, near his home in Peckham, south London. She had spent five and a half days giving evidence, hidden by a screen to protect her identity. But under cross-examination by Griffiths, her story disintegrated. At one point she pushed away papers that had been handed to her, swore under her breath and leaned back in her seat close to tears.

Bromley had made a 999 call a month after the murder; she didn't give her name, but the police traced her from the mobile number. She had been interviewed for 10 hours over a period of five weeks, and the video recordings of the interviews were played to the jury. But her account was fragmented and inconsistent; confronted with facts that contradicted it, she simply adjusted her story to fit. She had claimed that one of the four boys on trial had confessed to her, but in the witness box, her long list of lies was exposed.

The judge, Mr Justice Hooper, ruled that her evidence was unreliable, and the CPS withdrew the case against one of the defendants, who was then discharged. At the end of the prosecution case, a second defendant was also freed; the judge accepted he had no case to answer. On 25 April 2002, the jury found the two remaining defendants not guilty.

—

Murders of children get the most media attention, as we saw in the Robert Black case. There were other factors in the Damilola Taylor case that amplified this attention. That he had only been in the UK a few months added poignancy to his death; he had come to London to start a new life and it was violently taken from him.

There was another important aspect in this investigation that would drive the media into a frenzy: the reputation of the Metropolitan Police. Admired from afar, Scotland Yard is esteemed worldwide for crime investigation, with many notable and historic cases to their credit. But at home their reputation is more ambivalent, and attenuated by corruption scandals and incompetence. In 1993, the black teenager Stephen Lawrence was stabbed to death in a racist attack. The Met failed to deal with this case on every conceivable level.

The investigation into Stephen's death had used HOLMES, the police computer system introduced in 1984 after the equally disastrous Yorkshire Ripper investigation. In 2006, it was found that none of the previous investigations had used the system in accordance with correct procedure. The philosophy of HOLMES is that a systematic approach to an investigation requires all activities and information to be logged into the database so that nothing can be forgotten, lost or overlooked, and everything can be cross-checked. Staff trained in specialist roles are needed to run the system effectively. DCI Clive Driscoll[4] found that the HOLMES database in the Lawrence case was riddled with errors and gaps. Statements were missing, information had not been inputted or checked because the specialist staff required to run HOLMES effectively were not used. Failing to follow the recommended procedures, which is surprisingly common in police practice, meant that HOLMES was rendered ineffective.

This also reveals something else that is not well known: the police are not very good at using technology. Recent research[5] shows that throughout their history they have been slow to adapt to new equipment – cars, phones, radios, computers – because these are perceived as external factors that challenge their cultural practices and beliefs. Yet HOLMES retained an important role for the Met in the Lawrence investigation – it was symbolic. Reviews of the investigation, six of them, referred to the system as a means of reassuring others inside and outside the Met that the investigation had been thorough and up to standard.

The collapse of the case against those accused of murdering Damilola Taylor, a black child living in south London, resonated strongly with the failures in the Lawrence case and further questioned the competence and integrity of the Met, particularly in ethnic minority communities.

—

Damilola Taylor was born on 7 December 1989 in Nigeria. His parents had previously lived in England and had returned to Nigeria in the 1980s. Damilola's sister suffered from epilepsy, and because her condition was worsening, the family had returned to the UK. Damilola came to London in August 2000 with his mother and sister, while his father stayed in Nigeria to work. He was in Year 6 at Oliver Goldsmith School in Southampton Way, a short walk from his home on the North Peckham estate.

On 27 November 2000, Damilola went to the local library for an after-school computer club. He wore a grey or silver Puffa jacket over his school uniform: a maroon sweatshirt with the name of the school on the front, a pale blue polo shirt and grey trousers. He met some of his friends there and was in good spirits. When the club finished, he made his way home through the North Peckham estate. CCTV outside the library showed him leaving, and he was seen in Blakes Road at about 4.40 p.m.

Around 4.45 p.m., Bill Casal, a carpenter, spotted blood in the stairwell of a tower block as he made his way up to his office. On the first-floor landing he found Damilola with blood gushing down his left leg. He was leaning against the wall and then collapsed. Casal saw three black youths in the street below. One of them noticed him looking and made eye contact with him; he then drew his left hand across the top of his leg in a sideways motion.

Police were at the scene within five minutes and paramedics shortly afterwards. The first scene examiner arrived at 7.00 p.m. It was raining heavily, and SCSI Mike Nicholas was anxious to prevent loss of evidence. He quickly sampled a trail of bloodstains before they were washed away. He also found the broken, bloodstained remnants of a green bottle that had been covered to protect them from the rain by one of the police officers who had attended the scene earlier. Nicholas traced the blood trail from where Damilola had been found the short distance to where he had been attacked.

Damilola died of his injuries 90 minutes after arriving at King's College Hospital. A post-mortem examination, held later that day, established that death had been due to blood loss from a single stab wound to his left leg. It was later established that the wound had been caused by a shard of glass from the green bottle found at the scene. The pathologist, Dr Vesna Djurovic, concluded that the wound was due to a deliberate action. A second post-mortem concurred with these findings.

—

Bromley's evidence was not the only problem in the trial. The prosecution had planned to rely on a number of witnesses who had said that some of the defendants had confessed to them or admitted to being present at the murder. Unlike the Michael Stone trial, the judge ruled against the confession evidence, thus damaging the prosecution case. A conviction for murder, as opposed to manslaughter, would also have to prove that Damilola had been deliberately stabbed. But the defence found another pathologist – not a forensic pathologist – who said that the wound could have been an accident; Damilola could have fallen onto the glass. The lack of forensic evidence was an additional problem. A team of nine forensic scientists led by an experienced senior expert at the FSS had examined hundreds of items sent to them by the police. They had found fibres on the shard of glass that matched Damilola's trousers, but nothing to incriminate any of the four defendants or any of the other individuals who were suspects at the time.

Media and political interest, which had been intense during the investigation, became supercharged following the disastrous trial. The Met, still under the long shadow of the Stephen Lawrence case, instituted a review of their investigation. To bring some independent oversight to the review, they appointed a panel led by Dr John Sentamu, then Bishop of Stepney.* The panel also included senior police officers from outside forces to act as advisers, one of whom was Dave Stevens of Kent Police. The review report[6] was published in December 2002 and largely commended the actions and commitment of the Met in the investigation into Damilola's death. It went on to conclude that the Met had 'moved on since its unsatisfactory investigation of the murder of Stephen Lawrence in 1993'. My experience as the case unfolded suggested otherwise.

* Sentamu later became Archbishop of York before retiring in 2020.

The Met were the first force in the UK to set up a forensic science lab, which soon attained a worldwide reputation in the field. By the time I joined the lab at Lambeth in 1978, it was the largest in Europe, with over 300 staff. In 1989, I left the Met and moved to Edinburgh. In 1996, the year I moved to Kent Police, the FSS took over the Met lab. The rationale for the takeover was never clear to me, but the outcome was that the FSS had what appeared to be an unassailable monopoly of service provision in England and Wales. They also hijacked the worldwide reputation of the Met lab. Few, if any, in the Met Police or in the lab wanted this takeover, but they were politically outmanoeuvred by Janet Thompson, the CEO of the FSS at the time. I was present at the official launch of the new FSS London lab on 1 April 1996. Only hours before the opening ceremony, FSS staff had been scuttling around the building replacing official Met Police livery with FSS signage. The Met had refused to give up their lab to the very last minute.

The Met lab may have been administratively part of the FSS, but it was never fully integrated. It was much bigger than every other FSS lab and was culturally and operationally distinct. It was too big and too hard for the FSS to swallow. The relationship between the Met and the FSS in the Damilola Taylor investigation became the source of a bitter struggle between the organisations, and was one of many factors that led to the ultimate demise of the FSS.

—

'Why don't you call me ma'am?' said Janet Thompson. She was making the point that I had called the Chief Constable I had been talking to 'sir', and felt she deserved the equivalent when I spoke to her. She was standing squarely in front of me, dark-haired and diminutive, as if to stop me from passing until I answered.

Thompson was a notoriously difficult woman to deal with if the stories I had heard about her were true, but I didn't work for her. 'You're not a police officer, Janet,' I replied.

We were at the quarterly meeting of the National DNA Database Board, where I represented Kent Police. Thompson was a senior civil servant in the Home Office before she took over the FSS. She was a scientist but had no previous experience of forensic science. She came to the DNA board meetings with her senior team, including Dave Werrett, her deputy. Werrett had played a key role in the development of DNA profiling and the introduction of the DNA database. He was highly regarded as a forensic scientist.

In the late nineties, the New Labour government had caught the DNA bug. They saw DNA profiling as one of their tools for being 'tough on crime', as well as having the bonus of making them look tech-savvy and modern. Between 1999 and 2005, a vast amount of money – around a quarter of a billion pounds – was injected into a DNA expansion programme[7] to develop the DNA database in England and Wales. The rationale for this expansion was simple. Most criminals reoffend, so if their DNA is held in a database, this will allow quicker identification and arrest of repeat offenders, leading to more convictions.

When I arrived at Kent Police in 1996, my department had 85 staff; by the time I left in 2004, staff numbers had almost doubled, to 150. This growth was funded by the DNA expansion programme. The money was also used to buy equipment and vehicles; anything that could convincingly increase the collection of DNA samples for the database. The Home Office paid a lot of attention to what the cash was spent on, and everything had to be accounted for. How to measure the impact of the investment was much less clear, and to keep things simple, it was agreed that the number of crimes detected by DNA would be used as a yardstick.

It soon became obvious that counting detections was neither straightforward nor a good indicator of the impact of the DNA database. I was involved in the project and saw the data. Much of it was as accurate as could be expected, but some of it was just made up by police forces. Nobody seemed to care so long as the Home Office got a number from each force at the end of the accounting period. Nor was the money always spent wisely. Some forces were using low copy number (LCN) DNA profiling – a new supersensitive method of DNA analysis – in burglary investigations. At the time, LCN was slow, expensive and rarely gave a clear-cut result. It was a ludicrous thing to use in a burglary.

In 1995, about 40,000 samples from individuals had been submitted to the database. By 2001, over half a million samples had been submitted, and most of this work (and the accompanying cash) went to the FSS because they controlled the database. They now had more money than they knew what to do with and were expanding at a dizzying rate. Despite this, they couldn't cope with the rate at which samples were being submitted, and soon there were long backlogs. An obvious solution to this was to allow some of the new private suppliers to carry out some of the testing. But this was resisted at every turn as the FSS ruthlessly protected their monopoly. Still part of the Home Office, they controlled all the significant committees that related to forensic science, and also had access to the various policing committees. Not only were they controlling, they were predatory, and tried to get access to functions such as scene-of-crime investigations inside forces.

—

Early in 2004,[8] a new SIO, Detective Superintendent Nick Ephgrave, was appointed to the Damilola Taylor case. He had been based in Peckham at the time of the murder and knew the area well. Before joining the police, he had worked as a medical physicist in the NHS and believed that new developments in forensic science might solve the case. It was also decided that this work should be carried out in a different forensic lab and not by the FSS. Ephgrave was wrong about the role of new technology, but his decision to change labs was to prove crucial to the outcome of the investigation. It was also the cause of a high-level spat involving the Met, the FSS and the Home Office, and the lab that the items were sent to for examination, Forensic Alliance (FAL). The items from the case were removed from the FSS and gradually transferred to the new lab.

FAL was the new kid on the block, the brainchild of founder Angela Gallop, a highly experienced forensic scientist and author.[9] It represented the new world order of private forensic science that delivered what the customer needed quicker and slicker than the increasingly sclerotic FSS. FAL had notched up some notable successes, such as the reinvestigation of the notorious miscarriage of justice[10] associated with the murder of Lynette White in Cardiff in 1998. The first police investigation had resulted in the arrest and trial of five black and mixed-race men, three of whom were convicted in 1990. In 1992, the convictions were deemed unsafe by the Court of Appeal and quashed. The approach of FAL to this case exemplified a sophisticated blend of forensic and behavioural sciences that I had never seen before. It is inconceivable to me that such a level of cooperation between forensic scientists and investigators could occur nowadays in the desecrated landscape of forensic science that now exists in England and Wales.

—

In October 2004, I was appointed professor of forensic science at the University of Strathclyde. While working for Kent Police, I had expanded my experience into how forensic science and policing operated. I had been involved in and led many national projects, working with different forces around the UK and abroad. What I saw was a patchwork of practices, policies and structures that didn't seem to make sense. One of my hopes was that research in my new role would begin to explain some of this.

In May 2005, I was approached by the solicitors representing Ricky Preddie, who together with his brother, Danny, and another boy, Hassan Jihad, had been accused of murdering Damilola Taylor. A second trial was scheduled for January 2006. I was asked to review the fibres evidence in the case, while my colleague, Adrian Linacre, would review the DNA work. One of the first things we decided to do was establish how the evidence had been recovered when Ricky was arrested. Amongst the materials sent to us was a videotape of the raid on the brothers' home at Blackthorne Court on the North Peckham estate. Adrian set out to find a video machine somewhere in the university.

I was puzzled by what I saw in the video: men in suits going through clothing and other items in a bedroom. 'I think they've sent us the wrong tape,' I said to Adrian. 'Do you want to get in touch with the solicitors and get the right one?' I went back to my office.

A couple of hours later, Adrian knocked on my door. 'It's the right tape,' he said. 'None of the cops at the scene were wearing protective clothing.'

The Preddie brothers had been on the fringes of the first investigation into Damilola's murder. They had been arrested and interviewed but were never charged. Ricky was born on 25 June 1987 and was 13 years old at the time of the murder. Danny, his younger brother, was 12. They lived with their mother, Marion. Jihad was 14 years old at the time of the murder. His mother lived in Peckham, but he had spent some time in foster care, and at the time he was living with his aunt in Camberwell. Despite their ages all of the boys had criminal records and had been in and out of custody. All were well known to the authorities.

On Saturday 2 December 2000, Ricky Preddie had been asleep in the top-floor bedroom of his mother's flat. In the early hours of the morning he was awakened by shouts of 'Police, Police!' and the blinding light from a video camera. He was arrested at 5.57 a.m. and taken to Wimbledon police station.

At 7.10 a.m., two detectives arrived to search the flat for evidence. One of the detectives was the exhibits officer for the case. His role was to ensure flawless recording of every exhibit: exactly where it was found, who found it, who removed it from the scene, where it went next; its history from crime scene to court. In a murder investigation, these details will be pored over by defence teams looking for errors or anything that suggests the integrity of an exhibit has been compromised in some way, whether it be by poor storage, contamination or questionable police conduct. Amongst the many items seized by the detectives were a pair of old and worn blue Reebok trainers, a black Giorgio sweatshirt and a pair of dark blue Adidas tracksuit bottoms.

The police had expected to find Danny at the flat as well, but he was on bail for another offence and was living in a children's home in nearby Abbey Street. He was arrested later the same day and his clothing seized.

—

The first exhibits arrived at FAL on 12 June 2003, more than a year after the collapse of the trial and three and a half years after the murder. They continued to arrive in batches over a period of months. On 14 November, in the fourth batch of submissions, were the blue Reebok trainers, black Giorgio sweatshirt and blue tracksuit bottoms from Blackthorne Court.

A small team of experienced forensic scientists was assigned to the case, led by Ros Hammond. It was some months into their examinations before they reached the items from the Preddies' flat; they had found nothing of significance so far. Sheila Hilley, an assistant forensic scientist at the FSS, had already examined the Reebok trainers. Hilley was an experienced examiner and well regarded by her colleagues. She had found two stains on the front of the right trainer that looked like blood, and confirmed this with a chemical test.* She took two Polaroid photos showing the bloodstains and attached these to her examination notes. The two bloodstains were sent for DNA profiling; one matched Danny Preddie but the second test was unsuccessful.

On 24 March 2004, forensic scientist Alice Reynolds set out to examine the same trainers at FAL. She saw the two bloodstains on the right trainer that had been found by Hilley, and another stain on the heel that looked like blood. Not everything that looks like blood is blood, which is why stains are chemically tested. Reynolds tested the stain to double-check. It gave a positive reaction for blood. She looked at it again and retested it. Again it gave a positive reaction. The bloodstain was 4 mm by 9 mm; it seemed too big and obvious for someone to have missed it.

On 6 April, around two weeks after the trainers had been examined and all results had been double-checked, Hammond rang the SIO, Ephgrave, to update him on developments. The call would dramatically alter the course of the investigation; a DNA profile from the newly found bloodstain matched Damilola Taylor. The police now had solid evidence to link the trainer to Damilola. But who was wearing the shoe at the time of the murder? It had been found in Ricky's room

---

* The Kastle–Meyer test is the best known of a number of simple chemical tests used to indicate that a stain could be blood.

but had blood on it that matched Danny. And if the blood matching Damilola was so obvious, why had it not been found at the FSS? A few days later, there was more dramatic news for Ephgrave. A small area of blood staining had been found on the right cuff of the black Giorgio sweatshirt from Ricky's room. A DNA profile from the blood also matched Damilola Taylor.

In parallel with the blood examination, an extensive fibre examination was also in progress. The aim of this was to see if there were any links between Damilola's clothing and the clothing that had been found at the addresses of the Preddies and Jihad. By April 2005, this appeared to be yielding some interesting results, and Tom Callaghan, the forensic scientist who was leading on this part of the work, sent a memo to Ephgrave with a summary of his findings to date. The Giorgio sweatshirt was made of black cotton fibres that were too common to be worth looking for. However, on the tapings from the sweatshirt, a single red acrylic fibre had been found that matched the fibres of Damilola's school sweatshirt. Furthermore, when the missed bloodstain from the trainer was examined using a low-power microscope, some fibres could be seen embedded in the stain. The fibres were removed for more detailed examination. In late May, Callaghan contacted the exhibits officer, and told him that one of the fibres in the bloodstain matched polyester fibres from Damilola's grey school trousers.

By June, the investigation team had realised that they had a growing case against the Preddies and Jihad; now they wanted to put their foot on the gas. Detectives contacted Hammond suggesting they could speed things up if she used a larger team; money was no object. Hammond strongly resisted this, perhaps guessing what might have happened at the FSS with the missing bloodstain. She wanted to stick with a small team of experienced scientists and work through the case steadily and systematically.

The growing realisation that there could be a second trial in the case was tempered by concern about the newly found evidence. What had gone wrong at the FSS, and why? How could they have failed to find two critical bloodstains on two separate exhibits? This situation engendered many risks for the forthcoming trial. Clashes between forensics experts from the different laboratories was one concern. More worrying was the potential for the defence to suggest that the evidence had not in fact been missed but had been planted after the police had removed the items from the FSS. In many courts in the UK such an allegation would be dismissed fairly speedily as being incredible. London was different. When I worked in the Met dealing with armed robbery cases in the 1980s, 'planting defences' were common and sometimes successful because of the ambiguous reputation the force enjoyed.

It was imperative that detectives got to the bottom of why the bloodstains had been missed. The SIO, Detective Superintendent Ephgrave, and Gary Pugh, then Director of Forensic Services at the Met, travelled to FAL in Oxfordshire to see things for themselves. Amongst the various papers they were shown were the original FSS notes of the blood staining on the trainer. Attached to the notes was a Polaroid photo showing clearly visible blood staining that the FSS had missed and that now featured as critical evidence in the investigation.

Having taken the exhibits from the FSS, in December 2003 the Met then seized all the case files and accompanying paperwork. Sometime afterwards, forensic scientists from the FSS tried to get access to the files, but the Met instructed FAL not to allow this.

Despite the forensic breakthroughs, many difficulties remained to be resolved.

CHAPTER SEVEN

Silent Testimony – 'Every Contact Leaves a Trace'

I think you'll find it's a bit more complicated
than that.

Ben Goldacre[1]

'We're really worried about the fibres evidence,' said Charlotte
Kelly, a solicitor with the London law firm who were representing
Ricky Preddie. A second trial was now anticipated, more than
six years after Damilola's murder. The Preddie brothers could
not be named because they were under 18 years old at the
time, but Jihad was now 19. Kelly had flown to Glasgow to meet
me and my colleague Adrian Linacre. Since I had spoken to
her on the phone, I had quickly read through the forensic
statements about the fibres evidence the prosecution were
relying on.

'There isn't any fibres evidence,' I replied. That was the
short version, but my report would have to be much longer,
since I would have to unpick all the details that masked this
quite straightforward conclusion. There were five separate

statements about the fibres, amounting to dozens of pages, and I could see how the reader would be left with the impression that there was significant evidence, but for me there were many problems with such a conclusion.

On my desk were two ring binders, a box file and a lever-arch file full of documents: hundreds of pages of witness statements, scientific reports, HOLMES printouts, photographs and instructions to counsel. There were also numerous letters about the case between Dave Werrett, now CEO of the FSS, Gary Pugh of the Met, and the Home Office. Pugh had started his career as a forensic scientist in the FSS and risen to a senior management position. He had worked closely with Werrett in the past. It was rumoured that they had fallen out before Pugh had moved to the Met. I wondered what the letters would reveal, but for the moment they were peripheral to my work and would have to wait. The scientific statements covered the months and years as the case built up through the first trial and now into the second one. There were multiple statements from each of the witnesses. I scanned the papers to triage them: what was essential reading, to be read in depth and considered carefully; what might be relevant but could wait until later; what, if anything, could be safely ignored.

—

Analysis and comparison of fibres can be done with fairly standard scientific equipment, although there is no one way of doing this. Different labs work in different ways using a variety of equipment and techniques. A range of physical characteristics is tested, the most important of which is the type of fibre. Natural fibres like cotton and wool can be identified just by looking at them with a high-power microscope. Synthetic fibres need a more sophisticated analysis to identify the polymers* they are made of. A common way of doing this is to use another type of specialist microscope linked to an infrared spectrometer that uses some clever maths. A Fourier transform infrared spectrometer (FTIR) can identify microscopic fragments of textile fibres in seconds. If you can see the fibre under a low-power microscope and can lift it off the tape using forceps, it is big enough to be identified. Synthetic fibres also have microscopic features such as their cross-sectional shape (round, lobed) and diameter that can be compared. The colour of the fibre is another important characteristic. There are thousands of different dyes that can be used in seemingly limitless combinations to make an endless variety of colours. Analysing the colour and dyes in a fibre is a very useful way of matching a fibre to an item or excluding the item as a source.

The analysis in the lab is important, but what happens before the items arrive is equally important. Fibres are all around us in the textiles we wear and use; in our clothing, homes, offices, schools and vehicles. Some individual fibres can be seen with the naked eye, some are so tiny that they can't be seen without a microscope. Fibres can be transferred from item to item: clothing to clothing, clothing to furniture, clothing to weapon and so on. They are usually transferred by two items touching one another; what a forensic scientist would call direct transfer. They can also be transferred indirectly

---

* A polymer is a long-chain molecule made of repeating short molecules.

via an intermediary item such as another item of clothing or a seat. We also know that fragments of fibres can be left on surfaces such as tables or desks and then redistributed by air currents. This means that items for fibre examination must be recovered from crime scenes with great care in order to prevent contamination, and the details of their recovery must be recorded accurately and in detail.

I searched through the lever-arch files for statements from the officers who raided the Preddies' flat. The exhibits officer made a statement dated 9 May 2001 that was 49 pages long. It listed all of the hundreds of exhibits in the case; from the crime scene, the post-mortem examination, from each of the individuals arrested or charged, and from all of the premises that were searched. Most of the exhibits were items of clothing, but there were also mobile phones, digital media, documentation, knives and body samples. Following a briefing about the case, the exhibits officer went to Blackthorne Court with another detective and a senior crime scene investigator. He stated that they seized, packaged and logged items in Exhibit Book 6, but I could see from the paperwork that there were two exhibit books numbered 6; he didn't distinguish between them. This wasn't a good start. The exhibits officer went on to record that the blue tracksuit bottoms, black Giorgio sweatshirt and blue Reebok trainers were found in the top bedroom of the flat (Ricky's room).

In 2004, the exhibits officer made another statement. That one solely related to Blackthorne Court and listed a total of 69 items seized from that address. According to this statement, the Giorgio sweatshirt was found inside the wardrobe in Ricky's bedroom and the tracksuit bottoms were found 'in wardrobe in black bin liner'. He listed six other items of clothing – tracksuit bottoms and jeans – found in the same bin liner. The exhibits officer explained that before writing his second statement, he reviewed the video of the raid and saw that the blue Reebok trainers were found 'in the bin liner at the foot of the … bed'. He gave the bin liner an exhibit reference. This seemed to be a second bin liner, not the one found in the wardrobe. The copy of the exhibit book I had appeared to contradict this, recording that the blue trainers had been found in the '2nd floor bedroom … on right bed'. There was no copy of the other Exhibit Book 6 in the files, so I had no more information about the black Giorgio sweatshirt or the blue tracksuit bottoms.

The first statement of the other detective who raided Blackthorne Court was dated 14 January 2001; in it he described his role as part of a 'specialist search and exhibits team'. He corroborated much of what the exhibits officer stated, but there were some discrepancies. The detective said that the blue tracksuit bottoms were found in the wardrobe in a black bin liner and that the Giorgio sweatshirt was found in a bin liner from the wardrobe with the blue trainers. There were at least two bin liners, possibly three, but it was impossible to be sure about this from the records. The detective also made a second statement to correct his first one. He too had reviewed the video to remind him of what had occurred. In the second statement he suggested that a bin liner that he had previously stated was on the bed was originally on the floor. His explanation for this was that the bin liner was probably placed on the bed while the items were being packaged. There was no mention of the wardrobe, but he said the trainers were in the bin liner. He didn't specify which bin liner.

Having seen the video and read the statements, I was astounded. The 'specialist search and exhibits team' had operated in a completely haphazard manner in one of the UK's most prominent and controversial cases; they hadn't worn protective clothing, hadn't recorded their search fully, and in the process had muddled the continuity and integrity of three items that would be critical in the forthcoming second trial in the case.

The Sentamu report had commended the Met for learning lessons following the Stephen Lawrence case. All the arrests and property searches in the Damilola Taylor case had been fully recorded on video so that everything that took place could be demonstrated and independently scrutinised. All except the arrest of Ricky Preddie and the search of Blackthorne Court (there was a recording of the latter, but this was incomplete and did not cover the whole search). Where key items were found and who found them could not be demonstrated, nor could it be accurately established from the sworn statements of those involved. My initial fears on first seeing the video were proving correct: the recovery of the key items was at best chaotic and at worst incompetent. How this played out would depend on many factors, including what the defence tactics were and how the two detectives performed in court. I wondered whether it might cost them the case.

—

Some fabrics shed their fibres well and small fragments or individual fibres are freely available to transfer to other items. Other fabrics, particularly those that are finely woven or smooth, may not shed fibres at all. Smooth surfaces are also poor at retaining fibres; the fibres are lost from the item very quickly, sometimes within a few hours. A forensic scientist will take each case on its merits and decide what fibres are worth looking for based on the circumstances of the case and the types of fabrics involved. An ideal item for transfer would have fibres that shed well, are not too common, have a distinctive colour and are easily found under a low-power microscope. There also needs to be at least one item that will retain any transferred fibres.

Damilola's school sweatshirt was made of several fibre types, but the surface was composed mainly of red acrylic fibres that shed well. The sweatshirt would also retain fibres well. His jacket was neither a good source of fibres for transfer, nor would it retain fibres well on its smooth surface. His grey trousers were made of polyester and viscose fibres and would shed and retain fibres well.

Two red acrylic fibres had been found on items from Blackthorne Court; one on the tracksuit bottoms and one on the black Giorgio sweatshirt. Some cotton fibres matching the sweatshirt had also been found on Damilola's clothing, but these fibres were very common; too common to be a useful link. If the black cottons could be safely dismissed, the question for me was what was the significance of the two red acrylic fibres?

Although Danny had been arrested at a different address, he usually lived with Ricky at their home address. So any fibres found on his clothing could have a bearing on the significance of the two acrylic fibres found in Blackthorne Court. Thirteen red acrylic fibres matching Damilola's sweatshirt were found on items from Danny's temporary home at Abbey Street. Six fibres were found on a jacket, four on a sweatshirt and one on each of two pairs of jeans and a pair of tracksuit bottoms. Two viscose fibres matching Damilola's trousers were found on a jumper. One blue cotton fibre matching the same sweatshirt was found on Damilola's jacket.

Although I had no involvement with the third defendant, Jihad, I briefly reviewed the fibres evidence against him in case it was of any relevance. One red acrylic fibre matching Damilola's sweatshirt was found on one item of clothing from his address. One viscose fibre matching Damilola's trousers was found on a separate item. There was nothing to concern me here.

—

On 15 November 2005, I travelled to FAL, in Abingdon, Oxfordshire, to carry out the forensic examination of the exhibits. My plan was to re-read all the forensic statements on the flight and gather my thoughts for the lab work ahead. Looking through my paperwork, I rediscovered the correspondence between the FSS, the Met and the Home Office and started to read it.

On 24 November 2004, Dave Werrett had written to John Gieve, then permanent secretary at the Home Office. Werrett had become aware of the FAL forensic findings. The long letter was a heads-up about potential adverse publicity. He described the blood staining on the trainer and the sweatshirt that were missed by the FSS. Somehow he knew exactly where on these items the blood was found. He went on to discuss the fibres evidence: 'What we do know suggests that [the fibres] may not provide strong evidence of a link. The fibres recovered appear to be from a commonly worn school jumper.' The case file and the refusal by the Met to return it to the FSS was mentioned several times. Werrett believed the case file was 'one of the keys' to the mystery of why the FSS missed the bloodstain evidence.

I wondered what to make of all this. Then I recalled a rumour I had heard at a professional conference I had attended earlier in the year; that some people in the FSS believed that the 'missed' blood had been planted. This sounded like nonsense to me. It is very difficult to 'plant' blood and very easy to spot it if it has been planted.*

Werrett's letter had been passed to Mike Silverman, an old colleague of mine from the Met lab, now working at the Home Office. It was thought that the view of an experienced forensic scientist might be useful before the letter was sent to John Gieve. Silverman came to the immediate conclusion that it was disclosable.† Werrett, an experienced expert witness, had expressed an opinion that had cast doubt on the

---

* Even when forensic scientists mock up bloodstains for training purposes, it is very easy to spot that these are faked.
† The prosecution in a criminal trial are required to disclose certain evidence to the defence before trial. This includes evidence that supports the prosecution case and any evidence that undermines it.

prosecution's fibres evidence and therefore the letter had to be passed to the defence. The CPS were consulted and agreed: the letter and any related correspondence ought to be disclosed. This was how the documents came to be in my hands. The CPS also suggested that Werrett might be called by the defence as a witness. This would probably have no bearing on the trial but would be politically disastrous for the FSS and the Home Office. A series of phone calls and emails in the following days between senior staff in the two organisations culminated in a confidential note from Werrett, in which he tried to recover the position by stating that he was not acting as an expert and that all the information in the first letter was hearsay.

The situation rumbled on into the new year, and in March 2005 the Met entered the fray. A critical aspect of any trial is ensuring that the physical evidence can be accounted for at every stage of the process; from the moment it was found until it is presented in court, there must be a record of where an item was stored or who was in possession of it. This is called 'continuity' in the UK, although the US terminology, 'chain of custody', is often heard in TV crime shows. The hundreds of items in the case had now been handled by dozens of police officers and forensic personnel in two different forensic labs, and the Met were keen to ensure that no problems arose in court. They asked the FSS for a witness statement to cover continuity while the items were in their possession. The FSS replied saying they couldn't do this because the Met had seized their case file from them and wouldn't return it. The Met provided a certified copy of the file, but some of the pages were missing. The FSS said they still couldn't produce the continuity statement.

Months went by. In September 2005, the FSS tried another angle. With Werrett now under threat of being called as a witness, another senior member of the FSS management team wrote directly to the CPS attempting to sideline the Met and proposing that they themselves should review the Damilola Taylor case. The letter eventually got into the hands of Gary Pugh, Met Director of Forensic Services, who replied that although in his opinion the FAL findings demonstrated 'serious operational … failures by the FSS' and a review was necessary, it must wait until the case had been through the courts.

Meanwhile, the temperature had been rising in the Home Office, who were responsible for both the Met and the FSS. Stephen Rimmer, the Home Office Director of Policing, emailed Silverman, concerned that the whole debacle was going to backfire on the Home Office; the matter was 'extremely sensitive'. He wanted to distance the Home Office from any public row. What was never stated directly was the growing concern that the market value of the soon-to-be-privatised FSS could plummet.

I pondered the significance of all this. The FSS had fucked up big-style but couldn't accept this. Was this why someone had come up with the idea that the bloodstain was planted? The only way this could be proved was by looking at the case file that contained the photo. This would show whether or not the bloodstain had been on the trainer when the FSS examined it. This was why Pugh refused to return the file: he had seen the photo and the bloodstain was obvious. He knew it had been missed. Having failed to get the case file, the FSS came up with the wild idea of reviewing the case weeks before the trial. Apart from the obvious legal objections to this, there was a serious question about whether the FSS were capable of an independent review, as we will see in Chapter Ten.

—

I met Adrian at Heathrow. We picked up a hire car and drove north to Oxfordshire. When we arrived at FAL, we changed into blue scrubs – part of the routine anti-contamination measures necessary in modern forensic labs – before going our separate ways to examine items in different parts of the lab. Retained by the defence, my role was to review the evidence that would be used by the prosecution in the case. I would re-examine all the exhibits and the forensic evidence that had been found. This included a review and interpretation of the analytical findings. I would look out for any problems with the examination or results, but my hope was that there would be none.

There is always some anxiety around this review process. Having another scientist pore over your work in minute detail, especially in a high-profile case, can be an uncomfortable experience. Have I done all the right tests? Have I missed something? Is there anything in my notes that might look ambiguous? Nor is the procedure anxiety-free for the reviewing scientist, who is in an unfamiliar lab working with equipment they may have never used before and making decisions on the spot without the benefit of discussions with colleagues. Occasionally there are personality clashes or arguments about technical aspects of the analysis, but the disputed territory is usually not what the findings are, but what they mean.

—

'How did it go?' I asked Adrian as we drove back to Heathrow.

'Interesting,' he replied.

'What about the missed bloodstain on the trainer? Do you think it could have been planted?'

'Not a chance,' he said. 'I've mocked-up loads of bloodstains for teaching exercises – this was a real one. It was missed. How about you?'

'I checked all the fibres microscopically and all the analytical results; they were fine. I took some samples in case I need to do more work later.'

I wondered how all this would shape up. Nothing seemed to be straightforward, and in a case that was very high profile to begin with, the collapse of the first trial had raised the stakes further. The police and the CPS had already come in for criticism. The retrial would expose further failures: a critical bloodstain missed by the FSS and chaotic crime-scene management by the Met. I felt sure there would be further unwelcome surprises.

CHAPTER EIGHT

The Mystery Sweatshirt

There is always a well-known solution to every
human problem – neat, plausible, and wrong.

H. L. Mencken[1]

Making sense of what a fibre transfer means – how significant
the evidence is – can be more difficult than the scientific
analysis of the fibres. The evaluation involves a tangle of
scientific issues, logical reasoning, subjective experience and
uncertain information about the case. It's easy to list the factors
that need to be considered: quality of the analysis, numbers
and types of fibres, colour of fibres and dye types, whether the
transfer went from one item to another or from both items to
each other.* A crucial factor is how common the fibres are,
but there is no database that has this information like there
is for DNA. Nor would this be a practical proposition given
that production methods change and fashions come and go.

Callaghan, the forensic scientist who carried out the fibres
examinations at FAL, concluded: 'In summary, in relation to
the sweatshirt … and the tracksuit bottoms … the findings

---

* This is usually referred to as two-way transfer.

provide moderate support for the proposition that the wearer of these items were [*sic*] in some way, either directly or indirectly, associated with a burgundy coloured school uniform jumper supplied by [the manufacturer].'

My first impression on reading this was that it was so opaque as to be indecipherable. Evidence is something that helps you decide one way or another between competing versions of events; it should help you make your mind up. The allegation was that Ricky Preddie had stabbed Damilola Taylor or was present when someone else did so. The defence position was that he didn't stab Damilola nor was he there when it happened. Fibres associating Ricky with Damilola would tend to support the prosecution case, whereas absence of fibres would tend to support the defence case.* The important question was to what extent (if any) the fibres found connected Ricky to Damilola *at the time of his death*.

Callaghan's conclusion did not directly address this question, although you might argue that it was buried within it because it linked the fibres to their manufactured source and not the individual item. Textile fibres are not unique; most are mass-produced by the ton. One way of refining a situation so as to make findings more case-specific is to research how the items involved in the fibre transfer were produced and distributed. This gives some general idea of the numbers in circulation and can be used to hone the evaluation, but it also makes many assumptions, some of which may not be accurate.

---

* All other things being equal – which they usually aren't. For a variety of reasons, absence of fibres will not always support the assertion that there has been no contact.

Callaghan had made detailed inquiries into who had manufactured and dyed the acrylic fibres, how much had been produced and how they were distributed to suppliers. Oliver Goldsmith School had around 600 pupils, so hundreds of sweatshirts would be circulating in the area. The supply chain included five different companies that had manufactured and distributed garments containing the same red acrylic fibres as Damilola's sweatshirt. This would have amounted to many thousands of garments, mainly school uniforms, over several years. I didn't think it took the situation any further; in fact I thought it just complicated things unnecessarily.

If we were to take the conclusion at face value, what it said was that the two red acrylic fibres could have come from:

- any burgundy sweatshirt supplied by the clothing distributor
- two different sweatshirts (possibly at different times)
- different batches of these sweatshirts
- any other item that used the red acrylic source fibres
- any other manufacturer or supplier who also used the red acrylic source fibres produced by the manufacturer
- another manufacturer or source that matched by coincidence.

Finally, the conclusion said that the two fibres could be due to direct contact between two items or could have been transferred indirectly via another item.

Thirteen red acrylic fibres were found on Danny's clothing, and although this clothing came from Abbey Street, Danny usually lived at Blackthorne Court. What is not explicit in the conclusion is that the two fibres were found on items that were part of a bundle of clothing. The items were not seized individually, although they were eventually packaged individually. There were multiple potential explanations for these two fibres being found, but these explanations could not be disentangled.

My initial instinct about the fibres was sound. How incriminating was the fibre evidence against Ricky? Not incriminating at all. Was Callaghan's conclusion wrong? No, it was just unhelpful to the jury in addressing the specific issues before them. It was too indirect and multi-layered to expect any clear inference to be drawn from it.

Once you decide what your evidence means, it has to be put into words in the form of a report. These reports have a diverse audience: police officers, lawyers, judges, jurors, victims and accused persons. So they need to be clear, comprehensible and carefully crafted. Most forensic scientists believe that their reports are all these things and can be readily understood by their audience.[2] This belief is only true in the same way that we all believe we are better-than-average drivers. Lurking at the back of the mind of all forensic scientists (and sometimes not so far back) are two issues that heavily influence their writing: the mischief a lawyer might create in court, and what another expert, one on the opposing side, might make of it.

An expert's duty is to the court, not their client; they ought not to be taking sides. This is easy to say but can be hard to do. If you are in the midst of a murder investigation, working closely with the police, you can aim to be objective and independent, but it is impossible to remain uninfluenced, since all the information you receive will come from the police or prosecution. When you appear in court, you are called by one side or the other. In a tussle between the two sides, the law expects you to rise above partisan argument and walk a line that can be near impossible at times. In a report you have to fulfil this expectation in writing. Only in exceptional circumstances will there be a single explanation for a set of scientific findings. Courtrooms can be a fairground of alternative possibilities, of which as many as possible have to be anticipated at the time of writing.

—

Some weeks later, Adrian came to see me. We were both finalising our reports and he wanted to talk his over. It would also be useful for me to talk through what I had found. I listened while he summarised the DNA work.

'After they found the DNA matching Damilola on the black sweatshirt, they did a lot of tests to see if they could find DNA from Ricky. At first all they found was DNA matching staff from FAL. Then they found some skin flakes on the inside that gave a DNA profile that matched Ricky. Ricky denies all knowledge of the sweatshirt; it's not his and he has never worn it. So I took more samples for DNA analysis and to double-check the FAL findings. Everything squares up; my results confirm the FAL DNA findings.'

The DNA evidence provided a strong link between Ricky and Damilola that was all the more damning because Ricky had changed his story about the tracksuit bottoms, on which a DNA profile matching his had also been found. At first he had denied owning or having worn them, but then he backtracked and gave a complicated explanation about buying and exchanging them in a shop. From my perspective, the single red acrylic fibre found on each of these items added nothing.

Danny was also incriminated by DNA evidence albeit indirectly. He was believed to be the owner of the blue trainer from Blackthorne Court that had yielded DNA profiles matching him and Damilola Taylor.

—

On 26 January 2006, I got a letter from Charlotte Kelly, the solicitor who was leading on the case and had earlier come to see me in Glasgow. She explained that at a pre-trial hearing, the judge had directed that the two experts in the case (me and Callaghan) needed to meet for a 'round-table discussion' of their evidence. Could I come to the Old Bailey for this meeting?

On 2 February, I made my way to the Central Criminal Court. From Blackfriars Tube station, I took the short walk along Blackfriars Lane, past the Worshipful Society of Apothecaries and across Ludgate Hill into Old Bailey. This was my usual route when I worked in London and frequently gave evidence there.

At the peak of my activity at the Old Bailey, I gave evidence in three trials in one day: a serial rape and two murders. The first case went incredibly badly and I was accused of being unscientific and racist, neither of which was true. The former may have been a misunderstanding of my evidence; the latter was simply a personal attack. My only memory of the second case was being gently pulled up by the judge after commenting on the angle of a bloodstain where I hadn't taken everything into account. I have no recollection of the third case. I left the court utterly exhausted and made my way to the Tube station and home like an automaton.

On more than one occasion I had left this court swearing (literally) to change my occupation after yet another session where I felt I had been abused for sport. Punishment beatings weren't common if you kept your wits about you; however, they were a constant occupational hazard. Court was usually a forum for rational debate, but on occasion it felt like a playground full of school bullies with me as the class scapegoat.

Some of England's most senior and experienced lawyers were involved in the trial of the Preddie brothers and Jihad. Prosecuting was Max Hill QC, now head of the CPS in England and Wales. Orlando Pownall QC was defending Danny Preddie. Nigel Sweeney QC, now a senior judge at the Old Bailey, was defending Ricky. His junior was Benjamin Squirrel, a name surely straight out of a Dickens novel. Sweeney showed me and Callaghan into the small anteroom diagonally opposite the court. Despite my familiarity with the building, I had never noticed this room before. I suppose I was usually too preoccupied to explore my surroundings.

The plan was to discuss our reports and clarify where we agreed and disagreed. The judge wanted us to produce a joint report so that the court could focus on what was important and avoid unnecessary detail. These kinds of meeting have been recommended for many years in cases where there is important or disputed expert evidence, but they still happen quite rarely in criminal cases. Many lawyers are not keen to allow the experts to resolve their differences, because this can deprive them of tactical options for the trial.

There were many detailed differences in our reports, but only a few major ones. The first was that in Callaghan's opinion, there was evidence to link the clothing from Blackthorne Court to Damilola; my view was that there was none of significance. This crucial issue was one of opinion; we largely agreed on the facts. The second area of disagreement was more technical, and concerned how the dyes were analysed. My view was that there was an additional technique, thin-layer chromatography (TLC),* that could be used to analyse the dyes, and for me the analysis was incomplete. Callaghan felt TLC was unnecessary and was satisfied with the methods he had used.

We went through our reports, starting with the simple stuff. We agreed that Damilola's sweatshirt would shed fibres, that two matching red acrylic fibres had been found, that the black cottons were of 'extremely limited evidential value' and that we couldn't rule out the possibility that the matching fibres from Blackthorne Court could be there by chance. Then we started to get bogged down on what each of us meant by a 'chance match'; a match that was random and unconnected with the case. For me the chance of finding fibres that matched Damilola's sweatshirt was more likely in the local environment, where the sweatshirts were worn, compared for example to other parts of London. Callaghan appeared to agree with

---

* This is a technique that can be used to separate a wide range of chemical substances and is commonly used in forensic analysis.

this in principle but wanted to leave space in the joint report where he could express his own view.

From there we went on to the technical issues. It was obvious from the outset that we were not going to find common ground here. In essence, Callaghan considered his analysis complete and my criticism of not using TLC unfounded. I got the impression he thought I was out of touch with the newer methods of analysis he had used, but for me that was missing the point. The newer methods of analysis were just that, new. All the technical data showed that they were fine and useful, but I was coming from a different position. TLC had a long history of effectiveness and I would have backed up the newer methods with it. Did I think *scientifically* it would make any difference? No, I thought the dyes would match.* There was an 'extremely remote chance' of the dyes being different, as I recorded in my meeting notes. But if I was in Callaghan's position, I would not have gone into this retrial without closing that door.

—

Using Bromley as the key witness at the first trial had been a calculated gamble. She had repeatedly changed her story during interviews and there was always the possibility that this would happen in court. Her idiosyncratic performance in the witness box could not have been a complete surprise, although just how spectacularly wrong it all went could not have been foreseen. The problem that occurred in the second trial was as devastating as that in the first, but this one was completely

_____

* The dyes were subsequently tested and found to match.

unexpected. A case of Wagnerian proportions was about to be the subject of a subplot from *opéra comique*.

On 28 November 2000, the day after the murder, two detectives had been dispatched to Oliver Goldsmith School to get a sweatshirt so it could be photographed for the media pack being prepared for a public appeal. They drove to Southampton Way and were given a new sweatshirt still in its plastic bag. They then drove three miles to Greenwich mortuary, where the post-mortem examination was taking place and where there was a photographer available. There was no record of who had retrieved the sweatshirt. In the witness box during the second trial, one of the detectives who was believed to have been involved was asked which car was used to drive to the school. He couldn't remember. He was asked if the sweatshirt was removed from the bag before arriving at the mortuary. He couldn't remember. He was asked if the sweatshirt was left at the mortuary or taken elsewhere. He couldn't remember. Where was the sweatshirt now? He didn't know.

On 2 December, the same detective had been part of the team that arrested Danny Preddie. The team drove to Abbey Street in two cars and returned to the police station with Danny and the seized items of clothing. Had the duplicate sweatshirt been in one of the cars? No one knew. When the team arrived at Danny's address, Danny was in bed. None of the officers was wearing protective clothing. Unlike the team that arrested Ricky, who put him in a jumpsuit, Danny was told to put on some of the clothing that was lying on his bed. The rest was put into a single plastic bag and taken back to the police station. Danny was taken in one car and the clothing went in the other. No one could remember which cars were used. The clothing that Danny was wearing was not distinguished from what was found on the bed.

This new sweatshirt had never been logged into the inquiry exhibit system. It had now disappeared without trace and no one could remember where it had been, who had handled it, what cars it had been in or where it was now. Is this credible? I don't think so. Most detectives have very good memories, particularly about their individual actions in a murder inquiry. Is there an alternative explanation? Possibly. Fibres were not a significant feature of the forensic work at the FSS, and no incriminating fibres evidence was presented at the first trial.* Therefore, the duplicate sweatshirt was of no consequence. But when FAL found matching fibres, the free-floating duplicate sweatshirt was a potential problem; it had been kicking around since the start of the case and it was too late to formally log it in the exhibit system. Could it have been 'disappeared'; was *Life on Mars* alive and kicking in post-millennial London?

The trial seemed to lurch from one forensic disaster to the next. The assistant scientists who examined the trainer and black sweatshirt for the FSS were called to give evidence. In the witness box, Sheila Hilley, who no longer worked for the FSS, was handed the right blue trainer found at Blackthorne Court. She agreed that she could now see the bloodstain on the heel and that she must have missed it. 'I performed the tests as they are [recorded] in my notes. I do not have any

_____

* The FSS had found a tuft of fibres on the shard of glass that matched fibres from Damilola's trousers but this did not link any of the defendants to the murder.

other explanation.' Her colleague, Owen Gale, who missed the bloodstain on the black sweatshirt, was equally unable to explain how he failed to find the blood.

It's hard to believe even now that critical evidence was missed on not just one but two occasions in such an important case. But it is difficult not to be sympathetic towards these individuals; they were small cogs in a large machine who made honest mistakes. Mistakes for which they paid a heavy personal price.

The jury of seven women and five men deliberated for five days. On 3 April, they reached a unanimous agreement and found Hassan Jihad not guilty of murder and manslaughter. Jihad was discharged by the judge, Mr Justice Leveson. The jury memebers were unable to reach verdicts on the Preddie brothers, and Leveson told them that he would accept a majority verdict and directed them to continue their deliberations. They were still unable to agree, and later that day Leveson discharged them. The second trial ended with no convictions.

—

Having lost most of the potential witness and confession evidence during the first trial, the second trial was always going to turn on the forensic evidence. Despite our meeting, Callaghan and I never agreed a finalised joint report. I suspect this was overtaken by the events that now cast doubt on much, if not all, of the fibres evidence.

One can only guess how some of this testimony from police witnesses went down with the jury. Of the teams that recovered the crucial items, at least two officers had had to make second statements to correct errors in earlier ones. The seizure of the clothing from Blackthorne Court and Abbey Street had been carried out without protective clothing being worn, and there was a rogue identical sweatshirt in the system that no one could explain and that had now been lost. The exhibit management, so critical to the integrity of the forensic evidence, was chaotic.

At least one juror was so upset by what she had witnessed that she went public. She was staggered to hear how incomplete and incomprehensible the police answers were. 'In the witness box they kept saying: "I can't remember, I can't remember." But you would think that in such a high-profile case they would know exactly what had been seized and exactly what had happened to it.'[3] Yes, you would. This juror was unconvinced by the fibres evidence. It didn't matter whether I was right or Callaghan was right. The integrity of the evidence was completely compromised and could not be relied on.

—

Immediately after the trial, the police and CPS met to decide what to do next; four days later, it was announced that the Preddie brothers would face a retrial. Jihad had been acquitted, so the third trial of the case would feature only the Preddies, who were now old enough to be named. Another crucial change for this trial was that the murder charge was reduced to manslaughter. The trial began on 23 June 2006, and on 9 August, both brothers were found guilty. As the verdicts were read out, Ricky Preddie shouted at the jury: 'You are corrupt. You are nothing.'

We can have a sense of why the previous juries acquitted the brothers, because of the many problems that arose in those trials. But why did the jury convict them in the third trial? We can never really know; the deliberations of juries are never revealed. Perhaps the issues in the previous trials distracted the juries or raised doubts in their minds. Or was the evidence clearer third time around, having been pared to its essentials after two previous trials? But there was one key factor that was different in the third trial compared to the first two: it was for the lesser charge of manslaughter rather than murder.

—

With the legal proceedings over, questions about how the FSS missed the critical evidence began to take prominence. And with trust between the FSS and the Met now in terminal decline, the Home Office instituted an independent review.[4] Recognising that the apparatus of accusation had now been activated, the police alleged that there were many other cases in which the FSS had failed to spot blood. A list was passed to the review team, which looked into these cases and the full circumstances of the Damilola Taylor case, examining documentary evidence and hearing witness testimony.

In 1999, the police service had produced its first national guidance for investigating homicide – the *Murder Investigation Manual.* In December 2000, as the Taylor case was unfolding, Ian Johnston, the Deputy Assistant Commissioner of the Met, signed off the second edition, which included the following guidance: 'Investigators must work … in harmony with scientists and not in isolation of each other … The SIO must ensure the whole needs of the investigation are conveyed regularly and with clarity to the scientist so that any forensic information can be supplied as widely and as rapidly as possible.'[5]

Did the relationship between investigators and forensic scientists in the Taylor case meet these aspirations? Between the end of November 2000 and the end of January 2001, the police submitted 403 items to the FSS in 18 batches. All but three of these items were marked urgent. What were the police priorities here? And how did this murder rank against the other 200 homicides (and 200 rapes) that the London lab was working on at the same time? A strategy to do everything urgently is not a strategy, it is a fantasy. The FSS, deluged by the amount of work and the lack of clarity about priorities, suggested to detectives that some of the testing should be transferred to their other labs to spread the load. The Met refused to allow this, yet after the first trial they moved the work not only out of London but to a different forensic laboratory.

The situation was akin to what I faced in the Robert Black case, where the slow progress and the recognition that there was a shared responsibility compelled us to have the difficult conversation about what was important and what was less so. There were no such discussions in the Taylor case. Overwhelmed by the workload, the FSS were left on their own to take decisions about what ought to be prioritised. They responded by throwing resources at the problem. A highly experienced forensic scientist and a team of nine assistants were allocated to the case, an extraordinary number of assistants for a single investigation and something that would have been very difficult to coordinate. Even in the Black case, which had a similar if not larger workload, I only had three staff supporting me at any one time. The lead scientist and assistants on the Taylor case would also have been working on other cases at the same time. Hilley and Gale, who missed the bloodstains, were well trained and had good track records. They took adequate notes and could reconstruct their thoughts but could not recall every detail and could not explain their errors.

When the missed bloodstain on the trainer was examined at FAL, the chemical test for blood didn't work first time around and had to be repeated. Maybe the test also failed at the FSS, but was it repeated? This couldn't be established for sure. The bloodstain on the sweatshirt was small and on the inside of the cuff. It was much more difficult to spot. FAL only found it following a detailed examination using a low-power microscope.

The review found no systematic failings in the FSS practices or standards, either in the Damilola Taylor case or any of the other cases put up by the police. However, the lead scientist had failed to review the work of the assistants adequately, and if he had done so, the mistakes might have been prevented. The cause of the failures had already been established in the trial: human error.

The FSS also carried out an internal review that included a blind trial. A black sweatshirt with similar blood staining to that on the case item was secretly sent for examination to each FSS lab. Some of the labs outside London had maintained that the missed bloodstain was a London problem; they would never have missed it – but several of them did in the trial.

It took six years, two police inquiries and three trials costing an estimated £16m to bring the Preddie brothers to justice.[6] There were many distinctive and unusual problems in the case, but one aspect in particular gave me cause for personal reflection. Between the second and third trials a bundle of additional statements from various witnesses was served on the defence team. Individually, the significance of the statements wasn't always clear; some were only a few sentences. However, collectively they amounted to the prosecution tidying up, resolving problems, closing doors. In the bundle were several further statements from Callaghan, the FAL fibres expert. In one statement he dealt with the debacle of the missing sweatshirt: 'I have been asked to consider the impact of this proposition on the textile fibre findings,' he stated. He worked through the options systematically and dispassionately, ranging from no impact on his findings to complete negation of them. His analysis was careful and logical and his conclusions were clear. But it was an encore to a performance while the venue was on fire. What was unstated were the implications for forensic work more generally; the obvious and colossal gulf between the precision of the scientific analysis and the chaotic ineptitude of the police.

When I worked in the Met, I was a fibres expert. How many fibres cases had I done? Hundreds; some small, some big; some where I had found no fibres evidence, others with some evidence, and some where the fibres evidence was crucial. Every one of these cases relied on exhibit-handling procedures that even at the time were well known. Looking back, I wonder now how many of my cases were handled like this one. How often had I played an unwitting part in some incompetent or corrupt investigation?

CHAPTER NINE

On Wimbledon Common – the Murder of Rachel Nickell

Our tales are spun, but for the most part we don't spin them; they spin us.

Daniel Dennett[1]

The body of Rachel Nickell was discovered by Michael McIntyre, a retired architect, while walking on Wimbledon Common. It was a warm, bright summer morning; around 10.35 on 15 July 1992. At first McIntyre thought the partly undressed Rachel was a sunbather, something the common was well known for. Then he saw the blood, Rachel's glazed eyes and Alex, her two-year-old son, pulling at her, trying to get her up. Her body was 20–30 feet from open parkland and about 100 yards from a car park.

Dr Dick Shepherd,[2] the forensic pathologist who attended the crime scene, described similar feelings to those I experienced at the Russell crime scene in Kent: a sense of dissonance and incongruence, an ineffable tension between a violent death and the almost bucolic surroundings.

Rachel had been stabbed 49 times by a knife about 1.5 cm wide at the hilt and 9 cm long. A small number of these wounds were minor; they were used to control her, to ensure compliance with the demands of her attacker. One of the wounds had passed through her left hand while she was defending herself. No screams were heard because the deep incisions in her neck had prevented her screaming. Her T-shirt was bloodstained and her jeans had been pulled to below her knees. The jeans were muddy at the front and blood-spattered at the back, suggesting that she was kneeling at some point during the attack, before falling onto her front. She had then been stabbed 18 times in her back. The blood staining at the scene showed that her body had then been moved from where she was initially attacked, to an area under a tree where more blood staining was found. She was then stabbed in her front. Her killer continued to stab her after she was dead; the wounds to her heart and liver were post mortem. Finally, she was sexually assaulted. Shepherd estimated that it would have taken at least three minutes for all the stab wounds to be inflicted.

—

The small, cramped incident room at Wimbledon police station barely accommodated the team involved in the investigation. It had been established that about 500 people had been on the common around the time of the murder. Tracing, interviewing and eliminating these individuals was one of the first tasks to be undertaken. Two witnesses had seen a man washing his hands in a stream about 150 yards from where Rachel's body was found. Tracing this man was another important action. André Hanscombe, Rachel's partner and father of Alex, had been quickly eliminated; he had a cast-iron alibi.

Information from the public came at first in a trickle, then a flood as the news spread. Everything had to be added to the HOLMES database to ensure the information was current and available to the inquiry team. But there were not enough specialist HOLMES operators in the team. There never were in the Met.

There was no forensic evidence to speak of. The crime scene had yielded very little: one shoe mark in mud had been found, but nothing else. The pathologist had suggested that there was semen on the body, but so far the lab had found none.

Two weeks into the investigation, with no significant progress, a chief officer in the Met suggested to the SIO, Detective Superintendent John Bassett, that an offender profiler might be of some use. On 28 July, Bassett rang Paul Britton, a consultant clinical and forensic psychologist based in Leicestershire, who had advised the police in a number of very high-profile cases of violent and sexual crime, homicide and kidnapping.

—

My first experience of offender profiling and its imagined mindscapes of murderers was in the 1980s. 'Thinking like the offender' was a common trope; I had heard it often enough from detectives and even forensic scientists. But there was never any precision to this. No one ever told me how to go about this feat of mental exploration; nor did those who claimed to use the technique appear to have more insight than anyone else. Offender profiling was supposed to predict, amongst other things, the age, ethnic origin, occupation and criminal history of the offender. Detectives were ambivalent about the whole idea. They were caught between the seductive promises of novel 'science' and the audacity of psychologists who claimed to understand how to investigate crime, something they considered to be their reserved territory.

Four years before Rachel Nickell was murdered, on a bright Sunday morning in June, Pushpa Bhatti left her home to walk in Southall Park, London. It would have taken the 53-year-old mother of three no more than a few minutes to reach the park. She arrived around 6.00 a.m. Even at this early hour there were a few people in the park, but none reported seeing her or anything unusual. Her body, naked from the waist down, was found later that evening; she had been sexually assaulted, beaten and strangled.

Exhibits for forensic examination arrived at the lab a few days later and I set about examining samples from her body, clothing and items from the scene. Her handbag and some of her other belongings had been found near her body, together with a broken cider bottle that was thought to have been used as a weapon.

'We're using an offender profiler, Dr David Canter,' one of the detectives told me some weeks into the investigation. I had heard of Canter from my colleagues who had worked on the 'railway rapes',[*3] and I was curious about this new business.

---

* A series of rapes and three murders in and around London in the 1980s for which John Duffy and later David Mulcahy were variously convicted.

Canter had come up with an offender profile from his analysis of the crime scene and other information given to him.[4] The offender knew the area and was probably local. Although the attack had happened in a public park, he had chosen (and therefore had known) a secluded area. The body was only a few yards from a busy road, but it could not be seen because the offender knew where he could hide it. He had chosen the *location*, not the victim; Bhatti was in the wrong place at the wrong time. The attack was partly planned (the offender knew where it would happen), but it was impulsive; he did not know in advance that he was going to attack Bhatti. The violence and impulsiveness involved suggested that he had committed other crimes of violence and possibly sexual crimes before; he should have a criminal record. He was probably in his late teens or early twenties, not especially intelligent, and most likely did manual or unskilled work. It was also likely that there would have been some domestic instability in his background, possibly domestic violence. He may well have sexual problems.

So the offender was young, male and probably had a police record. On the face of it there was nothing new here; information like this often resulted in much scoffing by detectives. But what struck me immediately about Canter's interpretation was the clear links between his observations and inferences. For example, he accounted for the different locations of Bhatti's bag and payslip; they had been put there to hide them, and only someone who knew the area well would know where these things could be hidden. This type of clarity was not something I usually encountered with detectives. Their explanations were usually that something was obvious (to them) and needed no explanation; it was self-evident to anyone who understood such things. The detectives were drawing on the same information as Canter, but his reasoning was explicit and clear where theirs was intuitive and opaque. None of this made Canter right or the detectives wrong, but it made him easier to follow – rationality can be evaluated; intuition requires belief.

I worked my way through the items sent to the lab for forensic examination. There was a shoe print in blood on Bhatti's handbag, which provided the first real lead in the case. Amongst the exhibits was one of the oddest items I had ever encountered. This was a piece of paper rolled up into a tube about 10 cm long and 3 cm in diameter, with one end folded and closed off. Around it was a second piece of paper tied in a simple knot. The inside of the tube was heavily stained with semen. It seemed likely that the offender had ejaculated into this; it was a device to prevent him leaving semen at the scene. He had presumably intended to take it with him when he left, and that he had failed to do so was to be his downfall. I sent samples of the semen for DNA profiling.

On 25 July, a 22-year-old pregnant woman was raped in Havelock Cemetery, about a mile from Southall Park. The attacker covered her face with a jacket to prevent her from identifying him, but despite this, she managed to describe him. Police were led to the offender, Michael Ogiste, by her description and by tracing items that he had stolen from her and later sold. Ogiste had a previous criminal history, but detectives were not convinced he had murdered Bhatti; until DNA profiles linked the cases.

Most of what Canter had predicted was accurate. Ogiste was a local man around the age he had suggested; he did manual work and had a criminal history. But Ogiste was black and Canter had tentatively predicted a white offender. For Canter this had been a tricky problem, because data on the ethnicity of offenders was sparse and came largely from the USA – would it also be valid for offenders in the UK? His caution had been lost in translation, and as far as the police were concerned, he was wrong. This resonates with one of the common criticisms of offender profiling: what is the point of getting the generalities right if the specifics are incorrect?

On 1 December 1989, Ogiste pleaded guilty to rape, and guilty to manslaughter on the grounds of diminished responsibility. He told his lawyer that on the day of the murder, 'I was not my normal self. I was like a beast.' He was diagnosed with a psychopathic disorder and sentenced to be detained in a high-security psychiatric institution in Liverpool.

Amongst the most powerful influences on police practice – how they go about their job – are fashion and folklore. Apocryphal tales of new tactics, especially 'scientific' ones, travel around the country by word of mouth. A novel approach used successfully in one case is assumed to be useful in another, despite differences in the situation. In the late eighties and early nineties, DNA was the main fashion, but there was also a growing folklore around offender profiling. DNA analysis at the time was a slow, complicated and expensive process that could only be done in one backlogged lab in the country. It also needed more body fluids than were usually available in the average case, so didn't always work. Forensic psychologists and psychiatrists, however, were readily available and some were very keen to become involved in police work. Offender profiling also caught the public imagination, with its irresistible promise of seeing into the mind of a pervert or murderous stranger. In September 1993, the BBC launched the TV show *Cracker*, starring Robbie Coltrane as an entertaining but scarcely credible offender profiler. It was hugely popular, running for five seasons and viewed by tens of millions of people.

—

Paul Britton travelled from his office in Leicester to Wimbledon to be briefed about the Nickell investigation. He quizzed detectives about every detail of the case: the scene, the forensic work, the post-mortem examination. He also went to the scene and made a detailed interpretation of what he found there. He wanted to know about Rachel, too. He said he needed to know her 'as well as if she was sitting in the chair opposite. What's she going to say? What's she going to think? How's she going to respond in any given situation?'[5]

His desire for information was understandable; he could not allow detectives to make assumptions about what might be relevant. In my experience, it is usually easier to ask for every piece of information when trying to understand a case, in order to be confident that nothing has been overlooked. But was it really possible to know what someone might be thinking from a third-party description of them, no matter how detailed? Could he know what she was thinking even if she sat in front of him in real life?

Britton reflected on the information he gathered and created a profile: the killer was unknown to Rachel, aged between 20 and 30 years old, with poor social skills, of average intelligence and with a manual or unskilled job. He was single, socially isolated and lived alone, within walking distance of the common, a place he was very familiar with. His hobbies or interests would be solitary and unusual, possibly including the martial arts. There was a good chance that he would have a criminal record, although this might not be for similar or serious offences. He would have a powerful deviant sexual fantasy life, use pornography and was likely to suffer from some form of sexual dysfunction. He would have rehearsed the offence but not every detail; his choice of victim would have been driven by opportunity and impulsiveness.

This profile was almost indistinguishable from the profile of Michael Ogiste in the Bhatti case. But Britton added more: he was likely to kill another young woman.

—

On 10 August 1989, a young single mother was raped at knifepoint in her bedroom, while her children were downstairs. The attacker pulled her T-shirt over her face and secured it tight with wire. He was unable to get a full erection but did ejaculate. He then escaped through a break in the garden fence into the Green Chain Walk, which links 50 miles of branching, leafy pathways across otherwise disconnected fields, parks and woodlands in south-east London.

In September 1989, 23-year-old Robert Napper, an obsessively tidy, lonely and troubled man, lay in hospital having taken a drugs overdose. Why? his mother asked him. He told her he had raped a woman in south-east London. She passed this information to the police but they could find no report of a rape and took no further action.

On 10 March 1992, a 17-year-old girl was attacked in an alleyway in Plumstead, south London, on her way to visit a friend. Her attacker told her not to make any noise if she wanted to live, and dragged her behind some garages. He punched her several times and forced her to the ground. After raping her, he repeatedly kicked her in the head until she was unconscious.

A week later, a young girl stomped out of her parents' home in Eltham Palace Road in south London towards King John's Walk, part of the Green Chain Walk. She was standing admiring the distant view of Canary Wharf when a man suddenly appeared in front of her. He was wearing a balaclava but then took it off and forced her to her knees, threatening her with a knife. He pulled up her top and pushed the tip of the knife into her left breast. He then raped her. After he ejaculated, he moved the knife over her vagina.

In May the same year, a young woman pushing her two-year-old child in a buggy was attacked in King John's Walk. A rope was thrown around her neck from behind and she was jerked backwards so violently she almost lost consciousness. She was repeatedly punched and then raped.

As well as the geographic links in these offences, there were other common features: the attacker used a knife, his approach was similar, he was unable to achieve a full erection although he ejaculated each time. Crucially, forensic examination of the cases had established a clear link: the DNA profiles obtained from semen in each case matched. Dozens of other sexual assaults on women were also believed to be linked.

On 25 August 1992, police released an e-fit of the Green Chain Walk suspect compiled from descriptions given by the victims. A neighbour of Robert Napper reported him to the police a few days later. He said Napper's behaviour was a bit odd and he resembled the e-fit. Detectives interviewed Napper at his home. They thought he was too tall to be the rapist, but he agreed to come to the police station and give a DNA sample. He failed to appear, and the police failed to follow this up.

A few days later, a call to Crimestoppers* identified Napper as matching the e-fit. On 8 September, police called at his home again but he was not in. They left a letter asking him to come to the police station and give a blood sample for DNA testing. He never did.

In October 1992, Napper asked a local printer if he could supply him with Metropolitan Police headed notepaper. The printer was suspicious and reported this to the police. Napper was arrested and his flat in Plumstead was searched. A handgun, 244 rounds of ammunition, two knives and a crossbow were found. Napper was later convicted of firearms offences and sentenced to eight weeks in prison.

During the search, police also found a London A to Z, on which Napper had marked particular locations. No attention was given to this find.

---

* An independent charity that passes information about crime from members of the public to the police while retaining the anonymity of its sources.

In July 1993, police were called after a man was seen trying to climb into the flat of a young mother in south London. Robert Napper was found hiding in a nearby alley. The officers who spoke to him recorded his demeanour as 'strange, abnormal [and] a possible rapist',[6] but Napper convinced them he was just out for a walk and he was not detained.

—

The still unsolved Nickell case featured on BBC *Crimewatch* on 17 September 1992. It was hoped that this would break the deadlock in the investigation. An artist's impression of a potential suspect was broadcast. Amongst the 800 calls to the incident room following the programme, several people suggested that this was a local man called Colin Stagg, who walked his dog on the common most days.

Stagg had a previous conviction for a minor theft. He had also been convicted of possession of an offensive weapon – a set of martial arts rice flails – something that resonated with Britton's profile. Detectives considered this to be highly significant. Stagg was arrested the following morning and interviewed over a period of three days. During the course of the interviews, detectives were in constant touch with Britton for advice, but Stagg consistently denied any involvement in the murder. With no confession and no forensic evidence, the case against him was weak and circumstantial: he was local, he resembled the artist's impression, he walked his dog on the common and an eyewitness said she had seen him there near the time of the murder.

Around the end of September, detectives approached Britton with a new idea. The original aim of the offender profile was to prioritise potential suspects and give some idea what type of person the police were looking for. Detectives had noted that Britton also described in some detail a range of sexually deviant behaviour attributed to the offender, which he said was very rare. If Stagg exhibited similar sexual deviancy, could that prove he was the killer? And if so, could this evidence be gleaned by a police undercover operation? Although this idea was novel and unorthodox, the police were enthusiastic to explore it. Britton confirmed that the profile of the killer was very rare and the chances of more than one man living locally matching it were 'vanishingly small'. If Stagg fitted the profile, he was the killer.

Coached by Britton, detectives set in motion an undercover operation using an attractive young female police officer code-named 'Lizzie James'. James contacted Stagg by letter, then phone, and eventually met him in person. Her letters contained lurid sexual fantasies and she encouraged Stagg to respond with fantasies of his own. Amongst the wildest of her fantasies was that she had been involved in the satanic killing of a baby. Gradually she shifted the focus of the correspondence to Rachel's death, telling Stagg that she wished he had murdered her. Stagg responded to these advances in a way that was mundanely predictable. He was single, lonely, sexually inexperienced and was being lured by promises of sex from an attractive woman. But he was completely bemused by the nature of James's fantasies and made it clear he wanted a more friendly and loving relationship. On numerous occasions he said he had nothing to do with Rachel's death and knew nothing about it.

In August 1993, Stagg was rearrested and charged with the murder of Rachel Nickell. When he had been interviewed before, he had tried to answer questions honestly and explain himself. This time he took the advice of his solicitor and responded 'no comment'. At one point 'Lizzie James' walked into the interview room unannounced; Stagg realised he had been duped.

On 14 September 1994, Colin Stagg sat in the dock in Court 1 of the Old Bailey. The case against him was almost exclusively based on a police undercover operation. His defence team sought to have this evidence excluded from the trial. The prosecution had agreed that without the undercover evidence, the remaining evidence was not enough to convict him. It was all or nothing. If the judge was convinced by the defence argument, Stagg would walk free; if not, he would face trial for one of the UK's most notorious murders.

Mr Justice Ognall had taken several days to review the hundreds of pages of documentation and audio transcripts. He now began to give the court his decision. Most of what he said made little sense to Stagg. He couldn't tell if things were going his way or not, until his counsel, William Clegg QC, turned to him and subtly grinned. DCI Mick Wickerson and DI Keith Pedder, who had built the case against him, were optimistic about the prospect of a conviction, but grew increasingly anxious as Ognall went on. Now some way into his justification, the judge was scathing. The case against Stagg was based on 'a blatant attempt to incriminate a suspect by …

deceptive conduct of the grossest kind … [it was] a sustained enterprise to manipulate … designed, by deception, to … seduce him to reveal fantasies of an incriminating character, and to … admit the offence'.[7] After the judgement, prosecution counsel John Nutting QC rose and withdrew the case against Stagg. Outside the Old Bailey, Rachel Nickell's parents made a public statement: there had been a trial but there had been no justice.

The following day, the front page of *The Sun* newspaper carried a large photo of Colin Stagg accompanied by the headline 'NO GIRL IS SAFE'. It seemed there would be no justice for Stagg either.

—

On Thursday 4 November 1993, the bodies of Samantha Bisset and her four-year-old daughter Jazmine were found in their home in Plumstead, south London. It is a common trope to hear SIOs in media statements commenting on how terrible a crime is: 'The worst murder I have encountered in over 25 years …' But this crime scene was so horrific and bizarre that comparisons with the legendary crimes of Jack the Ripper were not exaggerations.

Samantha's body had been cut open and her internal organs theatrically displayed; worse still, it was obvious that her killer had taken his time and derived pleasure from doing this. There was very little blood at the scene because most of the mutilation had taken place after death. It was later discovered that part of her body had been removed as a trophy. Jazmine had been undressed, sexually assaulted, then re-dressed, before being placed in bed and smothered with a pillow. To those who saw her, she appeared to be sleeping. Few who attended the crime scene would have had any equivalent experience, and it was to be burned into their memories.

The SIO, Detective Superintendent Mickey Banks, contacted Paul Britton for offender profiling advice. He also asked Britton if the murders were linked to the Nickell case. Both women were young, blonde mothers, and were savagely attacked in the presence of a child. Britton's view was that how the children were treated distinguished the cases. Jazmine had been assaulted and killed, but Nickell's son Alex had not been attacked; it was not the same killer. He cited other differences too: Rachel had been killed in a blitz attack in the open air, while the murders of Samantha and Jazmine were much slower, deliberate affairs. On 8 February 1994, BBC *Crimewatch* broadcast a reconstruction of events leading up to the murders of Samantha and Jazmine.

Some months into the inquiry, there was a breakthrough. A fingerprint had been found on the handrail of the balcony outside Samantha's flat. The positioning of the print suggested that it had been left by someone climbing over the handrail. Apparently the mark was initially thought to have been from Samantha,* but closer inspection revealed it to match Robert Napper, who was arrested on 27 May 1994. While the squad went about investigating Napper further, another important question arose: could he have been involved in other offences that had happened locally?

---

* This is yet another error in the investigation that appears to have got lost among the many others.

—

In September 1994, the Met Commissioner, Sir Paul Condon, announced a review of the Nickell case. Detective Chief Superintendent Bill Ilsley, one of the Met's most experienced and well-respected detectives, would carry out this work. Ilsley would 'minutely examine all the evidence',[8] said Condon, and review the actions previously taken in relation to the 500 individuals who had been eliminated. He would also closely study the 7,000 files and 1,300 witness statements in the case.

The previous year, the Met had been compelled to review the murder of Stephen Lawrence due to immense external pressures from the Lawrence family, their representatives, the media and politicians. The review concluded that the investigation had been 'undertaken with professionalism and dedication by a team who have experienced pressures and outside influence on an unprecedented scale'.[9] This is reminiscent of the comments made by Hector Clark about the Yorkshire Ripper case (see Chapter One). The language was high-handed and patronising, and by implication blamed the Lawrence family for the lack of results. Murder reviews at this time were largely administrative affairs that defended investigations and lacked objectivity and independence.

There was another significant dimension to both the investigations and reviews of Lawrence and Nickell: the Met itself. I had worked with hundreds of Met detectives between 1978 and 1989 and was frequently reminded that the force was different. Everything *was* different: its operational structure, its ranks, its terminology and even its jargon. As the police force

for the capital, it was by far the biggest in the UK and one of
the biggest in the world. This and other factors shored up the
false belief that that Met was the best. Only rarely was this stated
explicitly. It didn't have to be said; how could it be otherwise?
If investigations in other forces came up in conversation, they
were often responded to with a smirk or a sneer. Later, when
I worked at Kent Police, I had many dealings with the Met. I
picked up the same signals from an organisation bathed in
unfounded self-belief, seemingly incapable of reflection and
inured to external criticism.

—

Robert Napper was tried at the Old Bailey for the murders of
Samantha and Jazmine Bisset, along with two rapes and two
attempted rapes from the Green Chain Walk attacks. He initially
denied the offences, but later changed his plea to guilty. On
9 October 1995, he was convicted of both murders, one rape
and two attempted rapes. The second rape was dropped due
to chain-of-custody problems; at some point samples involved
in DNA profiling had been transposed. He was sentenced to
be detained in Broadmoor secure psychiatric hospital.

Napper, born on 25 February 1966, had three siblings and
was brought up in a home where domestic violence was the
norm until his parents separated. At the age of 12, he was raped
in broad daylight in a local wood, an experience that changed
him dramatically. His teenage years were fraught and unstable;
his father occasionally returned to harass his mother, and he
was placed in foster care with his siblings. He was a habitual
liar, violent towards his siblings, and spied on his sister when

she was undressing and bathing. As an adolescent he was a vicious bully and thief; as a young adult he received regular counselling and professional support and was diagnosed with Asperger's syndrome and paranoid schizophrenia.

The Green Chain Walk attacks spanned four years, from 1989 until 1993, and ended when Robert Napper was arrested for the Bisset murders. We can't be sure how many attacks there were, because it is likely some were never reported, but the number could be as high as 100. Yet again, the errors in this investigation resonated with similar disasters in the investigation of the Yorkshire Ripper, Peter Sutcliffe.

On 20 December 1995, Napper was interviewed in Broadmoor in connection with the murder of Rachel Nickell. He denied killing her. The review team decided there was no evidence to incriminate him, and no further action was taken. Nothing came of the review. It was just one more failure to be added to a growing list.

—

It would be some years before the systems and culture of policing in the UK, and particularly the Met, were sufficiently mature to both confront their limitations and respond to the complexities of the public face of homicide investigation. Dealing with grieving families, building trust and managing the anger of victims, particularly in minority communities, needed new skills. Additional skills were also needed to help the police articulate their own position in a more nuanced and sensitive manner.

A second review of the Nickell case started in 2002. In the

decade or so between the first and second reviews, much had changed. The Lawrence case had exposed poor practices and compelled the police service to face up to the institutional racism that had dogged the investigation. The other big breakthrough was technological. Much of the focus in more recent reviews was on finding body fluids that could then be subjected to DNA analysis. If a profile was obtained, this could be used to search the DNA database. If no match was found, the work had been done; the profile was banked and awaited a match from someone who might offend in the future. Soon many police forces would set up case review teams that were separate from their primary homicide investigation teams, providing the necessary independence and objectivity that had been missing in the past.

The new review of the Nickell case would be carried out by the recently formed Met murder review group, and I was approached to advise them on forensic issues. This would draw me deeply into the technological and institutional aspects of DNA profiling, particularly the issue of DNA contamination.

CHAPTER TEN

Operations Edzell and Ecclestone

> Serial killers are extremely difficult to spot. They tend to look like just ordinary people [with] ordinary jobs. It's not so much that they lurk in the shadows as that they blend with the crowd.
>
> Professor Laurence Alison[1]

In March 2007, DCI Tony Nash, the SIO in the Nickell review, visited me in Glasgow. He was accompanied by Susan Bonnar, a senior prosecutor from the CPS. The review, which had now been ongoing for several years, had uncovered unexpected but highly significant forensic evidence. However, both the Met and the CPS had concerns about this evidence and they wanted an independent assessment of it.

A DNA profile had been found on a key item, but there was a chance that it could be due to contamination. The DNA profile matched Robert Napper, the man convicted of murdering Samantha and Jazmine Bisset and the Green Chain Walk attacks. In June 2006, Napper had been interviewed in

Broadmoor again about the Nickell murder. He refused to answer any questions, but made a written statement denying his involvement. He had not changed his plea to guilty in the Bisset murders and the Green Chain Walk attacks until the last minute. He was unlikely to confess to this crime until he was confronted with strong evidence of his involvement.

The DNA profile had been found on a taping from Rachel Nickell's body. Subsequently it had been discovered that samples from the Green Chain Walk attacks had been stored together with the Nickell tapings. Some of the Green Chain Walk items were stained with semen matching Napper. Worse still, the taping from Nickell had been examined in the same lab, on the same day, on the same bench and by the same scientist who had examined semen-stained items from Green Chain Walk cases.

At first the police and CPS thought that the contamination could only have been possible in the Met lab. But later the taping had been examined by a second FSS lab (although no DNA had been found there) and then in a third lab, where the DNA profile had been found. The more the police and CPS thought about it, the bigger the problem became. The highest chance of contamination was in the Met lab, but contamination would need to be ruled out in the other labs too. There was also the possibility of contamination outside the labs before the samples arrived, or as items were being transported between labs.

As the story unfolded, it became clear that the third lab was LGC, formerly the Laboratory of the Government Chemist, now a private company that supplied forensic services to many police forces in England and Wales. In 2005, LGC had acquired FAL, the lab that had found the missed bloodstains in the Damilola Taylor case. Were Nash and Bonnar aware of my involvement in that case? Were they aware of the contentious issues that had arisen and the questionable behaviour of the FSS senior management? If they knew these things, they chose not to mention them, but some familiar questions arose in my mind. Why had the Nickell case been transferred to LGC? Why had the DNA not been found at the Met lab in 1992? Folded into this question was another: why had the DNA been missed by the FSS? In the Taylor case I was on the periphery of the skirmishes between the FSS and the Met. But if I carried out this review, I could be caught in the crossfire. I could think of no obvious reason why the FSS would fail to find DNA when they examined the same item as LGC; but then they never found the bloodstains in the Taylor case.

'So what you want is a review of the chain of custody to see if there was a possibility of contamination of this taping?' I asked. 'A paper exercise to quality-assure the result?' As with all reviews, it's important that your precise role is nailed down at the outset.

'No, we want a complete review of all of the possibilities and any gaps filled,' replied Bonnar. 'If there is a realistic chance of contamination, there won't be a trial.'

You're fucked, I thought to myself. I didn't think there was any chance I could rule out contamination in these circumstances, and every likelihood that I would confirm it. I said nothing.

She went on, 'We've got a statement from the scientist at the FSS, who says that contamination is unlikely.'

I wasn't convinced by this either, given my previous experience in the Taylor case. Reviewing Operation Edzell, as it was called, would be interesting. It was a few years since I'd given evidence at the Old Bailey; this case looked like a sure bet for another appearance.

—

There is no universally agreed definition of 'contamination', but it is a concept widely understood to be a bearer of bad tidings. Portentous and vague, the word suggests multiple unwelcome possibilities: procedural failure, recklessness, ignorance, incompetence or misconduct. In court, the defence may throw up their arms in outrage, while the prosecution play it down or try to explain away the possibility. Sometimes the idea of contamination simply overwhelms rational argument.

Jill Dando was a popular TV broadcaster whose face was known to millions of viewers. On 26 April 1999, a man knocked her to the ground outside her home and fired a single shot into her left temple. The gun was a 9 mm semi-automatic pistol.

In a hundredth of a second, the firing of a gun produces a cloud of hot gases from the propellant and primer in the cartridge. The gases condense into minute particles that contain a distinctive combination of chemical elements: barium, antimony and lead. Tens of thousands of these particles are produced and are deposited onto the skin and clothing of the person holding the gun, as well as onto individuals and objects nearby. These gunshot residues (GSR) are easily transferred to other items after they are deposited, so their recovery requires complicated and time-consuming anti-contamination procedures.

Barry George was arrested in connection with the shooting a year later. Police seized a coat from his kitchen that he agreed was his. A single particle of GSR was found inside a right inside pocket of the coat.

George was an odd character, something of a fantasist and also a liar. He had photographs of himself hooded and wearing a gas mask while posing with a replica gun. He used false names, calling himself Barry Bulsara (implying a connection with Freddie Mercury) and Paul Gadd (Gary Glitter). When interviewed by detectives, he made up a false alibi. The case against him was based on the GSR particle and eyewitness evidence, supplemented by his perceived strangeness.

Orlando Pownall QC, one of England's leading barristers, opened the case against George, stating that the single GSR particle was 'compelling evidence' of his guilt. Michael Mansfield QC, another formidable legal figure, as we saw in Chapter Four, was defence counsel. Dr John Lloyd, an expert witness experienced in the interpretation of GSR, appeared for the defence. In his opinion, it was incredible that any significance could be put on a single GSR particle found a year after the shooting. He also raised the issue of contamination.

When the coat was recovered from George's flat, it was packaged to preserve evidence and prevent contamination. Later, the police removed it from its bag to photograph it, despite the fact that firearms officers were said to use the same studio where the photographs were taken. What was in the minds of these officers is difficult to know. I find it impossible to believe that they were unaware of the risk of contamination. Despite this, in an act of reckless indifference, they removed the coat from its protective packaging for photography. By the time it arrived at the lab, any trace evidence present was compromised.

Dr Robin Keeley of the FSS gave evidence for the prosecution. Amongst FSS experts in GSR at the time, the undocumented practice was that finding small amounts of GSR particles should be declared, but it should be stated that they were of no significance. Keeley didn't conform to this practice and said that, in his opinion, the particle was weak evidence of a link between George and a firearm. What was he thinking? Why did he not follow the practice of his colleagues?

The single particle of GSR dominated the proceedings. Keeley spent three days in the witness box dealing solely with questions about contamination. One by one he ruled out all the possibilities put to him by Mansfield, stating that each was 'remote'.[2] Confusion now crept into the court proceedings, and the debate about the particle led to a false dichotomy. If the particle was due to contamination, it should be ruled out; if it wasn't due to contamination, it was evidence to link George to the murder. This reasoning was fallacious because the particle meant nothing, as most experts believed at the time and do now. And if it was meaningless, what did it matter if it was due to contamination or not? Mansfield chose to focus on contamination; perhaps it looked like an easier target given the police actions, but he should have attacked the *significance* of the evidence.

At the end of the trial, the jury deliberated for almost six days before convicting George by a majority verdict. In 2007, the Criminal Cases Review Commission (CCRC) referred the case back to the Court of Appeal, who quashed the conviction and ordered a retrial. By this time George had been in prison for five years. At the retrial in 2008, the judge ruled the single particle of GSR as inadmissible and, in the absence of other convincing evidence, George was acquitted.

Almost every case in this book has an example of contamination, and it appeared to be that the Nickell case would turn on whether the DNA profile was due to contamination or not.

—

Serial offences can only be spotted with hindsight, after evidence or intelligence suggests links or an emerging pattern. Only at this stage can a forensic scientist look back over the cases to see if there have been any contamination problems. Then you have to look forward and plan for other possible cases that might follow. All of this adds another level of administration to track everything, as well as additional examination and storage areas for each case and each set of items from the victims and suspect. For these reasons, a common line of attack in court in serial offences is contamination; therefore, attention to detail in record-keeping is crucial.

The first of the Green Chain Walk cases arrived in the Met lab sometime in 1989. By the time the attacks were linked to the Bisset murders in November 1993 and Napper came into close focus, dozens if not hundreds of items from these cases had been sent to the Met lab for forensic examination. Items from the various cases were stained with semen matching Napper, but no one had known this. Several scientists would have been working on operations Edzell and Ecclestone* before the links were spotted, and so were unaware of the potential for cross-contamination between the cases. Samples from different investigations could have been stored in the same cupboards, fridges and freezers. Scientists could have worn the same lab coats in different cases or used the same scissors or forceps to cut out samples. Only a few cells are needed for a DNA profile these days, and a few cells could easily be transferred in these circumstances. Or so it seemed to me at the outset.

I could see why the CPS were so concerned, and above all I could see why the Met shared these concerns. After the disastrous Stephen Lawrence case, an epochal event for the force and perhaps the lowest point in their modern history,† the Nickell case was their next biggest public failure. Now the case sat on a knife edge. Even if I concluded that contamination was unlikely, the defence would have a field day. In most murder cases there is plenty of evidence: eyewitnesses, telephone records or CCTV. Some of this evidence will be lost in the process; witnesses may not live up to expectations or other evidence is

---

* The operation name for the Green Chain Walk attacks.
† This may have been eclipsed by Operation Midland, which was breaking at the time of writing. https://www.telegraph.co.uk/news/2019/10/06/nick-operation-midland-detectives-cleared-wrongdoing-inadequate/ (retrieved 7 October 2019).

less convincing than originally thought. But in most murders there is usually enough to convince a jury of a person's guilt. In this case it would all come down to an argument about a DNA profile from a single item taken from Rachel Nickell 15 years previously. The arguments would be detailed, complicated and highly technical. The presentation of the evidence by the advocates and the performance of the expert witnesses would be crucial. In the end it would be all or nothing; the jury would have to choose between two alternative accounts. If Napper got off the hook because of contamination, even contamination that was no one's fault, the Met would never be forgiven. It wouldn't matter that they couldn't have known about the contamination, because it would be perceived as the final error in an encyclopaedic list.

—

My first contact with DI Tom Sinclair, an experienced detective appointed as my liaison officer in the case, was in March 2007. I knew as soon as I met Tom that we would get on; he was an attentive, intelligent listener and quick to understand some of the technical issues we had to deal with. He also knew the cases inside out, knowledge I would have to develop before I could really get going.

At our first meeting we compiled a list of questions that needed to be answered to take things forward. Tom noted them carefully. Some he answered on the spot; others were being worked on. The remaining questions would need further investigation to track down detectives, scientists or others involved to get answers, copies of reports and statements. By the end of the meeting we had a long list of questions; a list that grew and receded as we progressed through the review. Some of the issues took weeks or months to be resolved; some were never resolved to my satisfaction.

The DNA at the centre of the case had been found on tapings from the genital area of Rachel Nickell's body. The first and obvious gap in information was exactly how the tapings had been taken, packaged and sealed at the scene in 1992. This wasn't clear from the documentation; I needed statements from those involved. Who took the tapings, who packaged them, what happened to them next? I needed every detail, every step of the way. Another obvious issue that concerned me was why the DNA profile had not been detected at the FSS. Tom explained that LGC had spent many months working on the samples and had used a new technique to get the results. What was the technique? I asked. Had it been validated? Was it accredited? These were issues that had not been raised before, and Tom had no answers at this stage.

New scientific techniques need to go through a rigorous testing process in the lab before being used in casework. If the technique passes muster at that stage, it moves on to the next: field testing. Many lab-based techniques fall by the wayside at this second stage; they simply don't deliver their promise when challenged by the demands of the real world. But if the technique still looks promising, is an improvement over the current one, or docs something new, it moves to the next stage. A new test might have a higher success rate or work on smaller samples, or it might be faster or cheaper. Once the technique has been validated,* it can be added to the formal list of accredited techniques used by that lab.

These procedures might seem obvious, but they are comparatively recent developments in forensic practice. The introduction of formal quality assurance in UK labs started in the eighties, but was accelerated in England and Wales following the quashing of the Birmingham Six's convictions in 1991.[3] In this case the forensic scientist had used a test that purported to detect traces of explosives. It was a poor test for this purpose and there were no documented standards for how to use it or how to interpret the findings. The scientist involved was also overconfident about the significance of the evidence. The traces of explosives were a key piece of evidence in the convictions, but were later exposed as erroneous and misleading.

If a new technique had been used in the Nickell case, I had to understand how it worked and how effective it was, especially if I was going to end up giving evidence at any future trial. This was a new angle to the review. If there was a problem with the method of analysis, the DNA profile might not be reliable. Like the Jill Dando case, if the evidence was meaningless, it didn't matter how it had got there. I also knew there was a backdrop of commercial and possibly personal rivalry between the LGC and the FSS. I didn't want this to get in the way, but I needed to find out why an analysis at one

---

* A whole range of questions have to be answered in the validation process. How accurate is the method? How precise is it? What is the minimum amount of substance it can detect? What interferes with it and might result in incorrect results? The aim of the validation process is a comprehensive understanding of how reliable the method is when correctly applied.

lab had been negative and yet in another had produced what appeared to be critical evidence.

In short, my task would be to examine the life history of the critical exhibit taken from Rachel Nickell to establish if the DNA profile found on it could be safely relied on in a criminal trial. I would need to break all the cases into individual elements to see where there was potential for contamination, and establish if it could have happened. I needed tangible and verifiable evidence for each stage. Could contamination have happened before the items arrived in the lab? Could it have happened in one of the three labs where the items were examined? Could it have occurred while the items were being transported to or from a lab, or while they were in storage before or after examination?

There were 15 years of records to review and gaps to be filled. I would need to track the tapings and all the items recovered by the police in every case connected with Napper; find out who had handled these items, where they were stored and which of them had been submitted to forensic labs. For items that were sent to labs, I would have to establish the lab submission dates, who had been in contact with the items inside the labs, and where they had been stored before, during and after forensic examination. I would also have to look in minute detail at all the individual lab examinations to see what procedures and equipment had been used to examine items. Were disposable instruments and lab coats used? Were benches cleaned before examination? The questions seemed to be endless.

Much work had already been done on the case before it came into my hands. A spreadsheet documenting the offences

Napper was connected to had been made by an intelligence analyst from New Scotland Yard. It listed eight individual offences, including the Nickell murder, over a period of three years, beginning in August 1989 and ending in January 1993. All the locations were in south London, most of them around Plumstead, Bromley and Eltham. Wimbledon Common stood out as an exception. The spreadsheet listed dates, crime locations, names of victims, police officers, CSIs, forensic scientists, forensic medical examiners (FMEs) and other individuals directly and indirectly connected with the cases. Hundreds of individual items from the cases were listed, as well as who had forensically examined them, and the movements of the items before and after they were sent to the lab.

I could see no obvious problems before items arrived in the Met lab. The victims were examined in different locations at different times and by different FMEs. The cases also involved different police officers and CSIs. However, the more I looked at the enormous spreadsheet of 22 columns and 398 rows (60 A4 pages printed out), the more gaps I spotted. Not all the relevant cases were listed; the most obvious missing one was the Bisset murders. One of the Green Chain Walk attacks was also missing.

There were other problems. The spreadsheet had been compiled from records made by dozens of different individuals in different places doing different jobs. Some of the data came from formal statements, but other entries originated from handwritten notes, call logs and phone conversations. There were ambiguities and possibly errors. For example, was the DC Parker noted in one case the same person as DC Porter recorded by someone else in the same case? Was this a discrepancy due to indecipherable writing or a misheard name in a phone conversation? There were also some entries based on standard procedures; in other words, there was no written record or even recollection but an assumption about what had happened. Would I be able to rely on this? The spreadsheet was a work in progress; I needed to finish it.

This problem also applied to the tapings. Although there was a record of who had taken them, I had no statement about exactly how this had been done and what had happened to them before being sent to the lab. I phoned Tom. 'I need statements from the lab sergeant* who took the tapings and the exhibits officer who packaged them,' I said.

'I knew you would,' he replied. 'It's already in hand. I've been promised them by next week.'

Over the course of weeks, I gradually accounted for all the movements of the tapings between 15 July 1992 and 11 July 2002, when they were received by FAL. There were 19 individual movements over the decade. Robert Napper had not been arrested until May 1994, and as far as I could see, the police had no samples from him before that date. I couldn't see how the tapings could have been contaminated before they got to the Met lab. There was one broken link over the whole period, when they were moved from one police station to another without a record. I left this with Tom to resolve. It

---

* As in many instances, the Met has different titles and roles from most other forces in the UK. The lab sergeants in the Met were specialist forensic personnel involved in most major offences; a cross between a forensic adviser and a scene manager. Part of the rationale for the lab sergeants was the assumption that only a police officer could truly understand how forensic work fitted with an investigation. This, of course, is untrue.

seemed that contamination before the tapings arrived in the Met lab could be ruled out.

The risk of contamination inside a forensic lab was more problematic. Items and samples are examined in detail, and handled repeatedly, sometimes by several scientists. Body fluid stains (the main sources of contamination) are removed by one scientist and passed to another for analysis. Different types of analysis take place in specialist units around the lab, with samples moving from place to place as required. However, all of this ought to follow standard procedures and be fully documented.

Identifying contamination that was a result of procedural problems was only one of the angles I needed to explore. There were a number of technical issues that also had to be considered. At least three different DNA profiling techniques had been used over the lifetime of these cases. Although DNA is either present or not in a sample, whether you detect it depends on what technique you use to look for it. Three forensic labs had been involved in the examination of the tapings. The first was the Met lab (as it was in 1992), and this was the obvious place to start. I needed to answer three questions: was there the potential for contamination? Did a sample exist that could have been a source of contaminating DNA? Was there a realistic mechanism for how this could have happened, e.g. did the item stay in a sealed bag in a cupboard or was it opened and exposed to other samples? If this was the case, how likely was it? Finally, if contaminating DNA had been present, would it have been detected by the DNA profiling techniques that had been used at the time?

—

I had left the Met lab in 1989, a few weeks before the first of the Green Chain Walk attacks had been sent for analysis – clothing and body samples from victims as well as anything found at the scenes. During my time there, I had examined thousands of items.

Nowadays, access to forensic labs is carefully controlled. Lab equipment is regularly cleaned and decontaminated, and high-grade certified DNA-free reagents and disposable equipment is used. Operators wear disposable gloves, headwear and lab coats. If you think about the kind of precautions taken and protective clothing worn by operators in the high-tech electronics industry, you will get a good idea of what goes on in a modern forensic DNA analysis lab. Movement of samples is also carefully controlled. Samples from people – suspects, witnesses and victims – and from clothing, weapons and scenes are examined in separate work streams by different people. These arrangements are routinely inspected both by internal staff and occasionally by the external and independent quality assurance body.* Breaches of procedure must be recorded and formally investigated. Even so, over the years, there have been a number of high-profile contamination problems, such as the instance in the Michael Stone case (Chapters Three and Four).

In 1992, Met lab staff and visitors could wander throughout the examination areas without protective clothing. There was no systematic cleaning of examination benches or

* The United Kingdom Accreditation Service.

exhibit storage areas. When I taught groups of detectives who came to the lab as part of their CID training, they sat around the same benches where I had previously examined blood- and semen-stained exhibits. Non-disposable lab coats were worn and there were no rules about laundering them. Some people never washed their lab coat until someone else complained about the state of it. No one wore masks or hats, and gloves were not always worn when handling items. The latter point is hard to credit nowadays; items stained with body fluids and all sorts of offensive stuff were sometimes handled with bare hands. Reagents (distilled water, chemical solutions and so on) were not DNA-free, and some details of the examination such as wiping of benches were not always documented.

This sounds like a recipe for ongoing, frequent and disastrous contamination problems, but that wasn't so. The DNA technique used in 1992 was called single locus probe (SLP) profiling. Although the technique was good enough for establishing whether DNA might match someone or not, it wasn't especially sensitive and needed much more material than current techniques. A bloodstain a few millimetres in diameter or the equivalent was required, and even then there was no guarantee of a result. So contamination was not a particular problem at the time; not because it didn't happen, but because it wouldn't be detected by the contemporary methods. Anti-contamination measures were very basic but sufficient.

The step change came with the introduction of polymerase chain reaction (PCR).[4] This was the basis of the new techniques for analysis, SGM Plus and LCN. SGM Plus was the standard analysis method, while LCN was a bespoke super-sensitive technique invented by the FSS. Tiny amounts of body fluids could be successfully analysed using SGM Plus, and invisible traces of DNA could be analysed by LCN. Anti-contamination precautions became much tighter and were monitored in more detail. These new techniques could detect traces of DNA left on equipment or which had been transferred to another item indirectly.

I reviewed the FSS case notes on the tapings. According to the notes, the tapings were packaged inside a brown paper envelope, inside of which was a piece of transparent acetate sheet with two pieces of Sellotape stuck onto it. The envelope and the acetate sheet were labelled with sufficient detail to unambiguously identify them. The notes told me who had examined the tapings, what they had looked for, and where and when they had done this work. The tapings were examined on a lab bench shortly after a pair of knickers from one of the Operation Ecclestone cases. The knickers were stained with semen matching Napper. The tapings were also stored in a drawer with items from two other Operation Ecclestone cases. A tiny square had been cut from the taping using a disposable scalpel. However, the sample had been picked up using non-disposable forceps, and the outer surface of the tape had not been cleaned before the sample had been removed. No sperm were found in this sample. After the taping was examined, it was put back in the drawer but it wasn't sealed.

Six of the Operation Ecclestone cases could be eliminated as contamination sources for a number of reasons. In some, this was due to the timing of the examination, either before the tapings had been examined or long afterwards. In others, no semen (or other body fluid) matching Napper was found. In one case the amount of semen found was so minute that it could not have been a realistic source of contamination. Three cases remained that were potential contamination sources, because they were the only ones where semen matching Napper had been found, and they were examined around the same time as the tapings. One of the factors that countered the likelihood of contamination was that the tapings were stuck down to the acetate sheet. Only one of them had been partly peeled back for examination. The underside of the tapes ought to be contamination-free.

—

'This guy targets women with children,' I said to DI Tom Sinclair at our next meeting. 'I've never come across a case like this before.'

'I've been told not to discuss that aspect of the case with you,' he replied, smiling.

I didn't press him further. The offender profiling in the case had already gone badly wrong. The last thing the Met would have wanted was to go down that track again. But it was hard to ignore this fact. Rachel had been with her son Alex when she was attacked, and Samantha Bisset had been killed with her daughter Jazmine. Some of the women in the Green Chain Walk attacks had also had children with them. Was it really that difficult to spot this and link the cases? There seemed to be an obvious pattern, though maybe this was with the benefit of hindsight.

'I've got the statements from the officers at the scene who took the tapings,' said Tom, handing the paperwork to me.

I quickly read the two short statements. 'That's odd,' I said. 'They both say the tapings were put into a poly bag, which was sealed and then sealed inside a brown envelope.'

'Isn't that how it's usually done?'

'Yes,' I replied, 'but there's no mention of a poly bag in the FSS case notes. That's a discrepancy someone will have to explain in court, but thankfully not me.'

I moved on. 'I need to find out how much contamination was going on in 1992,' I said. 'One way to do this is to track down samples that might still be stored in the lab from around that time.'

'We've already asked,' Tom replied. 'There aren't any.'

'That's a stock response, Tom, and I've heard it many times before in cases where I've later unearthed samples.' I've never been sure why this happens, but I imagine that getting rid of old samples is the last thing on people's minds. It's a boring job left to a junior scientist or technician who has plenty of other things to do. So there's no rush, it can always wait, and it's done at the end of the week or the end of the month, a Friday-afternoon job. If it doesn't get done properly, nobody notices. So the standard response is that the records show that the item has been destroyed. 'There's no point in asking if there's a record of existing samples. The only way we will find out is if someone searches the freezers. So we need to keep asking until someone tells us they've done this and there are no samples. And I'll need a statement from that person. I'm not willing to take this on trust.'

'I'll go back and ask them to search the freezers,' said Tom.

'They'll hate you for it,' I replied. 'Ask them to look for samples with the exact date of the examination.'

—

The only time I had been in the FSS Wetherby lab was when I examined the hairs in the Robert Black case in 1995. Around the millennium, that lab had become the FSS hub for LCN analysis, with samples being shipped from around the country.

LCN was the flagship DNA technique invented by the FSS, capable of profiling DNA that was hitherto impossible to detect. It could obtain results from minuscule amounts of body fluids and tissues, whether you could see a stain or not. It gave rise to the idea of 'contact' or 'touch' DNA, where invisible traces from the hands of an offender could be found and profiled. However, it was slow and expensive, so it was reserved for only the most serious cases. LCN analysis* was also technically more complex to carry out and more complicated to interpret. Only a small number of specialists could do this work. As word spread about cases where LCN had been successful, it attracted the attention of many detectives around the country who believed it could solve their case, and a backlog in the unit built up.

In November 2001, the tapings from the Nickell case had arrived at Wetherby for analysis. There had never been any samples from Napper or any of the Operation Ecclestone cases in Wetherby, so I could rule out contamination from these sources. I could also account for all the movements of

---

* LCN was based on a modification of the PCR process that used more cycles of amplification from minuscule amounts of DNA.

the tapings between London and Wetherby and there was no indication that they had been compromised. The only possible source of contamination was DNA that had been transferred to the outer packaging of the tapings when they had been in the Met lab. I would be able to rule this out if I could establish exactly how the examinations in Wetherby had been done. This turned out to be impossible, because the case notes were vague and sometimes contradictory. I couldn't establish from the notes which one of the two tapes had been examined. And although the tapings had been cleaned before they were sampled, I couldn't establish exactly what had been done. Requests for more details drew a blank; no one could add anything more to what was in the notes.

I couldn't categorically rule out contamination at Wetherby but it looked a pretty remote possibility. This left me with a burning question that was not strictly speaking within my remit. Why had DNA matching Napper been found on a taping by one lab (LGC) but not by another lab (Wetherby) that had examined the same taping earlier? This issue was the subject of an internal FSS review at the same time as my review, and I was beginning to get the impression that all was not well.

I had fallen into a pattern of regular communication with Tom by phone, email and occasional face-to-face meetings. He was still drawing a blank on samples from 1992 in the Met lab, which wasn't surprising, but some of the more straightforward questions that I was asking also seemed to be taking a long time to be answered. Tom was constantly chasing the FSS, and on one occasion where they continually failed to provide an answer it took a formal letter from a senior Met officer to the

FSS board to get the information. Tom's impression was that this was because some of the questions were highly technical and detailed. I wasn't so sure. Modern forensic science labs are highly procedural, constantly monitoring processes and collecting data to prove they are complying with standards. Almost all of the information I had asked for fell within this standard data collection regime. So why the delays? There had to be another reason.

CHAPTER ELEVEN

Lies, Damned Lies, and Statistics

> Tunnel vision is insidious … It results in the [police] officer becoming so focused upon an individual … that no other person … registers in the officer's thoughts.
>
> Peter de Carteret Cory[1]

In July 2002, the items in the Nickell case had been transferred to LGC, although it was not until 2004 that the DNA profile matching Napper was found. A cold-case review does not have the same time pressures as a live investigation, but I wondered what was going on for all this time. Surely they should have got to the tapings sooner than this? The answer to this question lay in how LGC had approached the case, particularly the DNA analysis, for which they used an in-house method called 3100E.*

---

* The name is derived from the model number of the instrument (ABI3100) that was in routine use for DNA analysis. The 'E' presumably stood for enhanced.

—

In July 2007, there was a breakthrough in my review. Despite the protestations and denials from staff in the FSS London lab, six samples that had been languishing in freezers for 15 years were found. Tom's persistence had paid off. Two of these samples had been examined on the same day and in the same location as the tapings. The other four had been examined very close to that time; two on the day before and two on the day after the tapings. The six samples came from three different cases unconnected with any of the cases that Napper was known or suspected to be involved with. None of the three were connected to each other. The samples could give us a snapshot of how much contamination might have been around in 1992. If contamination was widespread but was undetected by the primitive DNA methods of the day, modern DNA analysis would pick it up.

A total of 19 DNA profiles from nine different individuals were found in the samples. There was no cross-contamination. None of the DNA profiles from any of the cases were found in any other cases. Crucially, none of the DNA profiles matched Napper or Nickell.

I was astounded. My operating assumption had been that I was going to detect *some* contamination, I just wasn't sure how much. These results would be incredibly useful if I was to appear in court, because they were facts not opinions. If there was a weakness, it was that they fell short of a scientifically rigorous experiment; there were too few results for the findings to be statistically valid. But I could easily imagine how they could be presented during the trial. There would be no need for statistics. The findings from the six samples would be a bedrock that I could rely on.

—

On 18 September 2007, I met Tom at LGC for the final stage of the review: the examination of the tapings. As we were ushered into a waiting area, a scientist approached. 'Can I have a word?' he said to Tom, signalling that it was not for my ears. While I waited, I was given the LGC case notes to review.

Tom returned about twenty minutes later.

'What was that all about?' I asked.

'I'll tell you later,' he replied.

Two LGC scientists were present when I got to the lab. The item was packaged in a brown envelope, which was in quite poor condition and had been opened and resealed many times. Inside the envelope there was a clear polythene bag that contained an acetate sheet. The poly bag was opaque and appeared to be old. The statements from the officers at the scene were correct; the poly bag had somehow been missed by the FSS. There were two large pieces of Sellotape and one small piece stuck onto the acetate sheet. Everything appeared to be in line with how the tapings had been originally taken, labelled and packaged.

The critical tapings were stuck down inside a multi-layered package. Even if they had been in a cupboard unsealed, the chances of contamination appeared to be slim. But all this is easy when you are sitting in an office isolated from the determined counter-arguments of the courtroom. Of the thousands of cases I have been involved in, I have only given evidence in a tiny proportion of them, probably fewer than 10 per cent. Yet so much of what you do and think is focused on how it might play out in that theatre; who would be prosecuting, who would be defending, what would be agreed between the sides and what would be contested. Most forensic evidence is corroborative, but in this case I had already been told that what I found would be the deciding factor in whether to prosecute or not. This may have been an exaggeration for effect, to make sure I was willing to do the work and understood the significance of it, but it resonated with me and haunted me on a few occasions.

Afterwards, we went to the pub for lunch. 'So what was the secret squirrel stuff about?' I asked.

'You won't believe it; the 3100E technique that they detected the DNA with isn't fully validated yet.'

Tom was right, I couldn't believe it. Nor had I ever heard anything like it. All the work so far had been done on an unvalidated method of analysis. I had been asking Tom about validation for the last six months, and he had been asking LGC but had never got a straight answer until now. If the technique was not validated, the CPS would never allow the case to go into court; there would be no trial.

'They're going to validate it over the weekend,' said Tom. 'They've given me a cast-iron guarantee.'

—

Three types of DNA contamination are routinely monitored in modern labs: operator (scientist) to sample; sample to sample; and consumable to sample. We encountered operator to sample contamination in the Michael Stone case that led to a false DNA link. When the source of contamination is in reagents or disposable items (swabs, test tubes, etc.) used in DNA analysis, this is called consumable contamination. The most spectacular example of this type of contamination occurred in a case known popularly as the Phantom of Heilbronn. The phantom was thought to be a serial female murderer linked to cases in Germany, Austria and France that were being investigated between 1993 and 2009. But there was no serial murderer and the cases weren't linked. The DNA in each of the cases came from a factory worker who had packaged the swabs used to collect the case samples for analysis. In the Nickell case, the type of contamination I was interested in was sample to sample contamination – from a sample that matched Napper to a sample that came from Nickell (the tapings).

To reach a conclusion for my statement, I needed overall sample contamination data from the FSS and LGC. I got the data from LGC within a couple of days. The sample to sample contamination rate over four years was about 1 in 2000. This data covered the time of analysis of the Nickell samples. Tom continually chased the FSS for their data but they ignored him. It took repeated requests and weeks of waiting before eventually, and seemingly grudgingly, they supplied data for a three-month period in 2007. There had been seven contamination events of this type during that period in major crime cases. The FSS would have had years of data, but it seemed they would rather withhold this than pass it to me, despite the legitimacy of the request. This was data that they would have had at their fingertips, since it could be the subject of independent audit. I wasn't convinced they were being straight with me; they hadn't been so far. Based on that three-month period, I calculated that the rate of contamination in the FSS was about 1 in 3,000 cases. But this was for 2007, not 1992. It had to be an underestimate because anti-contamination procedures in modern labs were much more stringent.

—

There is a common misconception that DNA is incontrovertible evidence; that once you have it, you are home and dry. This is not true. In most cases, like this one, how the DNA came to be where it was found is as important as who it may have come from.* DNA profiles matching Robert Napper linked him to some of the Green Chain Walk attacks and Napper pleaded guilty to these crimes (as well as to the murder of Samantha and Jazmine Bisset). In these circumstances I could be satisfied that there was DNA from Napper in the lab. The DNA profile found on the taping from Nickell matched Napper, but how did it get on the taping; was it from contamination, or was it deposited by Napper when he murdered Nickell? I couldn't say categorically one way or the other. I certainly couldn't rule out contamination, so I had to decide which explanation was more likely, based on my findings.

* Strictly speaking, a DNA profile is never attributed to an individual categorically but as a probability. In court, a judge or jury can decide that a DNA profile came from an individual, but this is not a scientific judgement and it is usually based on the full circumstances of the case.

I had ruled out most of the potential avenues of contamination except from inside the Met lab. Evaluating DNA findings is usually done using Bayesian reasoning, so called after the man who came up with this idea, Thomas Bayes.* In this approach a ratio of two probabilities is used to estimate the likelihood of an event. If Napper was the killer, then I would expect the DNA on the taping to be from him. The probability in this instance would be 1, i.e. certain. Since I found no specific or direct means of contamination in the Met lab, the taping was no more likely to be contaminated than anything else in the lab. The probability of sample to sample contamination was somewhere between 1 in 2000 and 1 in 3000, according to the data I had been given from LGC and the FSS. The ratio of the two probabilities gives us something called the likelihood ratio, which is an estimate of the significance of the evidence.

The whole business of expressing probabilities is a tricky one. Scientists use formal statistical models and defined, consistent terminology when discussing such things, but this can all break down in the courtroom. At the extremes, there is usually not much of a problem;† if the chances of something happening are incredibly high or vanishingly small, this is usually easy to communicate and is readily understood. But the middle ground is more difficult; its greyness is unwelcome, harder to articulate clearly and easily misunderstood or manipulated. I was in grey territory here. There are other difficulties as well.

---

* Bayes was an 18th-century statistician, philosopher and cleric.
† Of course, there are examples like the Jill Dando case where even this breaks down.

There is plenty of evidence to show that most people are easily confused by probability, and there are all sorts of biases built into our brains that can lead to fallacious reasoning.* The courts also have a strong preference for words over numbers (unless the numbers are very low or very high); they like probabilities to be expressed in a verbal scale. So forensic scientists have come up with a series of phrases that aim to express the full range of probabilities using words. Using this scale, my conclusion was that the evidence (the DNA profile) strongly supported† the proposition that the DNA on the taping matching Napper came from the body of Nickell rather than being due to contamination.

This was not a conclusion I had expected to reach at the outset. Nor was it one that would be easily explained in court. While I drafted my statement, the potential lines of cross-examination popped in my mind like little firecrackers. Many of these questions were the usual suspects: could I rule out contamination in the lab? No. Could I rule out contamination where there were gaps in the exhibit record? No. These were straightforward answers. Other questions were much trickier. Had I definitively established whether one or two tapes had been sampled? No. Was contamination more

---

* Perhaps the best known of these is the 'gambler's fallacy'. After a run of reds on a roulette wheel, many people believe that the next spin is more likely to be black. But the earlier turns of the wheel have no bearing on the next; the probability of black and red remain the same. It is the same when tossing a coin. A run of (say) five heads in a row does not mean that tails is more likely on the sixth toss. The probability is still one chance in two (0.5).

† This is equivalent to a likelihood ratio of between 1,000 and 10,000. The full scale is: weak, moderate, moderately strong, strong, very strong, extremely strong.

likely in 1992 than in 2007, when I carried out the review? Yes. How much more likely? I didn't know. Was the data from the six samples from the FSS freezer scientifically valid? No. If not, how reliable was it? And so it would go on. The taping was either contaminated or not, but the circumstances and the evidence did not allow me to make binary judgements or give categoric answers. Yet black-and-white answers were what the lawyers would be after.

My review was based on incomplete information and relied on documents and information from others. This was not like giving evidence on work I had done personally. It was meta-evidence; evidence about evidence. My conclusion took all this into account, but the lines of cross-examination almost certainly would not. The questions would be narrow and specific and I would not be allowed to sweep them up into a general conclusion. It was also public knowledge that one of the rape cases against Napper when he was previously tried had been dropped because some samples had been transposed. It was unlikely that this would be used in court, because it revealed his previous convictions, but it highlighted how a single fatal error could result in the collapse of an entire case. There was a vast landscape of possibilities to explore; giving evidence on all of this would be like traversing a glacier in the knowledge that you were bound to slip at some point. Preparation was the key to a quick recovery.

—

The DNA profile was not the only evidence that linked Napper to the murder. A whole range of samples had been taken from her son Alex as well as from Rachel herself. Amongst these were hair combings to capture trace evidence. When the combings were examined in 2002, tiny fragments of red paint were found.

Following Napper's arrest for the Bisset murders, his flat had been searched and a red metal toolbox was found. The paint on the toolbox was flaking in places. The paint fragments found in Alex's hair were similar to the paint from the toolbox but were too small to be analysed fully. They couldn't be ruled out, but nor was there enough information to assess their significance. Even today, there are limits to forensic analysis.

There was also the single shoe impression that had been found in the mud at the scene. The impression matched one of Napper's shoes, but again the connection was weak. The DNA profile was pivotal.

—

You never know if you are going to be called as a witness. Even in cases where it seems you have crucial evidence, things can change at the last minute. I was convinced I would end up in the witness box in this case, but I was wrong. Around lunchtime on 18 December 2008, while I was arguing with a mechanic who was supposed to be fixing my car, my mobile rang. I answered it to break away from the discussion.

'Have you heard?' said Robin, a friend and colleague. 'Napper has pleaded guilty.'

Napper, now 42 years old, balding and pot-bellied, had appeared in Court 1 at the Old Bailey that morning. When the charge of murdering Rachel Nickell was read out to him, after some verbal stumbling he replied, 'Guilty to manslaughter by diminished responsibility.' He was standing in the same dock that Colin Stagg had stood in 14 years before. The judge, Mr Justice Williams, heard evidence from two psychiatrists that Napper was delusional and unfit to plead. The psychiatrists told the court of some of their findings: Napper believed that he had a master's degree in mathematics and a Nobel prize for peace, and that he was a multimillionaire from a family listed in *Who's Who*. Yet as in the Bisset case, he made no admissions until the evidence against him was overwhelming; was he really so irrational?

We can never know in any real sense what was going on in Napper's mind, or why he did what he did. Even if we did, it would be difficult for any normal person to understand. Napper is a sexual sadist who murdered Samantha Bisset and her daughter in a swirling vortex of hate. On Wimbledon Common in July 1992, he found himself with an overwhelming desire to humiliate and destroy a woman, any woman. Rachel Nickell was the unfortunate victim of his murderous rage that day.

Outside the Old Bailey, John Yates, Assistant Commissioner of the Met, apologised for the force's many failings. He acknowledged that the murders of Rachel Nickell, Samantha Bisset and Jazmine Bisset could have been prevented. Of Colin Stagg, he said, 'It is clear that he is completely innocent of any involvement in [the Nickell] case.'[2] With a cost estimated at £3 million, the murder of Rachel Nickell was one of the Met's longest-running and most controversial unsolved homicide investigations. But that wasn't the end of the story. Another parallel investigation had been going on for some time. Its aim was to find out why the FSS had failed to detect DNA on the taping where LGC later found a full profile matching Napper.

The answer to this question initially played out in a highly technical spat between the FSS and LGC. In the review documentation I had been given were some of the documents that set out their positions. The story from LGC's perspective was straightforward and credible: they had used standard DNA analysis to find the profile on the taping. The FSS had analysed the tapings using LCN, their bespoke super-sensitive DNA method. The LGC policy was to use standard DNA profiling wherever possible and only move on to LCN if there was no other option. This was because LCN analysis is more complex to carry out and more complicated to interpret. For LGC, if a standard DNA result was obtainable, this would be better evidence.

In DNA analysis, the amount of DNA in a sample needs to be balanced with a complex mixture of other chemicals if the reaction is to work properly. The first step is to test for the presence of DNA and measure the amount in the sample. The sample also needs to be free of interfering impurities that can inhibit DNA profiling. For example, indigo dye, which is commonly used to give jeans their blue colour, is a powerful inhibitor of the process. To avoid these problems, LGC* ran a series of cleaned-up samples at different concentrations. The first test was carried out on extracts from the tapings made by the FSS. This gave a mixed DNA profile that was largely DNA from Rachel with a trace of male DNA. Having picked up this weak trace of male DNA, they went on to purify and

---

* This work was actually done by a partner laboratory of LGC, Cellmark, who pioneered DNA profiling in the UK.

concentrate the sample and in the process developed a new technique. This was 3100E, the technique I had never heard of and for which I wanted proof of validation. It took them almost two years to perfect this technique, which explained some of the delays that had been puzzling me.

Exactly what had been done at the FSS was unclear. I couldn't reconstruct their analysis from their notes because they were inadequate. They had gone straight to LCN without considering standard DNA testing, but when this failed to detect any DNA, they just stopped. We also know that since the taping came from an intimate part of Rachel's body, it would have had her DNA on it. In what was one of the UK's most high-profile unsolved murders, no one paused to reflect on this odd result. No one wondered why no DNA was detected or whether another approach might get a result. Was that not what forensic scientists ought to do when they got an inexplicable result – ask why, enquire and try to get to the bottom of it? The FSS had missed out a crucial step in the process: they had not measured the amount of DNA on the taping. If they had done so, they would have detected DNA and things would have been very different. All of that was theory; now that the FSS found themselves in trouble again, they set about defending their territory.

—

The Met wanted to know why the FSS had not found the DNA.* They particularly wanted to know if this was an isolated event,

* As did other senior figures in the police service, the CPS and the Home Office.

a one-off error, or part of a bigger problem. Were any other cases affected? Their worst fears were to be fulfilled.

Amongst the papers I was given was an internal FSS report that purported to explain why they had not found DNA when the taping was tested at Wetherby. The report started with a series of falsehoods. First, that failing to find DNA on the tapings was 'not in any part due to error in the FSS examinations'. In a taxonomy of falsehoods we might consider this to be a classic bare-faced example. The kind of falsehood that is self-evidently untrue and is guaranteed to antagonise whoever is on the receiving end of it. It was a claim that required swagger and influence to carry off, and a credulous or trusting listener.

By this time, however, the FSS senior management had forfeited any swagger they had previously had and their influence was much diminished. And the Met were neither trusting nor credulous. Their memories of the errors in the Damilola Taylor case, and how aggressively the FSS had defended themselves and incriminated others, were still fresh. Even after the FSS had been proved wrong in that case, they continued to harass and bully[3] those who disagreed (but were actually right) and threatened others with legal action. Gary Pugh, Met Director of Forensic Services, said: 'The Met were astonished when they got a result in the Nickell case from LGC and it knocked their faith massively in forensic science.' Trust was at a very low ebb.

The false claims in the report continued, becoming more complicated, more folded into others and more technical: 'The [DNA] results can be explained entirely by a phenomenon known as PCR inhibition. At the time of the examination this was not known to the FSS.' This statement was designed to confuse the non-technical reader. But it wouldn't fool experts and was immediately and accurately refuted by LGC. It was a particularly inept claim because it didn't get the FSS off the hook; it simply raised a whole list of more difficult questions. When did the FSS first become aware of this problem? What had they done about it? Were any other investigations affected? If so, had the FSS told any of the police forces involved? The answers to these questions dragged the FSS into a scandal much bigger and more messy than the Damilola Taylor case.

In late 2007, the DNA problem came to the attention of ministers, who asked for a review to be carried out. The FSS initially refused to cooperate but were compelled to do so. The review identified 2,500 cases over a five-year period where LCN had been used but no result obtained. Was this because there was no DNA present or because the FSS procedure was flawed? The cases included murders, rapes and other violent crimes. This led to the re-analysis of around 5,000 samples, which yielded new results in 342 cases.

During my review, I had encountered constant resistance from the FSS to almost any query I raised. Some years later, I found out that every one of these requests, most of which related to technical or procedural issues, went to the FSS board before they responded. Looking back, this was an organisation in terminal decline.

—

Why did the Nickell case go so badly wrong? It started as a difficult investigation: a stranger murder, a blitz attack in a public place, no eyewitnesses, no weapon found, no forensic leads, a vast area to search and hundreds of people to eliminate. This was worsened by an extraordinary level of media and public interest. Hard-nosed reporters wept at the public appeal made by Rachel's partner André Hanscombe shortly after the murder. Yet the same media had earlier mobbed Hanscombe in a way that he described as 'primal, completely uncivilised' when he left the hospital where Alex was being treated. Initially supportive of the investigation, the media also stoked fear and public concern with their constant headlines. Later, their relationship with the police became combative when the *Sunday Mirror*[4] exposed the secret undercover operation to trap Colin Stagg. Yet when Stagg was acquitted, he was hounded and demonised by the press.

There have been more books written about the Nickell case than any of the other cases in this book. Amongst them is an account by Keith Pedder,[5] former DI in the Met and de facto SIO in the first Nickell investigation. He was later tried for corruption (ironically he was trapped by a covert surveillance), but the case against him was thrown out by the judge. Pedder retired early and his book appears to be directly based on the case papers. The text is jargon-packed; a real-life police procedural in all its dull detail, stuffed with superfluous acronyms and the tribal banter of the time.

Pedder's account is primarily self-serving, the main objectives being to demonstrate that the investigation was effective and that he was let down by the Met hierarchy and the judiciary. But the detail* lends a certain authenticity in terms of atmosphere and the day-to-day dynamics of the ongoing inquiry. What is revealed is an investigation that is overwhelmed not only with information and work but also with emotion and moral outrage. Sometimes the emotional responses are explicit; sometimes they are a subtext. Rachel's attractiveness is a recurrent theme, as are expressions of shock from detectives that such a beautiful young woman could possibly have been murdered. The sense of outrage is enhanced by the centrality of Alex in the case as a motherless survivor. The complexity and demands of the investigation fed a belief in the inquiry team that the case was impossible to solve.[6] It was also clear that detectives were under enormous pressure to solve it as quickly as possible; even the judge in the Stagg trial recognised this before condemning what had been done.

When the team lighted on Stagg, they were completely convinced he was the killer. Britton's profile was in line with what was acceptable for the time, but then he was drawn deeply into the investigation. Although he was an experienced forensic psychologist, he was naïve in his dealings with the police. It took months to plan the undercover operation and we can safely assume that by that time, those running the investigation had closed their minds to any alternative suspect.

If there was a single feature that dominated the investigation, it was the novelty of an undercover operation based on offender profiling. This fired the imagination and distorted

---

* Almost nothing is spared here: arrangements for overtime payments, extensive and detailed extracts from the post-mortem report, the offender profile, the surveillance operation and correspondence between Lizzie James and Stagg.

the judgement of virtually everyone connected with the case: the investigation team, police officers in the Met at every rank up to deputy assistant commissioner,* the CPS, senior prosecution counsel and even the FBI (Pedder had been in contact with them for advice).

Notwithstanding the voluminous detail in Pedder's book, there is a crucial area where he is silent. When Napper was arrested for the Bisset murders, Mickey Banks, the SIO in the case, thought he could be Nickell's killer. Banks invited the Nickell squad to Plumstead to discuss this possibility. By this time Stagg was on remand awaiting trial. 'They were convinced Stagg was their murderer – it was as simple as that,'[7] recalled Banks. There is no mention of such a meeting in Pedder's book. We are left with the impression that everyone believed Stagg was responsible.

Britton[8] also played his part in the disaster, with a cascade of serious errors in the conception and running of the undercover operation. He explained to detectives that sadistic sex murderers had deviant fantasy lives and that such individuals were rare. So if Stagg had such deviant fantasies, this would mean he was the killer. This assertion contains a number of embedded errors. It is both illogical† and confuses an individual's fantasy world with how they actually behave. The most significant misjudgement was the failure by Britton to link the Nickell and Bisset murders. He differentiated the cases because the children had not suffered the same fate. Alex, unlike Jazmine, was not harmed when his mother was killed. Despite stating

---

* The second-highest rank in the organisation.
† This is a classic reasoning fallacy often illustrated as follows: all dogs have four legs, my cat has four legs, therefore my cat is a dog!

this in his book,[9] he later blamed detectives and their 'tribal'[10] attitudes for ignoring his advice that the crimes were linked.

Here the profiling was being applied too rigidly. Britton knew that sexual killers were impulsive; might the killer not be reacting to the different circumstances in each instance? Napper had had time and privacy to murder Jazmine, but he could hardly act the same way in the open air of Wimbledon Common. Impulse and opportunity drove his behaviour on that morning, something Britton should have been alert to.

Despite his efforts to portray himself as such, Pedder was no scapegoat. It was Stagg who was the scapegoat. Pedder and Britton were Icarus and Daedalus soaring on the mythological winds of misconceived psychology.

The failures in this case were more deep-seated and longer running than a single flawed investigation. The Met as an institution also repeatedly failed. Numerous opportunities to arrest Napper were missed, and despite the collapse of Stagg's trial in September 1994, the Met remained fixated on him as the murderer. After the trial, the Commissioner, Sir Paul Condon, made a public statement that the police were not looking for anyone else; the standard coded language for 'We got the right man but the system let us down.' Only when the DNA findings in the reinvestigation of 2001 shattered this belief did they slowly begin to accept that this was untrue.

The Met mission statement at the time of my review of the Nickell case was to deliver 'total policing' to the people of London. The Nickell investigation, until it was resolved in 2008, was perhaps the nearest I have ever seen to the total and systematic failure of a police organisation over a sustained period.

CHAPTER TWELVE

The Cryptic Death of Gareth Williams

Secrets are thrilling and explosive and dangerous,
even if [you] don't quite know what the secrets
are finally about, or why it is that they are so
dangerous.

John Lanchester[1]

In the early evening of 23 August 2010, Gareth Williams, a
GCHQ cryptologist on secondment to MI6, was found dead
inside a large holdall in his flat at 36 Alderney Street, London.
These cardinal facts are amongst the few in this case that are
wholly reliable; they are neither contingent nor conditional
and are free from speculation, confabulation and conspiracy
theories. Why Williams died, when he died, how he died and
who, if anyone, was involved, remain mysteries.

Williams had been due to chair a meeting 10 days previously
at MI6 HQ, barely a mile from Alderney Street, but had failed
to arrive. He was also expected at another meeting a few days
later but did not appear for this either. No action was taken by

MI6 until they belatedly contacted GCHQ, who immediately contacted the Metropolitan Police.

GCHQ is the largest of the UK's intelligence organisations; bigger than MI5 and MI6 put together. Its forerunner was the unit at Bletchley Park famous for its spectacular and innovative code-breaking in the Second World War. Now based in the iconic doughnut-shaped building in Cheltenham, GCHQ sits at the centre of a vast worldwide signals collection and analysis system that provides intelligence for the UK government. It employs around 6,500 staff, including IT specialists, electronics and communication specialists, linguists, translators, mathematicians and code-breakers.[2]

MI6 is the UK's secret intelligence service, whose role is to prevent overseas terrorism threats, disrupt hostile states and maintain cyber security.[3] From their headquarters in London, they deploy officers around the world. By their own admission, they are spies, because their work has to be done in secret to protect both those involved and the country. In recent decades, both GCHQ and MI6 have sought to shed their gentlemen's club image acquired during the Cold War and present themselves as more open, modern institutions.

Within a few hours, the Met established that Williams was dead. The slowness of the UK's secret intelligence service (SIS) to act on his unexplained absence was an issue that was to spawn many conspiracy theories about the case. You may consider it to be incredible that one of the world's foremost espionage agencies would allow one of their men (a spy or otherwise) to go missing for 10 days without follow-up investigation. Alternatively, you may think that in the unreconstructed demi-world of the intelligence services, modern notions like duty of care might be rather low on the agenda. Make your choice. Whichever interpretation you favour, it is likely to condition what you make of this case: an international spy mystery complete with safe houses, sex games, undetectable poisons and sterilised crime scenes; or a terrible accident.

—

'Come to the meeting and make your decision then,' said Gary Pugh. 'You'll be working with Phil Shaw.' Phil was a highly experienced, recently retired detective with whom I had worked on a few occasions. He was intelligent and reflective and his involvement was reassuring.

'OK,' I replied, 'let's find a date.'

I put the phone down. Did I want to review this case? A case that was unresolved and ongoing, a complicated investigation involving the Met and the SIS with an inquest pending? The media coverage on the web looked like something from cyberpunk cinema; a bizarre combination of Cold War spy tropes and the mysterious new technological frontier of cyberwar.

A year into the investigation, the case was still live and unresolved. A case review needs independence; time and space between the original investigation and the review. If the sources of information for the review are those who are still working on the investigation, it can make it more difficult to be independent and objective. But I was outside the Met and had no stake in any particular outcome.

I could think of two other reasons for not doing the work. First, Williams worked for the security services; whatever his role, I could never be confident that I would be given all the information I needed. They would keep their secrets to themselves. I wouldn't be asked; someone would decide for me. Even if I had been security-cleared, I still wouldn't be confident that I was getting the full story.

The second reason was the shocking stories coming out of the Leveson inquiry into the phone-hacking scandal. The *News of the World* and some other newspapers had been hacking the phones of celebrities and others for salacious stories. This included the victims in some high-profile murders. I had known for many years that the police were constant sources of leaks, and I had also encountered unscrupulous behaviour on the part of the media. I'd naïvely thought that leaks were part of the horse-trading in the often complex relationship between detectives and the media during an investigation. The Leveson inquiry was highlighting something very different: links between the media and the Met at almost every level, and routine corruption. This reminded me of a conversation I had had with a senior figure in the Met around the time of the inquiry: 'I could be wined and dined by a journalist every night of the week if I wanted; many others are.' I wasn't sure this was an environment I wanted to work in. Maybe this was a case to let pass.

On 16 April 2012, I flew to London to be briefed about the Williams investigation. I would decide whether to take on the case depending on what I picked up at the meeting; not just the formal stuff, but the weaker signals about who was involved and where it might all go next. Phil would also be there. We would be briefed by Commander Simon Foy,

Head of Homicide and Series Crime Command, Detective
Chief Superintendent Hamish Campbell, and Gary Pugh, who
would chair the meeting. A notable absentee was DCI Jackie
Sebire, the SIO. I wondered why.

The tone was informal, with the detectives and Gary taking
it in turns to describe the current state of the case: inquiries
to date, pathology, lab analyses, digital forensics. There were
passing references to Vauxhall Cross (the location of MI6 HQ)
and some hints about difficulties. It also emerged that a new SIO
had been appointed. What they wanted from Phil and me was
an independent review of the investigation. They were looking
for us to provide some reassurance and also suggestions for
further work that might progress the case. I didn't ask many
questions, nor did Phil. I didn't get the impression that there
was any specific problem with the investigation, that it had
gone wrong somewhere, but I sensed that it hadn't all been
plain sailing either. After a couple of hours, Phil and I left to
talk privately in a meeting room provided for us.

'I'm not doing it if you don't,' I said.

'And I'm not doing it if you don't,' he replied. We laughed.

'We could be getting set up here,' I said. 'The case looks
unsolvable as it is, and who knows what is really involved. I
shouldn't have made that joke about Mossad; it didn't go
down well.' Phil smiled. 'If we take it on, we have to assume
that one day we'll be standing in the witness box in the Old
Bailey,' I added.

'Or worse,' Phil replied, 'it could be a public inquiry.'

It had never occurred to me that there could be anything
more testing than the Old Bailey, but I knew he was right.

'Let's go away and think about it,' said Phil. Gary had said he would send draft terms of reference in the next day or so. 'If we get the terms of reference right, we should be safe. If we don't like them, we can say no. Or we can redraft them and see if they're happy with our version.'

'OK,' I replied. 'Let's see what they come up with.'

—

If someone dies a violent, unnatural or traumatic death, it will be reported to the coroner.* Most deaths are not reported because it is reasonably obvious why they have occurred. If the coroner suspects or has good reason to believe the death is not due to natural causes, an inquest must be held; a public hearing in court where witnesses are called and evidence about the death is heard. If criminal activity is suspected (as in a murder), the inquest is usually opened and adjourned until after the police investigation and any trial has been held.

The inquest into the death of Gareth Williams began on 23 April 2012 at Westminster Coroner's Court in central London. The coroner was Dr Fiona Wilcox, who later was to lead the inquest into the Grenfell Tower fire.

Westminster Coroner's Court has a public mortuary tucked behind it out of sight. The post-mortem examination of Williams' body had been carried out there on 25 August 2010. I had been in this mortuary several times when I worked in London but I have only given evidence in the court on one

* In England, Wales or Northern Ireland. The legal arrangements are different in Scotland; there is no coronial system. A coroner is an independent judicial office-holder appointed by a local authority to investigate deaths.

very memorable occasion. Two prostitutes had been murdered in the course of a weekend in January 1987. I examined the crime scene in a lock-up garage in Chelsea where the body of Rachel Applethwaite had been found. She had been battered and strangled but I could see from the lack of blood staining around her body that she had been killed elsewhere. Marina Monti's body was found on waste ground in Willesden, north London. She had been strangled with a ligature. The victims' lifestyles and the fact that they worked the same area in west London appeared to link the murders, but not everyone agreed about this.

About a month after the deaths, an artist's impression of a man the police wanted to interview about the murders featured in a BBC *Crimewatch* programme. The following morning, Guillermo Suarez, the administrative affairs attaché at the Mexican embassy in London, walked into Kensington police station and identified himself as the man police were looking for. Suarez had been linked to Applethwaite, but there was no direct evidence that he had killed her. The head of the Mexican delegation in London was summoned to the Foreign Office and told that the UK would ask for diplomatic immunity to be waived, and the Mexican embassy agreed to cooperate with the investigation.

What followed has never been clear to me, but some months later there was an inquest into Applethwaite's death at which I gave evidence. This related to the amount of blood found on a bed sheet that Suarez had taken to a dry-cleaner's. His explanation was that the staining on the sheet was menstrual blood from his wife. His wife, safely in Mexico, was not available for comment. The police said the blood came from Applethwaite, and I was asked to adjudicate on this point.

My difficulty was that by the time I examined the sheet, it had been laundered; there was no blood to be seen. Detectives had then come to me with a drawing of the sheet made by a woman who worked in the dry cleaner's. I thought they were joking when they handed it to me. I was not going to get caught up with this mysterious bloodstain (if it was blood), how big it was and whether it was menstrual blood or traumatic blood, on the basis of what looked like a child's scribble. In a criminal trial, the sheet, the drawing and what it all meant would never have met the standard for evidence and would have been quickly dismissed. To my surprise, the coroner, Paul Knapman, pressed me to comment on the blood staining. I politely declined.

When I had finished giving evidence, I sat in court to watch the rest of the show. Knapman put several probing questions to Suarez about his possible involvement in the death of Applethwaite, directly or indirectly, and whether he had any information that could help the police with their inquiries. Suarez gave the same response to each question: 'I do not wish to answer that question on the grounds that it may incriminate me.' Shortly afterwards, he was whisked off to Mexico.

—

Most of what I knew about the workings of coroners had come indirectly from my experience in murder investigations. Working closely with SIOs, I could see how much of their time early in an investigation was spent on dealing with the coroner. My impressions were that coroners were powerful people, often demanding, sometimes patrician, occasionally capricious. Some had favourite pathologists and became upset if the police were using a different one. It was a situation that reminded me of regional procurators fiscal in Scotland. As a forensic scientist, I never set eyes on the fiscal from Edinburgh, who was a senior lawyer and public servant running a busy department. But outside the large cities, the fiscal was a big fish in a small pond. They were used to getting their own way and expected you to comply with their demands; their case was the only case that was important. Coroners seemed to be in the same mould.

The media interest in the Williams case was such that the coroner moved the hearing to larger premises in Marylebone Road to accommodate the numbers. It had become clear that full details of the case were unlikely to be heard in public before the inquest began. The Foreign Secretary, William Hague, had signed a public interest immunity certificate to prevent the release of official secrets. This information was to be withheld on the grounds of national security. This was understandable in the circumstances, but for conspiracy theorists it was more fuel for their fantasies.

The first day of the inquest was dominated by legal skirmishes between the various parties represented.* Vincent Williams, the barrister for the Met, wanted to block the public release of video footage that might be relevant to a later prosecution. He

---

* Those with direct interest in an inquest, such as the family of the deceased or the deceased's employer, can be legally represented at an inquest.

said there was a 'real possibility'[4] of an arrest and that 'a careful line must be struck between open justice'[5] at the inquest and the ongoing police investigation. Caoilfhionn Gallagher QC, a barrister whose interests included media law, represented a number of broadcasters and national newspapers who sought the release of photographs, video and documents believed to be in the hands of the coroner. The family of Gareth Williams, represented by Anthony O'Toole QC, objected to the release of a video that showed an 'expert' attempting to lock himself into the same kind of bag that Williams was found in.

—

Gareth Williams was born on 26 September 1978 in Anglesey, Wales, and was 31 years old when he died. He excelled at maths, obtaining his GCSE at age 11 and a first-class degree from Bangor University when he was 17. He later gained a PhD from the University of Manchester before being recruited by GCHQ in 2001 as a mathematician and cryptologist. He was on secondment to MI6 at the time of his death. His exceptional technical ability and knowledge was beyond doubt. He was described by some as nothing short of a mathematical genius and by others as 'world class'. At his funeral in September 2010, Sir John Sawyers, then head of MI6, described him as 'highly talented … very modest and very generous', a person who had done 'really valuable work … in the cause of national security'.[6] It was the first time that a head of SIS had attended a public funeral of an employee.

According to his friends and family, Williams was very conscientious and punctual: 'like a Swiss clock', according to one colleague. He also had a keen sense of humour; he was 'a good laugh'. His sister Ceri told the inquest that she thought he was a perfect big brother and something of a 'country boy'. Williams enjoyed the outdoors; he was a keen cyclist and a member of the British Mountaineering Council. He was fit and lithe.

—

It was the second day of the inquest before details of how the body was discovered were revealed. GCHQ called Scotland Yard and reported Williams missing. A PC Gallagher was dispatched to investigate. A neighbour let him in through the secure communal door, but there was no response from inside the flat. Gallagher was eventually given access by the letting agent for the property. The flat was clean and tidy, with no signs of forced entry. Gallagher searched the premises and came across a red North Face holdall in the bath of the en-suite bathroom on the upper floor. The zip opening of the bag was padlocked on the outside. Later, at the post-mortem examination, the key to the padlock would be found inside the bag underneath Williams' body. The door of the bathroom was shut and the light was off.

Gallagher lifted the bag up a few inches and saw red fluid seeping from it. Then he noticed a smell coming from the bag and called in for advice. Sergeant Paul Colgan arrived shortly afterwards and made a small cut in the bag. He saw that there was a body inside. Gallagher also noticed a 'lady's wig' on the back of a chair. Later searches found more wigs, women's clothing and shoes with an estimated value of around

£20,000. The SIO, DCI Jackie Sebire, described the clothing as 'an extensive high-value collection'. Her opinion from the outset had been that another person was involved in the death.

Three pathologists gave consistent views on the potential cause of death. The body was badly decomposed, which suggested that Williams had died shortly after he was last seen alive on 15 August. However, decomposition made it difficult for them to be definitive about the cause of death. Although no signs of bruising or injury were found, any that had been present could have been lost due to decomposition. Dr Dick Shepherd said that he believed Williams must have got into the bag himself, as it would have been extremely difficult to put a floppy dead body into the position in which it was found. But he conceded that Williams could have been sedated or forced into the bag at gunpoint. All three pathologists agreed that the most likely cause of death was hypercapnia due to the build-up of carbon dioxide in the bag. This would have rapidly inhibited breathing, causing death within two to three minutes. They also agreed that an undetectable poison was an alternative.

Shepherd had also come to the conclusion that the best explanation for how Williams came to be in the holdall was that he had been in engaged in some form of autoerotic experiment. This judgement was based on his previous experience of such deaths rather than direct pathological findings. He believed that Williams' solitary existence, his interest in women's clothes and his background as a mathematics geek all supported this. The coroner was enraged by this suggestion; 'incandescent',[7] as Shepherd later reported.

In direct contradiction to Shepherd, Peter Faulding, an expert in specialist rescue, said that Williams was dead or unconscious before he was put in the bag, and that he believed it was impossible for the bag to be locked from the inside.[8] Faulding had tried this himself hundreds of times, unsuccessfully.

William Mackay, an expert in confined spaces, had also tried to lock himself in the bag. Although unsuccessful, he was unwilling to exclude that this was possible.

—

The family and relatives of the deceased are a prime concern for the coroner. They have certain legal rights that must be fulfilled and they will have a close and particular interest in the details of the inquest and its outcome. There is also a legal requirement to complete an inquest within six months of the death,[9] although they often take longer, particularly in London.[10] If an inquest is not completed within a year, the coroner is required to explain this to the chief coroner. More than 18 months had elapsed between the death of Williams and the opening of the inquest.

The police investigation could be seen as having two phases. The first phase was characterised by the assumption of third-party involvement in the death. Two elements supported this assumption. The first was the view that it was impossible for Williams to have locked himself in the bag. The second was forensic evidence. On 24 September 2010, around a month after Williams had been found, there was a breakthrough. David Adams, a forensic scientist from LGC, phoned the crime-scene manager Paul Hinkel. A partial DNA profile had been obtained from a swab taken from the back of Williams' left hand. Hinkel immediately called the SIO to inform her. A meeting was quickly organised for the following day to discuss the significance of the result and the next steps. In the course of the following year, hundreds of items were sent for forensic examination, but nothing further was found; the DNA profile remained the most important lead in the case.

With a DNA profile capable of identifying a possible third party, the inquiry seemed to be heading towards some form of conclusion. The coroner had delayed the inquest in the hope that the mystery person who had left the DNA could be traced and the case resolved.

In August 2011, Adams was seconded to another position and Ros Hammond, a senior forensic scientist and cold-case specialist, took over the work at LGC. Hammond had worked on many high-profile and complex cases; she was the lead scientist in the Damilola Taylor case who found the missing bloodstains, and later played an important role in the final Stephen Lawrence trial that led to prosecutions. A case conference had been planned for 14 February 2012, and Hammond wanted to be fully prepared for it. She was aware of the significance of the DNA profile from Williams' hand and had reviewed all the DNA results. In the process of her review, she encountered a problem.

Like with fingerprints, it is important with DNA to exclude individuals who may have some connection with the case: police officers, scene examiners, forensic scientists and so on. Each forensic lab has a staff database against which all DNA matches must be checked before the results are forwarded to the police. Hammond asked for the DNA profile from Williams' hand to be double-checked. The result was a surprise: the DNA profile matched to 'individual 152',* a member of the Met Evidence Recovery Unit (ERU), the team who had sampled the hand swab. Puzzled as to how this error could have occurred, she checked through the paperwork. The components of a DNA profile are represented by a string of numbers, and these numbers are what the database stores. Single DNA profiles can be checked automatically, but mixed profiles are more complicated. The profile from the hand swab was a mixture of DNA from Williams and an unknown person. The unknown DNA components had to be selected individually and the numbers emailed to the database checkers. In the process of doing this, Adams had made an error, typing '25' instead of '23', resulting in a mismatch with the person from ERU and giving the impression that the profile was from someone else entirely.

On 9 February 2012, Hammond phoned Hinkel to give him the news. Hinkel immediately contacted the SIO. For everyone involved, the review meeting in a few days' time would be very different from what had been anticipated. A human error had caused the problem, but human attentiveness had discovered it. However, the apparent lead had vanished.

—

At the crime scene, there had been a tussle between different departments of the Met about who would investigate the

---

* Individuals from external organisations are anonymised in these databases.

death. Counter Terrorist Command, SO15, had claimed it, but it was wrested away by the homicide team. However, there remained a problem. The investigation would need information about Williams' background: his character, relationships and information from his colleagues at MI6 and GCHQ. How would this be achieved when none of the homicide team was security-cleared at this level? Having lost the argument about who was to investigate the case, SO15 insinuated themselves between the homicide team and MI6 on the grounds that they had higher security clearance. They would act as a conduit, between the homicide team and SIS. All inquiries relating to MI6 or Williams' work would have to go through SO15.

The inquest revealed that this arrangement was fraught with problems and that the investigation lacked coordination. For example, DC Hall was an SO15 forensics officer responsible for searching Williams' workplace. He found a holdall under his desk similar to the one in which Williams was discovered. He also found an iPhone in his locker. Was there anything in the holdall? he was asked. 'Stuff … of a sensitive nature,'[11] he replied. When probed further, he said couldn't remember what this 'stuff' was. The coroner asked him if he had considered seizing the holdall, since it might be relevant to the investigation. 'I was told there was nothing there about Gareth's death,' he replied. Who had decided what was relevant was unclear. If it was Hall, why didn't he remember? Was it the kind of memory lapse that had occurred with the detectives in the Damilola Taylor case?

Detective Superintendent Broster, the SO15 senior officer in the case, had been aware of the holdall but had not told the SIO. Later, it was also revealed that nine USB memory sticks had been found in a cabinet at Williams' workplace, and these had been handed to MI6 for analysis. The SIO did not find out about the existence of the memory sticks until the last day of the inquest. SO15 was more a firewall than a conduit. Broster was questioned further by the coroner. Had Williams' workplace been tampered with by SIS? He replied that he could not rule out that anything had been interfered with, although he had no reason to believe it had.

Anthony O'Toole QC, acting for the family, asked Broster why four days had elapsed before Williams' office laptop had been handed to SO15 by MI6. He was not satisfied with Broster's reply, and went on the attack: 'It was … under the old boys' act … They told you that and you accepted it.'[12]

The coroner also pressed Broster for an explanation about the laptop. His response made no sense; she described it as a 'total non sequitur'.[13] Could Broster rule out SIS involvement in Williams' death? Broster replied that he had seen no evidence that they were involved, but he couldn't exclude it; he just didn't know. O'Toole went on to suggest that if it was impossible for Gareth to lock himself in the bag, this must have been done by someone else, someone specialising in the 'dark arts of the secret services'.[14] This was a theme he maintained throughout the inquest, and the coroner accepted that the involvement of the SIS in Williams' death remained a legitimate line of inquiry. SIS was allowed to have secrets but they were not above the law.

O'Toole also quizzed Broster about how information about claustrophilia* and bondage websites had been leaked to the

* Abnormal pleasure derived from being in a confined space.

press. Broster could not explain this. The coroner speculated that it had been done by the SIS to discredit Williams.

Four anonymous SIS officers gave their evidence from behind screens. A contrite senior officer referred to as 'SIS F' acknowledged that they had failed to respond promptly to Williams' absence. 'We are profoundly sorry about what happened,'[15] she said. MI6 should have responded to the absence between two and four hours after it was noted. In an odd and ironic twist, one of the largest communications organisations in the world explained that their inaction had been due to a 'breakdown in communication'.[16] SIS F also said that an internal review had found that 'There was no evidence of any specific threat to Gareth and we concluded there was no reason to think his death was anything to do with his work.'[17]

By the time the inquest was complete, a more complex picture of Williams' character, lifestyle and situation had emerged. He may have been a country boy, but he liked the big city and fine shops like Harrods and Fortnum and Mason. He was also deeply interested in women's fashion and had completed fashion design courses at reputable institutions. He attended fashion shows and galleries.

His sexuality was unclear, but this was said to have no bearing on his work. Police found no evidence of a sexual partner. He had attended a transvestite act two days before his disappearance, and his web browsing included visits to bondage sites, but the coroner pointed out that these visits were 'sporadic and isolated' and only accounted for a tiny proportion of time he spent online.

Williams wasn't happy in London, according to his sister Ceri, who said that he was disillusioned with 'office culture, post-work drinks, flash car competitions and the rat race'.[18] But the GCHQ caller who reported him missing, when asked if there was any reason to be concerned, said that Williams had just been reassigned to GCHQ and may not have taken this well. His manager at MI6 thought a more likely explanation for him returning to GCHQ was that he was bored with the bureaucracy of process risk mitigation. Whatever the truth of this, it appears to confirm that he was doing a different job at MI6 from the one he had previously done at GCHQ, although the details were never revealed. All of this was far too complicated for the tabloids; they stuck to their caricatures – geek, spy, weirdo.

Williams was also a man with more than one identity, who called friends from one of several mobile phones and attended high-level international conferences about hacking with other technical experts and secret agents. When the family lawyer tried to explore this issue with one witness, the coroner intervened.

—

A criminal trial is an adversarial event; one side pitted against another, overseen by an impartial judge and adjudicated by a jury. Argument and confrontation are inherent parts of the process. In contrast, an inquest is inquisitorial, a process presided over and directed by the coroner, who decides which witnesses to call, what evidence to hear, leads the questioning and determines the verdict. The coroner is not bound by the criminal rules of evidence such as hearsay or the burden of proof beyond reasonable doubt. In this sense an inquest is a more open and less restricted search for the truth than a criminal trial.

Despite this, there were many aspects of this case in which the truth was unclear, or possibly unavailable because it was deemed to be secret. Multiple versions of events were contested by different parties to the inquest. The facts did emerge gradually and build towards clarity, but in fits and starts and from clashes at salient points between the coroner and witnesses who were attempting, usually poorly, to defend themselves and their institutions. SO15 were unable to justify their role in the investigation. Their actions or inactions appeared to have no underlying logic; they just got in the way. MI6 failed to convince the coroner of their version of events. The coroner was outraged because an apparent DNA lead had given false hope to the family, causing them distress and delaying the inquest. Forensic scientists and police were called as witnesses and compelled to apologise for the DNA mix-up. The coroner was equally outraged by the suggestion that Williams' death had an autoerotic element. There was continuing tension and drama during the hearing; 'it was a circus', according to one person who was present.

Amongst all this, the consistent line of the family's lawyer was that Williams had been killed and that MI6 knew much more about it than they were willing to reveal. MI6 were also in cahoots with SO15, who had deliberately obstructed the homicide investigation. O'Toole consistently evoked the 'dark arts', of SIS. If SIS were not directly involved in the death, they had exacerbated the family's grief by their reluctance and failure to assist the inquiry. I wondered what he meant. This seemed to me to be the vaguest of conspiracy theories and one that would gain no traction. For a court to pay any attention to this idea, he would need to be more specific. What was the nature of these dark arts, and how did they impact on Williams' death? On a few occasions the coroner had prevented O'Toole from taking particular lines of questioning on the grounds of national security. It looked to me as if the 'dark arts' approach was doomed to failure. Was this his brief? O'Toole had uncovered incompetence and possibly collusion, but that would have been an easy task in this inquest. I wondered if his approach had served the family well.

CHAPTER THIRTEEN

If In Doubt, Think Murder

... these speculations are too nightmarish. Better to feel 'I shall never know'.

Iris Murdoch[1]

Until recently, there was no standard guidance on how to investigate murder in the UK. In 1999, the first *Murder Investigation Manual* was produced, which was updated in 2006.[2] In cases where a death is odd, unusual or potentially suspicious, detectives are urged to 'think murder'. The rationale for this is simple: scaling down a potential murder investigation when a death is found to be a suicide or accident is easy. Deciding two or three days into a presumed suicide that it is a homicide may be a fatal error. 'Think murder' demands that attention and thought is given to cases whose immediate appearance suggests they are not suspicious.

The Williams case was different. Even to the most experienced homicide detective it would have appeared obviously and perplexingly strange. The location of the body was bizarre, the circumstances in the flat puzzling and the background of the deceased extraordinary. No one would have encountered such a death previously. It is in such situations, where there seem to be no normal footholds, that a forensic strategy is essential. It pushes the distracting details into the background and the important questions into the foreground. The answers to many of these immediate questions will be found by what are known as fast-track actions,* such as speedily recovering CCTV data or canvassing neighbours.

I found the forensic strategy for the Williams case in the review papers. It was jointly agreed on 23/24 August by the DI and the first CSM on the scene. It was clear and straightforward: identify the body in the holdall, establish how and when it got into the holdall (by pathological or scientific means), ascertain if third parties could have been involved, identify and trace those parties, establish the details of events in the days prior to the death, events leading to the death and events after the death until discovery. There was also a detailed action plan for 24 August and notes from a meeting attended by the SIO. We were off to a flying start.

No one in an investigation understands everything that is going on; it must be understood collectively through shared knowledge and experience. The role of the SIO is crucial to maintaining this understanding and retaining focus on the most productive lines of inquiry. As the fast-track actions progress the case, the forensic strategy moves into a new phase; from reflexive to reflective strategy. The answers will come more slowly and may be dependent on specialists such as forensic

---

* Any investigative actions that, if pursued immediately, are likely to establish important facts, preserve evidence or lead to the early resolution of the investigation.

pathologists, forensic scientists and digital experts. The reliance on these external specialists in different organisations and locations spreads and fragments activity; communication lines are longer, more complex and require more attention. The aim of the second phase of the strategy is to maintain focus and momentum in these circumstances.

The purpose of our review was to evaluate the forensic strategy, its adequacy, consistency and relevance to the investigation. We also agreed to identify any new opportunities for forensic work and any general improvements that could be recommended in policy or practice. Within the scope of the review were scene management, forensic pathology, DNA profiling, fingerprints and any other areas of forensic evidence.

—

In July 2012, I met Phil in Glasgow to develop a plan of action. We freewheeled on the case before getting down to the specifics. What might the lifestyle inquiries – shopping, cycling, holidays – reveal? What about Williams' job? A wildcard that had endless potential for distraction. As the themes popped up, I scribbled them down in my notebook. Was there any forensic evidence of anyone else having been in the flat? Was there any forensic evidence that might identify further lines of inquiry? We would need to audit any forensic work that had already been done to check it was up to scratch. We would need to check that the interpretation of any forensic findings by detectives was sound. Most of this would fall to me. The other big area of work was a review of the investigative decision-making as the case developed and a detailed analysis of exhibit management.

Much of this information would be in HOLMES and Phil, as an experienced user, would pick this up.

—

In August 2010, at the outset of the investigation, scene examiners had carried out the initial work, recovering items such as Williams' laptops and phones and beginning the search for forensic evidence such as fingerprints, shoe marks, bloodstains and so on. Great care was taken to prevent contamination; gloves, masks, suits and overshoes were worn. Stepping plates were placed on the floor to create a common approach path before the floor had been fully examined.

The Evidence Recovery Unit (ERU), a specialist Met lab team, had used additional technology to search for invisible evidence, including lasers, ultraviolet light and chemical enhancement techniques. The ERU can find and recover fingerprints, shoe marks and other traces that fluoresce when illuminated by certain wavelengths of light or are revealed by chemical treatments. Luminol* testing causes bloodstains to glow faintly, including traces of blood that have been cleaned up and are no longer visible. Seminal staining can fluoresce under UV light. The ERU also recover traces of DNA, hairs and fibres. The flat had been examined in minute detail. Many fingerprints and some shoe marks were found and removed for further examination. DNA swabs from the holdall and parts of the body were taken. Stains that tested positive for semen and bloodstains were also found and removed for analysis.

---

* Luminol is a chemiluminescent substance.

There was no evidence that the floors, walls or other surfaces in the flat had been cleaned to remove evidence. Nor were there any signs that the bag containing the body had been wiped or cleaned.

Scene examination is a demanding and tiring process, and when fatigue began to set in, the examiners had retired for the evening. The scene was secured and guarded by a police officer. When the team returned the following day, one of the ERU team was convinced that the stepping plates had been moved. There was no record of anyone having entered the flat.

Hundreds of items from the scene, including fingerprints, DNA and shoe marks, were now queuing in various locations as the forensic work in the case swung into progress. There were particular issues around the fingerprint examinations that were of concern, given the recent problems in the fingerprint world.

When I joined the Met lab in the late seventies, fingerprints and forensic science inhabited different and disconnected worlds. My earliest recollection of a fingerprint expert was while waiting to give evidence at the Old Bailey. He spent most of the time telling me how important his evidence was and how trivial mine was; his evidence was a conclusive fact, mine 'just an opinion'. When I asked him to explain why fingerprints were so powerful, he said he couldn't explain it to me because I wasn't a fingerprint expert. I relayed this story to colleagues back at the lab, who smiled knowingly. They had all had similar encounters. It also turned out that this particular fingerprint expert had form for this kind of grandstanding. But how does it all work in court? I asked them. They laughed; fingerprint experts didn't have to explain their evidence, they just proclaimed it and everyone believed them. It was some form of inscrutable and ineffable art.

This all changed in 1997 when a murder in Ayrshire, Scotland, led to a dispute about fingerprints that smouldered like a slow-burning fuse on a bomb before detonating over a decade later. The explosion permanently damaged the credibility of fingerprints as evidence; even today, the fingerprint community has yet to fully recover.

A fingerprint found at the crime scene was matched to Shirley McKie, then a serving officer with Strathclyde Police, who were investigating the murder. But McKie denied being at the scene. A year later, when the murder trial was over, McKie was charged with perjury and tried in the High Court in Glasgow. The only evidence against her was the fingerprint from the scene. The jury took just 20 minutes to reject the evidence of the fingerprint experts and find her not guilty. The case became an international scandal in the fingerprint world, which was divided about whether this fingerprint matched McKie or not. There were long-running public disputes in the media, and eventually, in 2006, a Scottish parliamentary inquiry, which I was appointed to advise.

I sat through the entire proceedings. The evidence given by the experts who matched the fingerprint to McKie was incoherent; none of them could explain the basis for their decision. Responses to questions from members of the inquiry were irrational, arrogant, defensive and in some cases simply ignorant. At the heart of the case was a simple error. But as with so many scandals, it was the denials and cover-up that had widespread repercussions, drawing in the police, the Scottish criminal justice system, the Scottish Parliament and the worldwide fingerprint community. The legal resolution finally came in December 2011, when a public inquiry determined that the print was not from McKie.

A similar scandal in the USA[3] emphasised that 'the Scottish case', as the McKie farrago was frequently referred to, was not a local issue but a worldwide problem with fingerprint practices. Fingerprints were first used in criminal cases in the UK in 1902; it seems that practices had not changed much since that time and had become fossilised articles of dogma.

One of the recurrent issues in fingerprint examination is police officers leaving their prints at crime scenes. Sometimes this can't be avoided; they may have to force entry or attend to an injured person. On other occasions it is due to sloppiness, handling items they ought to leave alone until a CSI arrives. Police officers' and CSIs' fingerprints are stored in a database against which any prints found are cross-checked. Inevitably, the level of scrutiny in these examinations is lower than for a fingerprint that might match a potential offender. A print matching someone who has legitimately attended the scene is generally of little consequence, and considered to be something of an occupational hazard.

The problem in the McKie case arose because, despite the fingerprint being matched to her, she denied having been at the crime scene. I suspected that a similar thing had happened in the Bisset murders, albeit with less serious consequences. The fingerprint matching Napper was not found until several months into the inquiry. The delay was explained[4] on the basis that his print resembled Samantha Bisset's. Perhaps, but only because someone did not examine it properly, as had happened in the McKie case. I wondered what I might encounter in the Williams investigation. I knew the Met did not have an unblemished record[5] in fingerprint examination.

A report summarising the fingerprint examinations in the Williams case ran to 44 pages of tabulated results. It listed 405 fingerprints* from the scene and items found at the scene. I scanned the report. It was colour-coded: prints matched to Williams highlighted in green and unidentified prints in pink. I thought the colour-coding would allow me to speedily review all the findings, but as I worked through the report, I noticed that it had been applied inconsistently. What, at first glance, looked to be helpful was actually misleading. I went back to the start and worked my way through the report again.

The point of such a report is to communicate concisely and accurately to the SIO the outcome of every individual fingerprint result so that their significance can be quickly grasped. This report was a sloppy compilation of results from six different fingerprint examiners who had used different formatting and colours to identify their results. Whoever compiled it was not thinking about the investigation; they were just collating a load of technical findings. I counted through the individual results and drew up a table. Most of the prints

---

* A significant proportion of these (122) were not of sufficient quality to be examined.

(237) were matched to Williams. Some prints were matched to two members of the Williams family and to two MI6 officers identified only by code.

The other problem with the report was more significant. A fingerprint on its own is useless unless you have someone to compare it with or a database to search. The main database in the UK is IDENT1 which stores fingerprints from around eight million people as well as prints from crime scenes. At the time of Williams' death, IDENT1 could be searched in different ways: local, regional and national. The various levels of searching were required to prevent the system being overloaded. Since most crimes are committed by individuals who live near where the offence took place, a local search is usually fine. In a potential homicide, a national search ought to be carried out.

There are other databases in addition to IDENT1: the UK Immigration database, a terrorist database, INTERPOL and the FBI. But which databases had been searched for each print by the six different examiners wasn't clear. Sometimes all the available databases had been specified as searched. Sometimes only one or two were listed. In other instances the results box just recorded 'checking complete'. It may be that everything possible in the fingerprint examinations had been done, but I wasn't reassured.

—

The HOLMES database containing the case records had been moved from its original location to the Met training school at Hendon in north London. Much of the material was sensitive, so Phil and I travelled to Hendon to review the documents. I worked through all the forensic reports, logs and communications.

Over 200 items had been sent to the forensic lab with the aim of establishing if someone else had been involved in Williams' death. The toxicology had drawn a blank. Extensive and detailed analyses had found no drugs or poisons. The bulk of the remaining items was for DNA testing: swabs and samples from Williams' body, the holdall and its surroundings, various stains from items and surfaces in and around the flat, fluorescent stains that may have been semen, and items of clothing. These items were accompanied by elimination samples from individuals who were known to have been or may have been in the flat at some time, including police officers, CSIs and forensic scientists as well as associates and relatives of Williams. Some of the samples were only identified by a code number to protect the identities of SIS staff.

I went through every item in turn. I wanted to know why it had been sampled and submitted to the lab, what tests had been done, what the results of these tests were and what the results meant to the investigation. Crucially, I wanted to establish if the results answered a question or closed or opened a line of inquiry, or whether further work was necessary or possible. For example, one item was labelled 'Quantity of white tissues (from kitchen bin)'. There were 25 tissues in all, from which 11 DNA profiles were obtained. Nasal mucus was visible on some of the tissues. Was this the rationale for the DNA analysis – only tissues that were stained had been analysed? Did the 11 DNA profiles come from 11 separate tissues or fewer? I wouldn't normally expect 25 tissues to be forensically examined, but this wasn't a normal case. If the tissues were in the bin, surely they had all been used? Was there more than one type of tissue, which might suggest that another person may have been present? I couldn't find the answer to any of these questions in the documentation. There were many items in this category, where something about the forensic examination needed to be clarified.

There were also many items that had not been examined, but it wasn't clear why. Apart from the potential these items might have as investigative leads, the lack of information was a possible hostage to fortune if there was ever to be a trial. A common tactic of defence advocates is to concentrate on what has *not* been forensically examined. There are two benefits to this for them. First, it avoids them repeating (and therefore reinforcing) the prosecution evidence. Second, although there are almost always more items seized than need to be examined, there still has to be a reason why something has not been examined. For example, a towel from the kitchen had been examined for semen but not a tea towel that was nearby. Why choose one and not the other? Were there fluorescent stains on one and not the other? If so, where was this recorded? Who knew and could explain this in court if necessary?

The final area where action was required related to the type of DNA profiling that had been carried out. There were many samples where partial DNA profiles had been found using one method, but a more sensitive method might have improved the result. All these profiles ought to be reanalysed using the most sensitive methods.

A great deal of DNA work had been done – hundreds of tests on dozens of samples. DNA profiles matching Williams were obtained from many areas of his body. The only exception to this was the sample from his left hand that was later found to be due to contamination from one of the scene examiners. DNA matching Williams was also found in many parts of the flat: near the kitchen doorway, in the bathroom, inside the bath, on items of clothing and on one of the iPhones. The only DNA profile found that could be attributed to someone other than Williams matched his sister, Ceri.

There were minuscule traces of barely detectable contact DNA from other individuals in a few samples from the flat and the bag. When working at these extremely low levels of DNA, it is standard practice to identify a component only if it can be positively confirmed by a second test. This is akin to corroborating evidence in a courtroom with a second, ideally independent, piece of evidence. This was not always possible, so some of the results were considered to be unreliable and could not be used. This is common in contact DNA profiling. In the few instances where the DNA components could be corroborated, there was still not enough information to identify anyone. This was the background DNA from unknown persons deposited at unknown times.

The holdall in which Williams was found was tested extensively. DNA profiles matching him were found in multiple locations on the inside, outside, opening flap, handles, padlock and zip. In most instances these were full profiles. On some parts of the bag, including the padlock, there were minute, indecipherable traces of DNA that could be from another person.

The impression that I was left with when I had completed this part of the review was that there were more questions than answers. It was as if the attention of investigators to some of the forensic work had simply petered out, and they had lost sight of exactly what was going on. No leads had been found, but many gaps and further potential remained.

Meanwhile, Phil had been examining the SIO's policy log and the exhibit databases. A total of 13 individual books had been used to log exhibits, which were also recorded in a number of Excel spreadsheets. The general principle is that the exhibit books are the settled, definitive record of *all* exhibits. Early in a case, the true situation might lag behind the actual one – for example, some exhibits may be taken directly to a forensic lab for urgent examination and the records will be updated later. At the stage we were at now, however, the list of items should be complete and accurate.

This wasn't what we found. Not all of the exhibits had been logged in the exhibit book. An exhibit is required to have a unique reference consisting of letters and numbers. The reference is usually made up of the initials of the person who creates it, with each item being numbered in sequence; AB/1, AB/2, etc. At least two of the crime-scene examiners had gaps in their numbering. We didn't know if there were exhibits missing or simply gaps in the sequence of numbers. There was also duplication of exhibit reference numbers, and at least one item, a hair from the crime scene, was not logged in the system anywhere. One way or another there was no definitive list of exhibits. With my previous experience of working on Met cases in mind, I asked Phil if the Met were just bad at managing exhibits. 'Not uniquely bad,' he replied.

Although the forensic strategy had not been updated in meeting minutes, there were detailed records of the decisions the SIO had made during the case. Her rationale for each judgement was recorded, albeit scattered throughout multiple documents and difficult to find. This meant that any follow-up investigation or review – like the one I was carrying out – would need to gather the fragmented aspects of the strategy from different sources, then link and cross-reference the information. A single repository of decisions and rationales for action would have been easier to consider, less prone to misinterpretation and harder to undermine by those so inclined in any subsequent trial.

—

Digital forensics is the new frontier in the forensic world. At first a curio, then of occasional relevance, it is now a central element in any death investigation. Mobile phones, laptops, tablets and satnavs are just some of the rich data sources that are routinely tapped into. Most of us use one or more of these devices every day, and it is increasingly difficult to be off grid. Whatever we do – banking, browsing or booking tickets – we leave a digital spoor on the device and on the remote servers it has connected to. Most of this data can be recovered and interrogated to reveal where we have been, who we have been in contact with; our hobbies, habits, histories and secrets.

It's not all plain sailing, however, and there are a number of issues that confront the digital investigator. First, there is a bewildering variety of ever-changing devices and operating systems that no one can keep up with. Second, there is a constantly evolving range of tools (software) for interrogating devices, and very few people actually understand how all these work. Third, the average laptop (and phone nowadays) will often have more data than can possibly be examined in a lifetime.* There is a need to focus by making decisions about what is relevant. In short, any device has to be examined by someone who understands how it works, has the correct tools and is asking the right questions. From a reading of the digital forensics reports, I wasn't convinced these conditions had been fully met.

Like any new frontier, digital forensics has attracted all sorts of hobbyists, buccaneers and self-proclaimed experts. My experience at the time of the review was that many of the police officers who were involved in digital forensics were simply cops who were interested in computers and had put themselves forward to do the work. Some of them had been trained, others had not. The training that was available was limited. And in a new area, working practices were variable; there were no agreed standards and few understood the detailed technical architecture of the devices or the tools used to interrogate them. This situation was not confined to the police. In the outside world I encountered 'digital experts' whose claims of expertise rested on nothing more than their ownership of a computer repair shop. Amongst

---

* 1 gigabyte is one billion characters. If this was printed out on A4 paper, it would produce a pile 50 metres tall. 400 gigabytes would produce a column 20 kilometres tall; two and a half times the height of Mount Everest.

these communities were a small number of individuals who had some real knowledge* of how the technology worked, and there were increasing numbers of highly knowledgeable experts who came from the world of computer engineering, the security industry and academia.

Williams had four iPhones and three MacBooks, and these were only the devices that were known about. The fourth iPhone was found in his work locker; one of the MacBooks also came from his workplace. He also had two SIM cards. All the phones were unregistered; they were not bought through a particular network provider. Although any of them could have been used with either of the SIM cards, that would not render them untraceable. Any outgoing calls would have the number of the SIM card, and this has to be associated with a network provider. When the SIM card is placed in the phone, there is a 'handshake', where information from the SIM card and phone will be exchanged. This combination of phones and SIM cards would not prevent tracking of the phones via cell sites or analysis of call record data, but it would make it more awkward, something that a spy would presumably know.

All the devices had been examined by specialist Met officers. One of the iPhones found in the flat had been reset at 23.30 on 15 August 2010. It was not established if this had been done remotely. There were very few contacts on the phones. One phone appears to have been used mainly for web browsing. Common browsing themes were cycling, IT software and

---

* This situation has improved – but not by much. Some organisations have formal standards and training and there are an increased number of knowledgeable experts. There are still plenty of hobbyists.

related stuff, women's fashion and accessories, models and drag queens. There were also a few fetish and bondage sites.

The police officer who led the examination of the devices other than the phones had fewer than three years' experience as a digital forensic examiner. I wondered why such an apparently inexperienced person had been allocated such a high-profile and potentially complicated case. Was this their most experienced expert? If not, why not? Would I allow a forensic scientist with three years' experience to lead on such a case? No. The MacBook from Williams' office contained only technical documentation. Some of the devices had to be outsourced to specialists because the Met did not have the facilities to access MacBook solid-state hard drives. The digital examiner concluded that there was no secret or confidential material on any of the devices, nor was there anything found that ought to have been secret, but he appeared to have been given little guidance about what to search for, and no keywords. He further concluded that the user of the devices appeared to have 'considerable technical knowledge'.

In contrast to the tyro Met digital examiner, Williams was a master of the digital world. It seemed likely to me that he was capable of manipulating and altering data on devices to create a digital miasma that would obscure his tracks. What struck me was not just the multiplicity of devices, but how little information seemed to be on them. Williams' last logged web browsing session was a cycle trials website on Monday 16 August at 1.03 a.m. In the same session he browsed a number of women's fashion and fashion gossip sites, and other sites about iPhone software tools.

There was no recorded digital strategy in the case. Given the potential importance of digital material to the investigation, it would have been desirable to either incorporate it into the forensic strategy or to have a separate strategy for the examination of all digital material. I wasn't convinced this part of the investigation was adequate. However, shortly afterwards I met the new SIO at an update meeting in London. It was clear that he was much more active on this issue and was outsourcing a number of the devices for examination by specialists.

—

The Williams case is a masterclass in how different institutions and communities attempt to make sense of evidence. Forensic scientists often have a luxury not afforded to others such as SIOs or jurors. Their evidence addresses narrower, more specific points, often a single issue such as whether a DNA profile is a match or a white powder contains a drug. They also have formal models for interpreting the evidence and determining its significance. A court is dealing with a multiplicity of evidence types: eyewitnesses, documentation, scientific data; direct evidence, circumstantial evidence. This is altogether more complex; there is no single approach that applies to all these evidence types. A particular feature of this case was the *absence* of evidence: no single definitive cause of death, no direct evidence of third-party involvement, no obvious investigative leads.

Gareth Williams was at the heart of this drama, and various facets of his character had been exposed at the inquest: country boy, respected colleague, friend and fashionista. For others, he came straight from a le Carré novel with a ready-made plot of twists and diversions. The combination of glamour and espionage, the bizarre manner of his death, his mathematical genius and uncertain sexuality were simply too much for some tabloids and web sources to resist. Some of the media isolated a single aspect of his character to frame their stories about a spy, a geek, an aberrant hobbyist. There was no evidence that he was a cross-dresser, a feature that attracted a great deal of media attention. Nor was he perfect. The inquest revealed that he had made unauthorised searches of MI6 databases, although the details were never revealed. His character was more complex and layered than reported but his main role now was as an object of inquiry and speculation.

Williams' job and lifestyle, the circumstances of his death and the uncertainty about the cause provided rich territory for the imagination, and there were many fantastical theses put forward in the media and on the web to explain the case. Many of these relied on the basic components of a conspiracy theory; that at the bottom of all this was some secret, powerful agency whose interests were served either by murdering Williams or covering up the real explanation for his death. The explanations relied on the central 'gotcha' of any conspiracy theory: *but you can't disprove it, can you?* Well, no, because conspiracy theories are not really theories at all. A real theory can be tested; evidence is gathered and this may contradict or support a hypothesis. Conspiracy theories are belief based, not evidence based.

In all of this there were some practical issues for our review. There were gaps in the evidence; many gaps. The cause of death was formally determined to be 'unascertained'; there was an explanation but it wasn't definitive. It seemed that at every point where there was a sensible answer – in this instance, hypercapnia – there was also an alternative that fuelled speculation – an undetectable poison. The route that we took through this miasma of possibilities was twofold. In our first conversation about the review, we agreed that we would proceed as if the case would one day end up in court. Courts operate on evidence; information that helps you decide between alternative explanations. Ideally, this is direct evidence; if that is not available, circumstantial evidence will do. Second, we limited the terms of reference to what we could personally access and make sense of. Our basic opening was that this was an unexplained death: suicide, accident or homicide. If it was homicide, it could be a murder.

Even so, some speculations could be quickly excluded in our view. A popular one was that some espionage agency from abroad (the enemy without) or MI6 (the enemy within) had killed Williams and then sterilised the premises so that there was no evidence of their presence. Yet there were hundreds of fingerprints in the flat and no indication that it had been cleaned or that evidence had been removed.

—

A coroner can reach one of several verdicts[6] about the cause of a death, the most common of which are 'natural causes', 'accidental death' and 'suicide'. Also open to the coroner is a narrative verdict, which records how the deceased met their death in more detail and includes the rationale for the decision. A narrative verdict can also apportion blame; for example, to a hospital or another institution that was involved in the death.

Dr Wilcox's summing-up lasted two hours. She ruled out natural causes; Williams was young and fit and the post-mortem exam had not revealed any organic disease. Suicide was also excluded; there was no evidence to support this, nor was there any history suggesting it was likely. She rejected the idea that Williams got into the holdall willingly, because he was risk-averse and would have taken a knife with him. Nor did she believe that the death was connected with autoeroticism; she was scathing about suggestions that Williams was a cross-dresser and the leaking of his browsing habits to the media. She was also critical of the police, particularly SO15, and MI6.

Wilcox concluded that a third party was involved. This person had placed the bag in the bath while Williams was inside and probably alive. He had then died of hypercapnia. His death was therefore unlawful and criminally mediated, but there was no evidence that he had died at the hands of spies. She also said that the highly unusual circumstances of the death had led to 'endless speculation', one of many factors that had hampered inquiries. Despite a 21-month police investigation and seven days of evidence at the inquest, Dr Wilcox concluded that 'most of the fundamental questions in relation to how Gareth died remain unanswered'.[7]

—

Until Williams was attached to MI6, he had worked at GCHQ as a mathematician and cryptologist. He had applied for operational field work at MI6 but failed the training at his first attempt, although he later passed. What was his role at MI6? Was he a spy – someone who spends their life undercover handling assets? Given his personality and background, this seems unlikely, and it would probably have been a waste of his talents. But that doesn't mean he was not operational. It seems that his role was somewhere between spying and backroom. In July 2010, he attended the Black Hat[8] and DEFCON[9] conferences in Las Vegas. A DEFCON badge was found in his flat when it was searched. It was confirmed at the inquest that he was involved in covert operations in the months before he died. If he was a spy, he was a new kind of spy; not a Cold War spy but a cyberwar spy.

—

At the time of our review, the investigation was ongoing and advanced. Most lines of inquiry had been extensively investigated. Almost everything that could be done had been done – almost. Although we found further potential forensic work, none of it suggested that it would lead to a breakthrough, though it might definitively close doors that had been left ajar. We found no major problems, no 'smoking gun'. However, the investigation wasn't completely smooth-running. SO15 hampered the homicide team; they were not adequately tasked and controlled by the SIO. The poor explanations for their actions and decisions should have been challenged during the investigation rather than at the inquest. What was being investigated was an unexplained death, and MI6, as Williams' employer, had information that could be relevant and that would have been sought in any other case: his role, employment history, any reason to believe his death may have been connected to his work. None of the information was secret; it was all ultimately revealed by MI6 managers at the inquest. MI6 were under fire from the outset due to their failure to respond adequately to Williams' absence. Cooperation with the homicide investigation might have softened this criticism.

The forensic strategy was another area that was not fully under control. Although adequately defined at the outset and regularly monitored, it was not fully recorded or communicated. The theory of a third-party involvement – that someone else must have been involved in the death – gradually became embedded in the minds of the investigation team as the sole explanation, to the detriment of other possibilities. The basis for this appeared to be the belief that it was impossible to lock the bag from the inside. We weren't convinced this was true. It was accepted that two individuals had tried to achieve this hundreds of times and failed, but neither of these individuals was Gareth Williams, nor had they completely ruled it out.

We proposed that the investigation team ought to reconsider all of their lines of inquiry more deeply and more imaginatively; the processes were fine but the thinking could be improved. By doing so, it might be possible to reject some potential explanations. We gave two examples to illustrate this point. The first related to the pathology results and the cause of death. The formal cause of death was 'unascertained' – that is, the cause could not be established. Taken at face value, this took the investigation nowhere, but it was possible to interrogate this further, as had happened at the inquest, to reveal the likely cause of death (suffocation) agreed by the pathologists. This did not completely resolve the situation, however, because of the possibility of an undetectable poison.

The second example we raised related to autoerotic activity. Had this been fully investigated? Williams had seven Apple devices, three of which contained evidence of web browsing on subjects such as bondage, self-bondage or sexual fetishes. His remaining devices contained no similar material, although one of them had been reset and no data had been extracted from it.*

The coroner rejected an erotic experiment connected with bondage on two grounds: that Williams' browsing in these areas was limited, and that he was risk-averse in his work and lifestyle. Perhaps the homicide team shared this view, but again we were not convinced. It is true that the browsing that was found was limited, but the complete extent of his browsing on these topics was never likely to be discovered. Williams' technical knowledge suggests that he was capable of erasing such data and rendering it undetectable.† One of the websites he visited had extensive information about self-bondage, and a previous incident involving bondage appeared to us to be salient. In 2007, Williams, who was tied to his bed in his boxer shorts, had to be set free in the early hours of the morning by his landlady's husband. Both husband and wife were of the view that this was a sexual act. One of the bondage websites included advice on safety,

---

* This was the situation at the time of our review. However, iPhones are notoriously difficult to extract data from generally, and this is still the case.
† Deleting a file or browsing history does not completely remove data from a device. Traces of the data will remain and can be recovered.

particularly ensuring that keys were available if locks were involved. But even if Williams had followed this advice (the key to the padlock was found in the holdall), he could not have known how quickly he would have suffocated when the holdall was closed. It is difficult to see the connection between a risk-averse lifestyle and sexual behaviour that the coroner drew. A common element of sexual behaviour is the risk associated with it, as many public scandals show.

The police and the coroner had taken a view that another person was involved in Williams' death. We took a different view, which was that there was no evidence of this. Hundreds of fingerprints had been found, the majority of which had been attributed to Williams. Of those remaining, all could be explained by individuals with legitimate access to the flat. The situation with DNA was similar. Taken together, these findings also scotched one of the wilder speculations about evidence being removed by cleaning.[10] Not only was there no evidence that the flat had been cleaned, there was extensive evidence in the form of DNA and fingerprints that it had not. What remained was the central puzzle in the case: if no one else was involved, how did Williams manage to lock himself in the holdall?

What was needed was for the Met to reconsider the investigation and clear up the many loose ends we had identified. It might be that some of these would lead to evidence of a third party; alternatively it would confirm the current position. In short, our main recommendation to the investigation team was to go back and think again, look in detail and be as open-minded as possible. The involvement of a third party could not be excluded, but if there was ever a trial, it would be decided on evidence, and there was none.

—

Some months after the review was completed, I saw Gary Pugh at a business meeting. 'Look out for an announcement in that case,' he said quietly during a lull in the proceedings.

On 13 April 2013, Deputy Assistant Commissioner Martin Hewitt, a former colleague of mine from Kent Police, gave a press briefing. He acknowledged that the original investigation into Williams' death had had deficiencies and said that the approach in the reinvestigation had been different and had clarified some aspects of the case. Following the inquest, SIS had allowed the Met direct access to GCHQ and MI6 staff, personnel files and other records. Twenty-seven of Williams' colleagues were formally interviewed. The Met were unable to identify any motive for causing him harm and were satisfied that his death was not connected with his work. It was not possible to exclude the involvement of a third party. However, it was now accepted that it was possible to lock the holdall from the inside. After three years of investigation, the force concluded that no other person had been present when Williams died. Echoing the words of the coroner, Hewitt concluded that many questions about the death were left unanswered.

CONCLUSION

The Killer of Little Shepherds

The public feel they have a reasonably clear sense of how the police organisation works. That they … are generally misinformed is largely a consequence of the ways in which the institution, its officers and its working methods are presented in the media.

Tim Newburn[1]

In nineteenth-century France, a series of horrific murders terrified the public, bamboozled police and lawyers and drove the media into a frenzy. Joseph Vacher, a vagabond former soldier, murdered at least 11 people between 1894 and 1897. Most of the murders were committed in the south-east of the country. Many of the victims were young shepherds whom Vacher stalked in the open fields while they tended their flocks. He killed children and adults of both sexes, stabbing his victims dozens of times and often disembowelling and raping them. He was dubbed 'the killer of little shepherds'.

He was caught by the husband of a woman he had attacked in a field in the Ardèche and taken to the police.

There was little evidence against Vacher, but he confessed to the murders and claimed he was insane. A number of doctors examined him and concluded that he was sane. He was convicted, sentenced to death, and was executed by guillotine on 31 December 1898.

One of the doctors who examined Vacher was Alexandre Lacassagne, then professor of forensic medicine at the University of Lyon. Lacassagne instituted many of the procedures that we now take for granted in crime investigation: controlling crime scenes, attention to detail and logical thinking. The investigation of the murders coincided with the birth of modern policing and the invention of what we now call forensic science. Lacassagne and his colleagues shrugged off many of the mythologies created by previous generations. In an excellent account of the Vacher case, Douglas Starr[2] tells the story and provides a contemporary context: France and Europe were on the threshold of the modern world.

What struck me about the account of this investigation was how strongly it corresponded to my experience of murder investigation over a century later in the cases recounted in this book. There were many difficulties in the Vacher case, too many to go into here. They included: a mobile offender avoiding detection by operating across administrative boundaries (Robert Black, Robert Napper); the failure of the authorities to recognise a highly distinctive *modus operandi* (Black and Napper); the willingness of the police to light on an individual and build a case around them (Colin Stagg, Stephen Downing);

a lack of evidence when the expectation was that it would be found (Michael Stone); and police incompetence (Damilola Taylor, Robert Napper).

Most of the issues that bedevilled the Vacher case and which are seen throughout this book can be linked to the culture of police organisations. Culture in this context is the personality of an organisation, institution or occupation. And like real personalities, it varies enormously; some cultures are relaxed, some cooperative, some like to dominate. Imagine the differences between a theatre group and a law firm, or a primary school and a factory. Culture is largely intangible; you sense it more than you see it, but it can be observed in the structure of an organisation, how power is wielded, and in rituals, procedures, symbols and language.

Police culture can be summed up in four words: mission, action, pragmatism and control.[3] Policing is considered to have a moral imperative; it's not just a job, it's *the* job* – a job primarily about action, as we have seen. A job that can only be understood and experienced from the inside by those in the know. Action is based on pragmatic concrete choices and decisions, not theory or reflection. The focus is getting the job done, getting through the next few days or sometimes hours. There is limited time for reflection and no time for research.

The police have a strong need to control groups and individuals from outside the organisation, such as forensic scientists and other experts, particularly if they have knowledge of policing and criminal justice. The academic literature refers

---

* *The Job* was the title of the Metropolitan Police weekly staff newspaper, which is still available as a free monthly magazine.

to such individuals and groups as 'challengers', because their independence and potential for non-compliance is seen as problematic by some police officers. Trapped recently in Edinburgh airport waiting for a delayed flight, I fell into conversation with a fellow traveller, a former police officer, now a psychologist. 'There's nothing a police officer likes less than someone who isn't a police officer talking back,' I said.

'Or someone who knows what they're talking about,' she replied.

—

Almost all my experience of murder investigation has been through the twin lenses of science and technology. For around 10 years I was associate director of the Scottish Institute for Policing Research, and during that time I met many researchers and police officers from around the world. On one occasion I was invited to observe a session in Pearls in Policing, a 'global think tank where top executives in law enforcement meet to discuss the strategic and personal challenges of their organisations'.[4] The session was the final presentation from one of the workshops, whose task had been to choose a policing problem of international significance and present a solution.

The group involved had chosen Somalian piracy,* an issue of some significance if you lived, worked or travelled (especially by sea) in that part of the world. But how many people did this affect? I wondered. Was it the biggest issue facing international policing at that time? What about human

_____
* Somalian piracy has significantly receded but it was near its peak around the time of the conference in 2011.

trafficking, transnational cybercrime or the drugs trade? Why choose Somalian piracy over these other global issues? I was puzzled until I saw the presentation. A solution to the Somalian problem had to involve action, risk, drama and emotion, as well as helicopters, guns and materiel of all sorts. As I watched, I imagined the choppers moving in on the targets and black-clad strike teams dropping from the sky onto ships amid stun-grenade blasts and gunfire. Somalian piracy was topical and exciting.

The group's choice of problem highlighted for me two crucial aspects of police culture that I have experienced throughout my career and that we have seen repeatedly in the cases in this book. First, the need for action, ideally immediate action and the type of thinking that goes with it: fast thinking, intuitive thinking, emotional thinking. Second, the belief in technological solutions when there may be more effective alternatives, even when the technology is not fully understood. Does everyone in policing think like this? Of course not, but it is there in the mentality that influences policing at an institutional level. The day-to-day equivalent of Somalian piracy is the rapid reaction to crime reports that have virtually no effect on detection rates,[5] and over-the-top responses with multiple police vehicles at minor crimes. It wastes resources and solves nothing, but creates drama. Is this a new problem? No.

—

Throughout my career, I have been engaged with detective training at many levels. A very common question at the end of these sessions is: what science is new; what can give us an edge over the bad guys? There are many false assumptions embedded in this question. That something new will be more effective than what is already available, that it will be applied effectively, and that it will give the police an advantage over criminals. On this last point, only rarely can technology be used to get ahead of the bad guys, because the bad guys are almost always lighter on their feet and more entrepreneurial than conservative, hierarchical police organisations. If this is a war, it's an asymmetric war. Police culture conditions what technologies the police use and how they use them. The culture is so strong that it can override technology even when imposed from the outside.

This can be illustrated by two high-profile miscarriages of justice that arose because of the persistent desire of detectives to obtain confessions from suspects. Maxwell Confait was a male prostitute who was murdered in south London in 1972. His body was found in his burnt-out flat. Three youths* were arrested and convicted variously of manslaughter on the grounds of diminished responsibility, murder, arson and burglary. All confessed to their crimes.† None of the boys was legally represented and it was later found that the confessions were obtained by police oppression. The convictions were quashed.

The Confait case was one of several that led to major legal reform‡ to protect the rights of arrested persons. Amongst a number of protections introduced was the use of tape-recorded

---

* One of the boys was 18 years old but had a mental age of 8.
† There was forensic pathology evidence about the time of death that ought to have eliminated the boys, but the pathologist changed his opinion in the witness box.
‡ In England and Wales: the Police and Criminal Evidence Act 1984.

interviews in police stations. Although the boys' confessions had been challenged at trial, the police had stuck to their version of events and had prevailed. The introduction of tape recording was anticipated to resolve arguments about what was truly said during interviews and so prevent miscarriages of justice. The assumption was that the technology – a recording of the interview – would resolve the issue.

In 1988, Lynette White was murdered in Cardiff, and in 1990, three black men were convicted of her murder. In 1992, the convictions of all three were quashed following appeal. One of the reasons for the convictions being overturned was oppression on the part of the police during interviews, despite the fact that they were recorded. According to an appeal court judge, the interviews involved so much bullying and hectoring that they should never have been admitted in evidence. A decade or more after the introduction of taped interview recording, the approach of the police had not changed; the technology had not resolved the problem, because how it was used was determined by institutional practices.

This is only one example, but if you have any doubts about the importance of something as vague as culture, it may be worth recalling that for over a decade, the world was plunged into a financial crisis that was largely due to institutionalised cultural practices within banking.

A more recent example of culture defeating technology is how the Met used HOLMES in most of the cases in this book. The point of the HOLMES system is to log, track and therefore not lose sight of critical connections and evidence in major crime investigations, especially murder cases. HOLMES requires a number of specialist staff for it to be run effectively, yet the Met appear to have had a policy of not staffing HOLMES adequately. In these circumstances it cannot possibly fulfil the role it was designed for: a safeguard against the failures that occurred in the Yorkshire Ripper investigation. In these circumstances technology is nothing more than a symbol, like a flash car parked in a driveway and never driven.

—

How the police use forensic science is set in the same overall context of how they understand, use or ignore technology. It has become obvious to me over a long career that the police do not understand forensic science. I am not alone in this view; it is shared by most other forensic scientists. Quite apart from those cases that come to the attention of the media and the public, there is plenty of documentary evidence of this issue too.

In 1996, the year I joined Kent Police, the police service and the FSS published a joint review[6] of how forensic science was used in England and Wales. The report stated that forensic science and forensic science labs were seen as something separate from investigations, and that communication between forces and labs was 'often poor'. It went on to say that awareness of forensic science* was also poor and often insufficient for purpose; that is, detectives didn't have adequate knowledge of forensic science. In 2000, there was a follow-up review,[7] which found that few forces had bothered to read the first

---

* The report uses the phrase 'scientific support', but for our purposes we can take this to be cognate with forensic science.

review, and concluded that 'ignorance of its contents was widespread'. In relation to police training and knowledge of forensic science, the report stated: 'A recurrent theme ... was the lack of awareness *at all levels*, particularly the operational levels.' In 2002, a third audit was carried out.[8] This was a much slimmer document, much of which consisted of repeating the recommendations from previous reports. It concluded: 'Overall this [report] has revealed a mixed take-up of the recommendations [in previous reports].' Knowledge and training in forensic science were not mentioned; the issue had been dropped.

In 2005, I gave evidence to the parliamentary inquiry* into forensic science.[9] Amongst other things I said, 'The evidence ... is consistently clear, [police] knowledge [of forensic science] needs to improve and ... their training needs to improve.' In March 2011, there was a second parliamentary inquiry.[10] The opening line of the report described forensic science in England and Wales as 'in a near constant state of flux for over a decade'. Amongst many observations in my written submissions to the committee, I made it plain that police knowledge of forensic science, on the basis of reviews carried out by the police themselves, was not fit for purpose. This was put to the chief constable who led on forensic issues at the time, Chris Sims; he disagreed, although he accepted that the levels of knowledge were variable. I guess the police just don't know what they don't know. Or the reports I cited were conveniently forgotten.

---

* This parliamentary inquiry and the others referred to below relate solely to England and Wales.

There was a third parliamentary inquiry in 2013.[11] By this
time the institutional structures of forensic science in England
and Wales were falling apart. The FSS had closed and the
police service acted like supermarkets, controlling the market,
driving down prices and commoditising services. The forensic
science labs were the farmers. The single dominant rationale
in the police contracts was price. It was, in the words of one
individual from the Home Office, 'a race to the bottom'.
In 2019, there was yet another select committee inquiry.[12]
Amongst other things, it heard evidence that understanding
of forensic science by lawyers and judges was variable and
juries overestimated its significance. It would seem that the
criminal justice system is a knowledge-free zone when it comes
to forensic science.

—

The cases in this book are spread over almost half a century,
but many of the problems described appear to have existed for
at least twice as long; since the creation of police forces in the
late nineteenth century. The breakthroughs that Lacassagne
and colleagues made in the investigation of crime were a small
part of the major developments, fractures and upheavals of
modernity. In technological terms, it seems we are approaching
a similar large-scale change as we enter the third decade of
the twenty-first century.

Developments in AI, biometrics and big data will change
the world in ways that cannot be foreseen, despite the many
claims to the contrary. These technologies are likely to have
legitimate and practical uses for criminal justice, but there is

a widespread lack of understanding of how they operate and the level of risks they present. There is much excitement in police circles about how they might be used to fight crime and disorder, largely through new surveillance mechanisms and automated forms of identification, yet there is no evidence that these technologies are sufficiently mature or reliable for use in such an important environment. And there is growing evidence that the police understand neither how they work, nor the risks or ethical issues associated with them. It appears that these new technologies will creep into the criminal justice system as they are, with few safeguards and limited evidence of their operational effectiveness.* Black boxes in a brave new world; quantum technologies in a Newtonian system.

The law is a social creation, crime is a social event and murder investigation is a human system. Whatever technologies are deployed, they will be deployed into this human system. Every component of the system is reliant on the others, and no single individual or institution understands all their moving and colliding parts. The limits of the criminal justice system are not technological, but human. How do we make this work?

The orthodox response to a problem of this type, particularly from scientists, is that there is a need for knowledge; more training and education in science and technology. If only those involved understood science, these difficulties would vanish. I'm sure more knowledge would go some way to improve things, but a little reflection shows that this is neither the

---

* There is a biometrics commissioner in England and Wales and one is about to be appointed in Scotland. These roles will be crucial in determining how new technologies will be used and what safeguards are necessary.

problem nor the solution. How many people will we train? For how long? In what subjects? How will we keep them up to date? How much will it cost? Who will be doing their job while they are being trained?

Another angle on the issue of scientific knowledge is illuminating. We are in the midst of a worldwide measles crisis, with increasing numbers of parents choosing not to have their children vaccinated, resulting in a loss of herd immunity. Is this a knowledge problem? I have a degree in life sciences and spent much of my career working as a professional biologist. Do I fully understand the risks for and against inoculation? I'm not sure, but I trust the advice of the professionals around me and make the decision on that basis. Trust is the problem, not knowledge.

In a recent cold-case investigation[13] of a 30-year-old sexual murder, detectives arrested a man on the basis of a DNA profile. The profile had been generated in 1994 and was constantly upgraded as new techniques became available. The original profile had been done by the FSS, but the police were now working with one of the newer private forensic labs. The DNA was a mixed profile, and any interpretation and calculation of its statistical significance would have been complicated and time-consuming. The police arrested the man before the match calculation had been carried out and arrived at the lab demanding that it be done instantly. They also specified that they needed a result of 'a billion',* magical thinking that revealed their ignorance of the science and the role of the scientist as

---

* Expressing the evidential significance of a DNA profile often involves the use of very large numbers – a billion being the largest.

much as their desired outcome. The scientist responded that it was a complicated piece of work and would take some time. And the statistical probability would be whatever the calculation produced; it was not something that could be tailored to the wishes of an investigator. The detectives simply threatened to take the work to another private lab, compelling the scientist to do the work immediately. The incident shows the staggering level of ignorance of some detectives, and their willingness to bully professional colleagues.

When I look back at my experience of working in London, Edinburgh and Kent, what I find is that when I worked more effectively with detectives it was not because they were more knowledgeable (although this was often the case) but because I found them to be more trustworthy. Trustworthiness and knowledge are not unrelated. Individuals who are perceived to be knowledgeable and competent are more likely to be trusted than those who lack these characteristics. When it comes to the effective use of forensic science in the investigation of a crime, providing advice to a prosecutor or defence lawyer in a case conference, giving expert testimony in court or advising a parliamentary inquiry, knowledge is necessary but not sufficient. The primary currency of such transactions is the trustworthiness of those involved.

Afterword

It was widely believed that Robert Black had killed more children than those he had been convicted of, and investigations continued after he was imprisoned.

In 1981, nine-year-old Jennifer Cardy was abducted as she was cycling to a friend's house in County Antrim, Northern Ireland. Her body was found six days later in a reservoir 16 miles away. She had been sexually assaulted and strangled. In 2011, Black was convicted of her murder and sentenced to a minimum of 25 years in Maghaberry prison.

Genette Tate was 13 years old in August 1978 when she went missing while delivering newspapers in Aylesbeare, Devon. At the time of my involvement in the Black investigation, I recalled some of the details from the Tate case. The photograph of her bike in the road gave me the immediate impression that she had been snatched, like most of Black's victims. In 2000, I met detectives from Devon and Cornwall Police who were investigating her disappearance. My files from the Robert Black case had been passed to them by Lothian and Borders Police and they wanted to discuss some of the details in my notes. I spent the whole day with them, but nothing much came of the process. Sometimes I thought they were reading too much into my abbreviated scribbles; on other occasions, despite the written record, I couldn't recall exactly what the meaning of my note was. In December 2016, when Devon and Cornwall Police were about to submit their files in the case to the CPS, Black died in Maghaberry.

Black was also thought to have been responsible for the murder of 14-year-old Patsy Morris, a case I had worked on as an assistant scientist in London. There were other child murders in Ireland, Germany, the Netherlands and France where he was a suspect.

—

In 2017, Michael Stone applied again to the Criminal Cases Review Commission. The basis of his application was that Levi Bellfield, who had already been imprisoned for multiple murder,* was the true killer. Stone's legal team claim to have identified forensic evidence from the scene that corroborated an alleged confession by Bellfield. The CCRC provisionally rejected the application, a decision that was confirmed on 2 December 2019.[1]

—

In 2019, Don Hale published a third book[2] on the Downing case. The changes to the book are largely presentational; there is more detail, although this is often background information. Again Hale ignores the critical comments made

---

* Bellfield was convicted of the murders of Milly Dowler, Marsha McDonnell and Amélie Delagrange. He also attempted to murder Kate Sheedy.

by appeal judges that Downing's conviction was unsafe but that they had not considered whether he was guilty. Hale also repeats his view that the reinvestigation was 'expensive, half-hearted – and … totally inadequate', but he is careful to refer to it as the 'allegedly inconclusive and unsuccessful reinvestigation'. He fails again to confront the issues raised during the reinvestigation – the elimination of all the potential suspects other than Downing. The fact that the inquiry was independently scrutinised and that Downing confessed his guilt to a number of individuals, including his father, is ignored. There are no new arguments; Hale simply ignores anything that counters his predetermined view.

—

In September 2010, Ricky Preddie was released after serving four years of his eight-year sentence. The following year his brother Danny was released. Ricky was returned to prison a number of times due to bail violations and for committing further offences. He was finally released in 2013 after serving his full sentence.

—

André Hanscombe complained to the Independent Police Complaints Commission (IPCC)* in November 2009. The IPCC concluded that if the Met had acted adequately, the deaths of Samantha Bisset, Jazmine Bisset and Rachel Nickell,

---

* In January 2018, the IPCC was replaced by the Independent Office for Police Conduct.

as well as a number of sexual assaults and rapes, could have been prevented. The Met apologised unreservedly for the failings. Hanscombe sought compensation from the Met, but there was no legal basis for this. His son Alex was awarded £90,000 by the Criminal Injuries Compensation Authority. They had lost a mother and a partner and their family had been irreparably damaged.

The IPCC also identified the gross errors of judgement in the misdirected investigation that had focused on Colin Stagg. In 2008, Stagg was awarded £706,000 compensation by the Home Office.

'Lizzie James', the undercover officer involved in the Stagg honey trap, was awarded £125,000 by the Met in an out-of-court settlement. She had been on sick leave for 18 months suffering from post-traumatic stress disorder. She is no longer a police officer.

Robert Napper remains in Broadmoor Hospital.

—

In 2010, Gareth Williams was posthumously awarded the Sir Peter Marychurch award,* which is given annually for work in international cryptology. Following the attempted murders of Sergei and Yulia Skripal, interest in the Williams case was rekindled in some quarters and there were calls to reopen the investigation. No further developments have come to my attention.

—

---

* This title of this award appears to be widely misquoted in the press as the Mary Church award.

There were many factors that led the Home Office to close down the Forensic Science Service towards the end of 2010. Some of these arose from the operating environment in which the FSS found themselves; an increasingly competitive and shrinking market that led to price wars. But there were also internal factors that contributed to their demise. The Damilola Taylor and Rachel Nickell cases were self-inflicted wounds; damaging no doubt, perhaps severely damaging, but not fatal in themselves. What took the FSS from a progressive dwindling of their performance and reputation into terminal decline was how the senior management responded to these mistakes. This was characterised by a symphonic sense of self-regard and an aggressive belief that everyone else could be blamed without any comeback. They had pioneered DNA profiling and given the world its first DNA database; how could they be wrong? So instead of digging themselves out of the problems they had caused themselves, they dug deeper; misleading ministers, trying to con senior civil servants, threatening legal action and accusing chief police officers. The last of these was their downfall. The police, more politically astute in these circumstances, outmanoeuvred them.

The FSS management never believed the Home Office would pull the plug on their financial recklessness. In the endgame they were losing £2 million a month. The more scurrilous accusations against the FSS around this time included using the DNA database for illegal purposes and rewriting the Wikipedia page of Sir Alec Jeffreys to big up their own involvement in the discovery and development of DNA profiling. The FSS had built and sustained an international reputation as leaders in the field over decades. This reputation was based on their 1,600 skilled staff, most of whom lost their jobs. A significant UK asset had also been lost. The case for the privatisation of the FSS had been flimsy at best, an ideological decision papered over with a superficial analysis of a very unusual market* that was not understood by those who made the decision. The main benefits expected to arise from privatisation never appeared. But privatisation alone was not the cause of the FSS failure.

---

* When the decision was made, the FSS had 95 per cent market share and essentially a sole customer: the police. It was a monopoly, monopsony market.

Notes

Author's Note

1   Malcolm, J. (2004). *The Journalist and the Murderer*. Granta, London.

Preface

1   Auld, R. (2001). *Review of the Criminal Courts of England and Wales: Report*. Stationery Office Books, London.

Introduction

1   This case was some years ago, but I know of recent similar examples. Police Scotland determined that Brian McKandie's fall was an accident until a pathologist opened the body bag a few days later and identified multiple injuries. Crucial opportunities had been lost by that time. https://www.bbc.co.uk/news/uk-scotland-north-east-orkney-shetland-46994189 (retrieved 17 November 2019). Another example is the Stephen Port case, the 'Grindr killer' who was ultimately convicted of multiple murder. At the time of writing, there was an ongoing inquiry into why the Met had failed to spot links between the deaths. https://www.bbc.co.uk/news/uk-england-london-48882145 (retrieved 27 December 2019).
2   https://www.gov.uk/government/publications/forensic-pathology-audit-report-3 (retrieved 27 December 2019).
3   Summerscale, K. (2009). *The Suspicions of Mr Whicher*. Bloomsbury, London.
4   Cohan, S. (2008). *CSI: Crime Scene Investigation*. Palgrave MacMillan, Basingstoke.
5   McNamara, M., *I'll Be Gone in the Dark*. Faber & Faber, London
6   Kirk, P. (1953). *Crime Investigation*. Wiley, New York.
7   Research in Scotland (and my experience elsewhere) shows that very often the front line do not know what is required of them because policies are not communicated to them. Here is one example: Ludwig, A. and J. Fraser. (2014). Effective use of forensic science in volume crime investigations: Identifying recurring themes in the literature. *Science & Justice*, 54(1): 81–8.

8   States, Bert O. (1985). *Great Reckonings in Little Rooms: On the Phenomenology of Theater.* University of California Press, Berkeley.

Chapter One: Robert Black, The Killer of Childhood

1   Starr, D. (2011). *The Killer of Little Shepherds – The Case of the French Ripper and the Birth of Forensic Science.* Simon & Schuster, London.
2   The report was considered to be so sensitive by the authorities that the full version was not released by the Home Office until 2006, in response to a Freedom of Information request. It is now available at https://www.gov.uk/government/publications/sir-lawrence-byford-report-into-the-police-handling-of-the-yorkshire-ripper-case (retrieved 20 December 2019).
3   Clark, H. with T. Johnston. (1994). *Fear the Stranger: The Murders of Susan Maxwell, Caroline Hogg and Sarah Harper.* Mainstream Publishing, Edinburgh.
4   The functionality of HOLMES has been considerably updated and HOLMES 2 was introduced in 2001. http://www.holmes2.com/holmes2/whatish2/ (retrieved 4 September 2017).
5   *Fear the Stranger,* p.77.
6   Wyre, R. and Tate, T. (1995). *The Murder of Childhood: Inside the Mind of One of Britain's Most Notorious Child Murderers.* Penguin, London, p.143.

Chapter Two: The Many Roads to Justice

1   Twain, M. (2015). *Pudd'nhead Wilson.* Vintage Classics.

Chapter Three: The Chillenden Murders

1   Kermode, F. (1979). *The Genesis of Secrecy: on the interpretation of narrative,* Charles Eliot Norton Lectures. Harvard University Press, Cambridge MA.
2   I am indebted to my colleague Peter Stelfox for his comments on motive.
3   Russell, S. (2000). *Josie's Journey.* BBC Worldwide Ltd, London.
4   Ibid.

Chapter Four: The Trials of Michael Stone

1   Frayn, M. (2007). *The Human Touch.* Faber & Faber, London.
2   https://www.telegraph.co.uk/news/uknews/1358539/Stone-guilty-of-Russell-murders-for-second-time.html (retrieved 11 December 2019).
3   Russell, S. (2000). *Josie's Journey.* BBC Worldwide Ltd, London.
4   Stone, R. v [2001] EWCA Crim 297 (14 February 2001) http://www.bailii.org/ew/cases/EWCA/Crim/2001/297.html (retrieved 29 June 2020)

5 https://www.independent.co.uk/news/witness-in-stone-trial-says-i-lied-1180916.html (retrieved 12 December 2019).
6 Ibid.
7 Clegg. W. (2018). *Under the Wig*. Canbury Press, Kingston upon Thames.
8 https://www.theguardian.com/uk/2001/oct/05/audreygillan.nickhopkins (retrieved 23 January 2019).
9 https://www.telegraph.co.uk/news/uknews/1358539/Stone-guilty-of-Russell-murders-for-second-time.html (retrieved 23 February 2019).
10 https://www.irishtimes.com/news/most-horrific-crimes-ever-heard-of-earn-man-three-life-sentences-1.206980 (retrieved 23 February 2019).
11 *The Chillenden Murders* (BBC 2, June 2017) [TV documentary] https://www.bbc.co.uk/programmes/b08sxrj1 (retrieved 21 December 2019)

Chapter Five: The Murder of Wendy Sewell

1 Sterne, L. (1759). *The Life and Opinions of Tristam Shandy, Gentleman*, Vol. 2. Penguin Classics, London.
2 http://netk.net.au/UK/Downing.asp (retrieved 12 December 2019).
3 https://www.scotcourts.gov.uk/search-judgments/judgment?id=e2988aa6-8980-69d2-b500-ff0000d74aa7 (retrieved 12 December 2019).
4 Hale, D. (2002). *Town Without Pity*. Century, London.
5 *Homicide Investigation and Forensic Science* was a major study funded by the Leverhulme Trust of 44 homicide investigations in the UK between 2015 and 2018. https://criminology.research.southwales.ac.uk/news/2019/homicide-investigation-and-forensic-science-project-hifs/ (retrieved 30 April 2020).
6 https://web.archive.org/web/20061022081608/http://www.derbyshire.police.uk/news/26.html (retrieved 27 May 2020).
7 Gardner, A. 'Downing a "bloody fool" says his friend', *Sunday Mirror*, 2 March 2003.
8 https://www.telegraph.co.uk/news/uknews/1441408/Campaigner-for-Stephen-Downing-admits-to-errors.html (retrieved 15 March 2019).
9 Hale, D. (2002). *Town Without Pity*. Century, London.
10 Clark, C. and Tate, T. (2015). *Yorkshire Ripper – the secret murders*. John Blake Books, London.
11 Downing, R v [2002] EWCA Crim 263 (15 January 2002). http://www.bailii.org/ew/cases/EWCA/Crim/2002/263.html (retrieved 28 May 2020)

Chapter Six: The Murder of Damilola Taylor

1 Eagleton, T. (2003). *Sweet Violence: The Idea of the Tragic.* Blackwell, Oxford.
2 https://www.theguardian.com/uk/2002/feb/05/ukcrime (retrieved 12 December 2019).
3 https://www.telegraph.co.uk/news/uknews/1386257/Damilola-judge-rejects-witness-as-a-liar.html (retrieved 12 April 2019).
4 Driscoll, C. (2016). *In Pursuit of the Truth, My Life Cracking the Met's Most Notorious Cases.* Ebury Press, London.
5 A good up-to-date summary of this topic is the work of Cynthia Lum in the USA: Lum, C. *The Impact of Technology on Modern Policing.* James Smart Memorial Lecture, Scottish Institute for Policing Research International Policing Conference (2014) available http://www.sipr.ac.uk/archive/presentation/lum.ppsx (retrieved 29 June 2020)
6 Sentamu, J., et al. (2002). *The Damilola Taylor Murder Investigation Review: report of the oversight panel.* London.
7 Wilson, T. (2005). *Life Beyond the DNA Expansion Programme: The Forensic Integration Strategy.* University of Teeside Conference.
8 Silverman, M. (2014). *Written in Blood.* Bantam Press, London.
9 Gallop, A. (2019). *When the Dogs Don't Bark: a Forensic Scientist's Search for the Truth.* Hodder & Stoughton, London.
10 https://www.theguardian.com/uk/2012/sep/17/cardiff-three-five-wait-justice (retrieved 12 December 2019).

Chapter Seven: Silent Testimony – 'Every Contact Leaves a Trace'

1 Goldacre, B. (2015). *I Think You'll Find It's a Bit More Complicated Than That.* Fourth Estate, London.

Chapter Eight: The Mystery Sweatshirt

1 Mencken, H. L. (1921). *Prejudices,* Second Series. Jonathan Cape, London.
2 According to some recent research, the reading level of many forensic reports requires master's-level English comprehension. See Howes, L. M. et al. (2014). 'The readability of expert reports for nonscientist report-users: reports of forensic comparison of glass'. *Forensic Science International, 236,* 54–66.
3 http://news.bbc.co.uk/1/hi/uk/4775217.stm (retrieved 22 December 2019).
4 By Alan Rawley QC and Brian Caddy, professor emeritus in forensic science at the University of Strathclyde.
5 *Murder Investigation Manual.* Association of Chief Police Officers, 2000.
6 https://www.theguardian.com/uk/2006/aug/10/ukcrime. sandralaville1 (retrieved 22 December 2019).

Chapter Nine: On Wimbledon Common – the Murder of Rachel Nickell

1 Dennett, D. (1993). *Consciousness Explained.* Penguin Books, London.
2 Shepherd, R. (2018). *Unnatural Causes.* Penguin, London.
3 https://www.telegraph.co.uk/news/uknews/1320832/They-were-like-two-bodies-with-one-brain-raping-and-killing-for-kicks.html (retrieved 23 December 2019).
4 There is a full account of how this profile was developed in Canter, D. (1995). *Criminal Shadows.* Harper Collins, London.
5 Pedder, K. (2002). *The Rachel Files.* John Blake, London.
6 Britton, P. (1998). *The Jigsaw Man.* Corgi, London.
7 Pedder, K. (2002). *The Rachel Files.* John Blake, London.
8 Ibid.
9 Cathcart, B. (1999). *The Case of Stephen Lawrence.* Viking, London.

Chapter Ten: Operations Edzell and Ecclestone

1 Alison, L. and M. Eyre. (2009). *Killer in the Shadows: The Monstrous Crimes of Robert Napper.* Pennant, London.
2 For a more detailed account of this case, see Fraser, J. (2020). *Forensic Science: A Very Short Introduction.* (2nd edition, Oxford University Press, Oxford).
3 https://en.wikipedia.org/wiki/Birmingham_Six (retrieved 18 September 2019).
4 This is the method invented in the eighties that allows the amplification of tiny amounts of DNA until there is sufficient for analysis. For a fuller non-technical explanation, see *Forensic Science – a very short introduction.*

Chapter Eleven: Lies, Damned Lies, and Statistics

1 Quoted in Rossmo, D. K. (ed.) (2009). *Criminal Investigative Failures.* CRC Press, Boca Raton.
2 https://www.theguardian.com/uk/2008/dec/19/police-errors-rachel-nickell-murder (retrieved 10 October 2019).
3 There is an account of one of these encounters in Gallop, A. (2019). *When the Dogs Don't Bark: a Forensic Scientist's Search for the Truth.* Hodder & Stoughton, London.
4 Pedder, K. (2002). *The Rachel Files.* John Blake, London.
5 Pedder published two virtually identical books on the case under different titles: *The Rachel Files* (John Blake, 2002) and *Murder on the Common: The Secret Story of the Murder That Shocked a Nation* (John Blake, 2003).
6 André Hanscombe in interview with Fergal Keane on *Taking a Stand,* (BBC Radio 4, 16 November 2010) [Radio broadcast]
7 *Crimes that Shook Britain,* TV documentary broadcast 11 March 2012. https://www.youtube.com/watch?v=PwpHqxVjxVY2012 (retrieved 23 December 2019).

8   Britton insisted that the covert methods used were a 'splendid investigative technique' providing officers handled them properly. https://www.telegraph.co.uk/news/uknews/law-and-order/3867783/Criminal-profiler-says-Rachel-Nickells-killer-could-have-been-arrested-within-half-an-hour.html (retrieved 14 September 2019).
9   Britton, P. (1998). *The Jigsaw Man.* Corgi, London.
10 Interview for Sky News (Sky, 18 December 2008) [TV broadcast]

Chapter Twelve: The Cryptic Death of Gareth Williams

1   Lanchester, J. (2007). *Family Romance.* Faber & Faber, London.
2   I follow Aldrich's usage of this term from his comprehensive account of the official history of GCHQ. Aldrich, R. J. (2019). *GCHQ.* William Collins, London.
3   https://www.sis.gov.uk/our-mission.html (retrieved 2 November 2019).
4   https://www.walesonline.co.uk/news/wales-news/spy-gareth-williams-family-say-2048518 (retrieved 27 December 2019).
5   Ibid.
6   https://www.bbc.co.uk/news/uk-wales-11380079 (retrieved 7 November 2019).
7   McDermid, V. *Forensics: The Anatomy of Crime.* Profile Books, London.
8   https://www.telegraph.co.uk/news/uknews/crime/9232552/MI6-spy-inquest-Gareth-Williams-was-dead-or-unconscious-before-he-went-into-the-bag.html (retrieved 27 December 2019).
9   Coroners and Justice Act 2009.
10 Ministry of Justice Statistics (2019). *Coroners Statistics 2018: England and Wales.*
11 https://www.independent.co.uk/news/uk/crime/coroner-criticises-mi6-investigation-into-spy-gareth-williams-death-7703546.html (retrieved 6 November 2019).
12 https://www.theguardian.com/uk/2012/may/02/gareth-williams-inquest-police-mi6 (retrieved 28 March 2020).
13 https://www.theguardian.com/uk/2012/may/01/gareth-williams-murder-police-mi6 (retrieved 27 December 2019).
14 https://www.telegraph.co.uk/news/uknews/crime/9175962/Was-MI6-spy-in-a-bag-Gareth-Williams-killed-by-secret-service-dark-arts.html (retrieved 27 December 2019).
15 https://www.itv.com/news/wales/2012-04-26/mi6-witness-we-are-profoundly-sorry-about-what-happened/ (retrieved 27 November 2019).
16 https://www.telegraph.co.uk/news/9229214/Gareth-Williams-relatives-break-down-as-inquest-hears-MI6-did-not-notice-codebreaker-missing.html (retrieved 27 November 2019).
17 https://www.theguardian.com/uk/2012/may/02/gareth-williams-key-unanswered-questions (retrieved 28 November 2019).

18 https://www.telegraph.co.uk/news/uknews/crime/9221161/Spy-found-dead-in-locked-bag-hated-flash-car-and-drinking-culture-of-MI6-inquest-hears.html (retrieved 27 December 2019).

Chapter Thirteen: If In Doubt, Think Murder

1 Murdoch, Iris (1999). *The Sea, the Sea*. Vintage, London.
2 Association of Chief Police Officers/Centrex. (2006). Murder Investigation Manual. National Centre of Policing Excellence, Wyboston.
3 https://oig.justice.gov/special/s0601/exec.pdf (retrieved 27 December 2019).
4 Alison, L. and M. Eyre. (2009). *Killer in the Shadows: The Monstrous Crimes of Robert Napper*. Pennant, London.
5 See for example https://www.independent.co.uk/news/fingerprinting-errors-could-free-dozens-1266202.html (retrieved 15 December 2018).
6 Bass, S. and S. Cowman. (2016). Anaesthetist's guide to the Coroner's Court in England and Wales. *BJA Education, 16*(4), 130–3.
7 https://www.telegraph.co.uk/news/uknews/crime/9240940/Death-of-MI6-spy-Gareth-Williams-may-never-be-explained-says-coroner.html (retrieved 27 December 2019).
8 Black Hat is an international security conference. https://www.blackhat.com/about.html (retrieved 30 December 2019).
9 DEFCON is an international computer hackers' conference that is also attended by members of the security services from many countries. https://www.defcon.org/index.html (retrieved 30 December 2019).
10 Rumoured at the time of the review but later made public by the *Daily Mail* was the idea that an agent from an unknown secret service broke into the victim's flat through the skylight to destroy or remove evidence. https://www.dailymail.co.uk/news/article-3199587/Agents-killed-body-bag-spy-got-flat-skylight-destroy-evidence-New-theory-solve-mystery-five-years-later.html (retrieved 1 April 2020).

Conclusion: The Killer of Little Shepherds

1 Newburn, T. (2016). Revisiting the classics: Robert Reiner: the politics of the police. *Policing and Society, 26*(7), 841–9.
2 Starr, D. (2011). *The Killer of Little Shepherds: The Case of the French Ripper and the Birth of Forensic Science*. Simon & Schuster, London.
3 Reiner, R. (2010). *The Politics of the Police*. Oxford University Press, Oxford.
4 https://www.pearlsinpolicing.com (retrieved 19 December 2019).
5 This is just one example of police tactics that are feted (by police and public) but don't work. For more examples see Gash, T. (2016). *Criminal: The Truth About Why People Do Bad Things*. Allen Lane, London.

6   Association of Chief Police Officers/Forensic Science Service/ Audit Commission. (1996). *Using Forensic Science Effectively.* HMSO, London.
7   Her Majesty's Inspectorate of Constabulary. (2000). *Under the Microscope: Thematic Inspection Report on Scientific and Technical Support.* Home Office, London.
8   Her Majesty's Inspectorate of Constabulary. (2002). *Under the Microscope Refocused: A Revisit to the Thematic Inspection Report on Scientific and Technical Support.* Her Majesty's Inspectorate of Constabulary, London.
9   House of Commons Science and Technology Committee. (2005). *Forensic Science on Trial.* HMSO, London.
10 House of Commons Science and Technology Committee. (2011). *The Forensic Science Service,* Vol. 1. The Stationery Office Limited, London.
11 House of Commons Science and Technology Committee. (2013). *Forensic Science Second Report of Session 2013–14,* Vol. 1. The Stationery Office Limited, London.
12 House of Lords Science and Technology Select Committee. (2019). *Forensic Science and the Criminal Justice System: A Blueprint for Change.* House of Lords, London.
13 This case was part of a recent ethnographic study of homicide investigation in the UK. One of the conditions of access to the research was that the police forces involved had to be anonymised. You can find out more about the project here at https:// criminology.research.southwales.ac.uk/news/2019/homicide-investigation-and-forensic-science-project-hifs/ (retrieved 29 December 2019).

Afterword

1   https://www.dailymail.co.uk/news/article-7654075/Murderer-Michael-Stone-loses-bid-freedom-claims-Levi-Bellfield-killed-Lin-Megan-Russell.html (retrieved 30 December 2019).
2   Hale, D. (2019). *Murder in the Graveyard.* Harper Element, London.

Acknowledgements

I am indebted to many people for their support and advice in the writing of this book. Chief amongst them are Gary Mead, who steered the idea into a publishable form, and Robin Williams, who reviewed the manuscript. Both have made many valuable comments and observations, for which I am grateful. I also received valuable advice and comments from my editor James Nightingale at Atlantic Books and copyeditor Jane Selley.

Many others helped with advice, comments, materials and information, refreshed and challenged my memory, or provided their own recollections of these cases. They are (in alphabetical order) John Armstrong, Dave Barclay, Fiona Brookman, Brian Caddy, John Clark, Roger Cook, Rajan Darjee, Ian Evett, Chris GanTicliffe, Jim Govan, Steve Griffiths, Gary Holcroft, Adrian Linacre, Chris Mills, Ann Priston, Gary Pugh, April Robson, Geoff Roe, Craig Russell, Derek Scrimger, Angela Shaw, Mike Silverman, Gerry Sinclair, Peter Stelfox and Ben Swift.

Index

A Note About the Author

Jim Fraser is a Research Professor in Forensic Science at the University of Strathclyde and a Commissioner of the Scottish Criminal Cases Review Commission. He has over forty years' experience in forensic science and has worked on many high-profile cases as an expert witness and case reviewer. He has advised many public agencies including police organisations in the UK and abroad, the Home Office, the Scottish Parliament and the UK Parliament.